A STUDY GUIDE FOR THE CRTT EXAM

The Bare Basics of Respiratory Care

Karl L. Gettis, BS, RRT

AN ASPEN PUBLICATION®
Aspen Publishers, Inc.
Gaithersburg, Maryland
1997

Library of Congress Cataloging-in-Publication Data

Gettis, Karl L.
  A study guide for the CRTT exam: the bare basics of respiratory
care/Karl L. Gettis.
      p.   cm.
  Includes index.
  ISBN 0-8342-0924-1 (alk. paper)
  1. Respiratory therapy—Examinations, questions, etc.
                                                                 I. Title.
  [DNLM: 1. Respiratory therapy—Examinations, questions. WB 18.2
G394s 1997]
  RC735.I5G48 1997
  615.8'36'076—dc21
                                                               DNLM/DLC
for Library of Congress
                                                                 96–45157
                                                                      CIP

Copyright © 1997 by Aspen Publishers, Inc.
All rights reserved.

Aspen Publishers, Inc., grants permission for photocopying for limited personal or internal use.
This consent does not extend to other kinds of copying, such as copying for general distribution,
for advertising or promotional purposes, for creating new collective works, or for resale.
For information, address Aspen Publishers, Inc., Permissions Department,
200 Orchard Ridge Drive, Suite 200, Gaithersburg, Maryland 20878.

Orders: (800) 638-8437
Customer Service: (800) 234-1660

About Aspen Publishers • For more than 35 years, Aspen has been a leading professional publisher in a variety of disciplines. Aspen's vast information resources are available in both print and electronic formats. We are committed to providing the highest quality information available in the most appropriate format for our customers. Visit Aspen's Internet site for more information resources, directories, articles, and a searchable version of Aspen's full catalog, including the most recent publications: **http://www.aspenpub.com**
      Aspen Publishers, Inc. • The hallmark of quality in publishing
         Member of the worldwide Wolters Kluwer group

Editorial Resources: Lenda Hill
Library of Congress Catalog Card Number: 96-45157
ISBN: 0-8342-0924-1

Printed in the United States of America

1 2 3 4 5

This book is dedicated to all of those respiratory therapy professionals who have blazed the trail, making respiratory therapy an honorable and necessary profession, and to all of those practitioners yet to follow, who will build upon a solid foundation based on caring, compassion, knowledge, and excellence. Additionally, I would like to dedicate this effort to Melissa, without whose support and understanding I would have not been able to complete this project.

Table of Contents

Preface xi
Acknowledgments xiii

PART I—A Review of the Basic Foundations of Respiratory Care 1

    1—Essential Basics, A Short Review 3
        Respiratory Care Pioneers 3
        Temperature and Pressure Conversions and a Review of Definitions 3

    2—A Basic Review of the Anatomy and Physiology of the Cardio-Respiratory System 7
        External Respiration 7
        Internal Respiration 7
        Cardiac Output 8
        The Airways 8
        Control of Ventilation 9

    3—Hemodynamics Review 11
        RCPS and Hemodynamics 12

    4—Hypoxemia 13
        Definition 13
        Cardiovascular and Respiratory Symptoms of Acute Hypoxemia 13
        Physiologic Causes 13
        Oxygen Therapy 13
        Cyanosis 13
        General Notes about Hypoxemia 14

    5—Pulmonary Pathology Review 17
        Asthma 17
        Status Asthmaticus 17
        Adult Respiratory Distress Syndrome (ARDS) 17
        Atelectasis 18
        Bronchitis: Acute and Chronic (Blue Bloater) 18
        Bronchiectasis 18
        Empyema 18

Emphysema (Pink Puffer)	18
Flail Chest	18
Smoke Inhalation/Carbon Monoxide (CO) Poisoning	19
Pulmonary Embolism	19
Pneumothorax	19
Pneumonia	19
Pleural Effusion	19
Sleep Apnea	19
Obstructive Sleep Apnea	19
Central Sleep Apnea	19
6—Pediatric Pulmonary Pathology Review	**21**
Croup or Laryngotracheo Bronchitis (LTB)	21
Epiglottitis	21
Foreign Body Aspiration	22
Bronchiolitis	22
Status Asthmaticus in Children	22
Infant Respiratory Distress Syndrome (IRDS): Newborns	22
Bronchopulmonary Dysplasia (BPD)	22
7—The Major Gas Laws and Other Indispensable Academic Baggage	**25**
Gas Laws in English	25
The Major Gas Laws and Other Indispensable Academic Baggage	25
8—Acid–Base Balance	**29**
Definitions	29
Pathology	29
Non-Respiratory Parameters	30
Metabolic Acidosis	30
Metabolic Alkalosis	30
Parameter Regulation	30
Compensation	30
Correction	30
Normal Values	30
Henderson-Hasselbalch Equation	30
Miscellaneous Considerations	31
Blood Gas Analysis	31
Blood Gas Interpretation Notes and Caveats	32
9—A Review of the Oxi-Hemoglobin Dissociation Curve and O_2 Transport Considerations	**33**
Curve Shifted Left, Causing Increased Affinity	33
Curve Shifted Right, Causing Decreased Affinity	33
Know the Factors	34
10—Pathogenic Organisms and Respiratory Care	**35**
Diagnostic Tools, Techniques, and Indicators of Pulmonary Infection	35
Some Thoughts Regarding the Treatment of Respiratory Infections	35
The Secrets of Sputum and Some Organisms that May Lurk Within	36
Types, Characteristics, and Disease	36
Gross Blood	36
11—Algebra, Respiratory Care, and You	**39**
Cylinder Duration	39

Alveolar Air Equation	39
O_2 Content Formula	39
A–V Difference	39
A-a Gradient	40
A/A Ratio	40

12—Examining the Chest and Assessing the Patient's Respiratory Status 41
    Inspection 41

PART II—Oxygen Therapy 45

13—Flow Regulators and Flowmeters 47
    Flow Regulators 47
    Flowmeters 47

14—Oxygen Delivery Systems 53
    Low Flow Devices 53
    Remember the Following When Dealing With Any Type of Humidity 54
    High Flow Devices 54
    Some Thoughts 55
    Air Entrainment Considerations 55
    Humidity Fun Fact 55

15—Aerosol Generators and Humidity 57
    Things You Should Remember 57
    Ultrasonic Nebulizers (USN) 57

16—Equipment Cleaning and Sterilization Review 63

17—Government Regulations and Bulk Oxygen Systems 65
    Cylinder Markings 65

PART III—Treatments and Medications 67

18—Respiratory Pharmacology 69
    Review of the Nervous System 69
    "Hot" Drugs Currently Used in Respiratory Care 70
    Appendix 18-A—Respiratory Medication Quick Statistics 73

19—Intermittent Positive Pressure Ventilation and Human Physiology 75
    Work of Breathing (WOB) 75
    Clinical Goals of IPPB 75

20—The Secrets of IPPB 77
    Desirable Physiologic Effects of IPPB 77
    Elastance, Compliance, Flow, and Resistance 77
    Mean Airway Pressure 77
    The Bird MARK 7 78
    Indications for IPPB 79

21—Incentive Spirometry Breathing 81

22—Aerosol Therapy with Small Volume Nebulizers 83
    Aerosol Therapy Treatment 83

23—CPT and Postural Drainage **85**
    Goals of Chest Percussion 85
    Percussion Do's 85
    Percussion Don'ts 85
    Some Contraindications of Percussion 85
    Postural Drainage 86
    Clinical Indications for Percussion and Drainage 86
    Some Thoughts Regarding Drainage Positions 86
    CPT and Postural Drainage Notes 86

24—Cuffed Endotracheal and Tracheostomy Tubes and Airway Suctioning **89**
    Thoughts on Tube Size 89
    Endotracheal Tubes Versus Tracheostomy Tubes 89
    Cuff Characteristics 90
    Types of Tracheostomy Tubes 90
    Cuff Pressure 91
    Some Notes on Intubation 91
    Some Notes on Suctioning 91
    Suctioning Pressures 91
    Types of Catheters 91
    Airway to Catheter Size Ratio 92
    The Procedure 92
    Signs of Hypoxia 92
    Miscellaneous 92

25—Oxygen Analyzers **95**
    Physical Analyzers 95
    Electric Analyzers 95
    Chemical (Scholander) Analyzers 95
    Mass Spectrometer 95
    Electro-Chemical Analyzers 95

PART IV—Mechanical Ventilation or the Art of Respiratory Therapy **97**

26—Ventilator Classification **99**

27—The Modes of Ventilation **101**
    Control Mode 101
    Assist-Control Mode 101
    Assist Mode 101
    Intermittent Mandatory Ventilation Mode 101
    Synchronized Intermittent Mandatory Ventilation Mode 102
    Pressure Support Ventilation 102
    Flow-By 103
    Auxiliary Airway Maneuvers 103

28—Ventilator Alarms **105**

29—Basic Ventilator Controls **107**
    Basic Controls 107

30—Indications, Effects, and Complications of Mechanical Ventilation **109**
    Increased by Ventilation 109

Decreased by Ventilation	109
Increased by PEEP	109
Decreased by PEEP	109
Indications for the Institution of Mechanical Ventilation	109
Signs of Acute Respiratory Failure	110
Causes of ARDS (Schock Lung)	110
Signs of ARDS	110
Chronic Respiratory Failure (As Seen in Patients With COPD)	110
Calculating Compliance	110
Complications of Ventilation	110

31—Implementation of Mechanical Ventilation and Ventilator Checks 113
    Before Patient Goes on Vent 113
    Some Tools for Setting Flow Rates 113
    Ventilator Checks 114
    Airway Resistance 114

32—The Ventilator Set-up and Fine Tuning the Vent to the Patient 115
    Ventilator Set-Up 115
    Fine Tuning the Vent to the Patient 115
    Compliance 116
    Ideal $\dot{V}_E$ 117

33—Troubleshooting Tips 119
    Patient Assessment 119
    Assessing the Ventilator 119

34—Weaning the Patient from the Ventilator 121
    Weaning Parameters 121
    Weaning Techniques 121
    Termination of Weaning Trail 122
    Tools to Help Patients Stay off the Vent 122

35—Pulmonary Function Testing 125
    Restrictive Lung Disease 125
    Obstructive Lung Disease (COPD) 125
    Asthma 125
    Advice 126
    Fluidics 126
    Thoughts on Home Care 127

The Self-Assessment Tests 129
    Self-Assessment Test 1 131
    Test 1: Answer key and category breakdown 143
    Self-Assessment Test 2 145
    Test 2: Answer key and category breakdown 157
    Self-Assessment Test 3 159
    Test 3: Answer key and category breakdown 171

Index 173

Preface

Each time I reached a new level in my career, it felt like another door opened, creating new and wonderful personal and professional possibilities, while making all those things I once only dreamed of a bit more possible. Although each college degree and my registered respiratory therapist credential mean a great deal to me, I never felt as confident or proud as the day I found out I passed my CRTT exam. I felt like I had finally "arrived." Having my CRTT meant that I had advanced from the ranks of unskilled labor to the level of professional. My certified respiratory therapist technician (CRTT) credential said to the world that Karl Gettis, CRTT, knows how to do something that very few know how to do, and that no matter where he goes he will be accepted into a very small professional community without question. My life changed completely. The CRTT credential opened the first door for me and I've been kicking doors open ever since. Now it's your turn!

The most recent door to open for me was the one with education behind it. Someone asked me if I could put together a study guide to help graduate respiratory therapy technicians (GRTTs) study for their CRTT exams. I began to think of how nice it would have been to have such a thing when I took my exam. I remembered how confused and insecure I was going into the exam because of the blizzard of facts that was swirling about in my brain. What an opportunity! I pondered the questions of what information should be included in a study guide and how should it be presented so that it would not seem so overwhelming.

What you are about to read is the product of carefully thought-out research and experimentation. The major problem when preparing for these exams is that we overload ourselves with data before the test, resulting in discarding common sense when we answer the questions. We have a tendency to over-analyze everything; this is any wonder, when one considers the amount of information we have absorbed in school. One of the big hurdles we encounter while taking the test is that now we must tie all of the information together and apply it practically in a high-pressure exam setting. The data are no longer a collection of random facts that can be recited within the context of a particular chapter. Now, the combination of these separate facts is the tool that you will use to solve the various problems encountered while taking your exam and, ultimately, to care for your patients. Your patients are people who will totally rely on your expertise to relieve their suffering.

To successfully pass the exam, you must be able to tie every fact you've learned together. Relating these facts to one another is the primary focus of this study guide. Your chance for success on the exam will improve dramatically if you can look at the bigger picture, rather than become bogged down in details.

I hope to help you tie up some of the loose ends and increase your understanding of the information you've learned in school. To do this, I have selected specific topics and then have broken these down into the simplest explanations I could devise. While explaining each topic, there may be some discussion about how each ties into other subjects, along with the occasional helpful hints that have been learned through years of experience. Regard this book as if it was a conversation with a therapist you know giving you his or her slant on what it takes to pass the CRTT exam and how he or she views the facts overall.

I have tried to minimize the dialog. I am not trying to teach you anything; you already have learned it. I am simply tying up the loose ends and reinforcing the facts you have learned in school. Much of what you will encounter will simply point out that certain things should be committed to your memory for the exam. It's all stuff you know, I'm just pointing you in the right direction.

The overall goal you should set for yourself when you take the exam is to approach each problem or situation as a puzzle, putting together your solution piece by piece. You are doomed to mediocrity if you attempt to practice your chosen medical art by simply reciting facts and formulas; by the way, this will make you a boring person, too.

Finally, you shall have the opportunity to test yourself against the ample self-assessment section included in this book. The questions you'll encounter in this section are similar to those on the CRTT exams regarding wording and difficulty. When you read these questions, remember that all the hints you need to solve the puzzle are in the question. By the time you work through this book, you should have a strong understanding of the information you need to pass your exam.

I have tried to make your task as simple and painless as possible; but let's face it, preparing for this exam is not going to be high on the list of life's little pleasures. Remember that knowing something and understanding it are two different things, and here, understanding is our goal. Stay focused on your goal and give this endeavor everything you've got! Good luck.

Acknowledgments

I thank James H. Connor, CRTT, who believed in me when I did not and set the stage for this project being what it is. I also thank Randy Dick, BS, RRT, for his encouragement and support—HEALTHSOUTH is lucky to have a manager like him. Not least of all, I thank my friends and colleagues in the Respiratory Services Department of HEALTHSOUTH of Mechanicsburg, Renova Facility, for their patience, help, and input both professionally and personally, and especially Ronald Rostalski, Jr., RRT. Finally, I thank Luzie Maria Raab-Gettis, my mother, for her help, support, and prayers.

Part I: A Review of the Basic Foundations of Respiratory Care

- Essential Basics, A Short Review
- A Basic Review of the Anatomy and Physiology of the Cardio-Respiratory System
- Hemodynamics Review
- Hypoxemia
- Pulmonary Pathology Review
- Pediatric Pulmonary Pathology Review
- The Major Gas Laws and Other Indispensable Academic Baggage
- Acid-Base Balance
- A Review of the Oxi-Hemoglobin Dissociation Curve and O_2 Transport Considerations
- Pathogenic Organisms and Respiratory Care
- Algebra, Respiratory Care, and You
- Examining the Chest and Assessing the Patient's Respiratory Status

1

Essential Basics, A Short Review

Here is where your journey into the mysterious world of respiratory therapy begins. You are about to embark on the wildest ride of your life, traveling into the realm heretofore inhabited only by the secretive respiratory gods. In this chapter, we shall review some basic information just to be sure that we all understand some of the basic data that we will build on later. Don't pass over the historical review, because these names may show up on the exam. Where deductive reasoning is concerned, Hercule Poirot will have nothing on you by the time you finish this book.

RESPIRATORY CARE PIONEERS

I have taken the liberty of listing some of the historical figures who have contributed to the evolution of the field of respiratory care. This is by no means a complete list. The following are some of the more prominent philosophers and scientists who pondered the problems of respiration circulation and oxygenation:

Hippocrates: Circa 410 B.C., he is considered to be the "father of medicine" and advised ailing persons to take "fresh air" as treatment.

Aristotle: Circa 350 B.C., he showed that an animal will die without access to air.

William Harvey: About 1615, he described the circulation of blood throughout the body.

Robert Boyle: Around 1660, he demonstrated that the lowering of air pressure causes death and bubbles in the tissues. He also developed "Boyle's Law."

Hooke: About 1670, he demonstrated that blood turns red after passing through the lungs. (I shudder to think about how he accomplished that.)

Joseph Black: He was the first real, quantitative chemist. He discovered CO_2 around 1770.

Antoine Lavoisier: Around 1780, he, with others, demonstrated that during respiration, the body absorbed oxygen and CO_2 was given off. (By the way, he had a beautiful, young wife who divorced him and married the Count von Rumford.)

Hering and Breuer: In 1868, they demonstrated that there is an inhibitory effect on lung inflation that, when stimulated, causes lung collapse, facilitating exhalation.

Paul Bert: He published "Barometric Pressure" after his 1878 experiments demonstrating the relationship between altitude and air pressure changes.

Joseph Priestly: He discovered O_2 around 1774. This is definitely a name to remember! He, along with Haldane, advanced the theory that arterial CO_2 controlled respiration.

Torricelli: He devised the first mercury barometer around 1600. The unit of measurement mm Hg is also called torr in honor of Torricelli.

Thomas Beddoes: In 1798, at Bristol—where he had his Pneumatic Institute—he became the first to recommend treating diseases with inhaled gases. He also developed a system of one-way valves to prevent rebreathing of CO_2. He is considered the father of respiratory care.

Karl von Linde: He developed the technique of "fractional distillation" to extract pure O_2 from air. He opened his first commercial plant, which used this technique, in 1907 in Buffalo, New York.

Bennett: He developed the first intermittent positive pressure breathing (IPPB) machine between 1945 and 1950.

TEMPERATURE AND PRESSURE CONVERSIONS AND A REVIEW OF DEFINITIONS

In this section, the goal will be to hit the high points, so to speak, providing you with a basic review of temperature and pressure conversions and a few basic definitions of fluid characteristics. This information should help you gain insight into basic concepts regarding why gases and liquids act the way they do. Who could ever tell Mother Nature what to do? The best we can hope for is to understand her (or him, whichever you prefer). Anyway, here we go!

Temperature Conversion Formulas

Remember that you must convert temperatures to Kelvin to use the gas laws.

C = 5/9 (F − 32)
F = (9/5 × C) + 32
K = C + 273
Temperature conversion data: 32° Fahrenheit (F) = 0° Celsius (C) = 273° Kelvin (K).
0 K = −273 degrees Celsius.

Pressure

Pressure = Force/Unit Area
Units of pressure: e.g., psi, cmH₂O, mm Hg, etc.

Barometric Pressure and Molecular Activity

1 atmosphere of pressure (atm) = 14.7 psi; 760 mm Hg; 760 torr; 1034 cmH₂O; 29.9 inhg.

These measurements all reflect barometric pressure at sea level. Barometric pressure decreases as altitude increases.

As temperature increases, molecular activity also increases.

Definitions Regarding Fluid Characteristics

Melting Point: solid goes to liquid.
Freezing Point: liquid goes to solid.
Boiling Point: liquid goes to gas.
Evaporation: point below boil that liquid goes to gas.
Vapor Pressure: force necessary, when molecules hit surface of a liquid, to allow liquid to vaporize.
  a. Mass attraction of molecules decreases with increase in temperature.
  b. When vapor pressure exceeds pressure of outside gas, H₂O evaporates.
Critical Temperature: temperature at which you have the last chance at a liquid, not above.
Critical Pressure: pressure needed at critical temperature to go liquid.
psig: gauge reading + 1 atm (or whatever gauge calibration is).
psia: absolute pressure; actual atmospheric pressure included within gauge reading.

Pressure Conversion: mm Hg to cmH₂O

1.36 cmH₂O = 1 mm Hg

760 mm Hg = x cmH₂O

$$\frac{760 \text{ mmHg}}{1} \times \frac{1.36 \text{ cmH}_2\text{O}}{1 \text{ mm Hg}} =$$

$$\frac{x}{760 \text{ mm Hg}} \times \frac{760 \text{ mm Hg}}{1} = 1034 \text{ cmH}_2\text{O}$$

The previous information consists simply of straightforward facts that you will need to solve more complex problems later. Know this information, but above all, understand it.

The following is a list of abbreviations commonly used in respiratory therapy and throughout this book. You will see these over and over again! If you do not understand their exact meanings, you shall, most likely, misinterpret the information you are dealing with and come to the wrong conclusions. The bottom line is, know these abbreviations as well as you do your social security and phone numbers.

General Abbreviations

P   Pressure
f   Frequency of an event per unit of time
V   Volume in general
V_T Tidal volume, aka normal resting breath (It's just like the ocean tides that flow in and out smoothly at regular intervals.)
$\dot{V}_E$ Minute ventilation
F   fractional concentration of a dry gas
t or T   Time or temperature
α   Alpha, first letter of the Greek alphabet and symbol used to signify a type of receptor in the sympathetic nervous system that, when stimulated, causes vasoconstriction
β   Beta, second letter of Greek alphabet—also used to signify receptor types found in the sympathetic nervous system
Δ   Delta (change)
/   Per, which is the same as "divided by" (e.g., miles/hour).
÷   Divided by
+   Plus, excess, acid reaction, or positive
−   Minus, deficiency, alkaline reaction, or negative
±   Plus or minus
×   To multiply
=   Equal to
≠   Not equal to
>   Greater than
<   Less than

≤	Less than or equal to	PEFR	Peak expiratory flow rate
≥	Greater than or equal to	R	Resistance
:	Denotes a ratio, or "is to"	C	Compliance
∴	Therefore	B	Barometric as in P_B
≈	Approximately	STPD	Standard temperature and pressure of a dry gas. Condition of gas $0°$ C, 760 torr, and no vapor
≅	Approximately equal to		
↑	Increase or increased	BTPS	Body temperature and pressure, saturated with H_2O vapor
↑↑	Greatly increased		
↓	Decrease or decreased	ATPD	Ambient temperature and pressure of a dry gas
↓↓	Greatly decreased	ATPS	Ambient temperature and pressure, saturated with H_2O vapor
→	Left to right or direction of a reaction		
←	Right to left or a reaction's direction	atm	Atmosphere = 14.7 psi
↔	To and from or a reaction's direction	psi	Pounds per square inch
$2°$	Secondary to or due to	psia	A = absolute = PSIG + 1 ATM
max	Maximum	psig	G = gauge or 0 psi @ 1 ATM
min	Minimum	L	Lung
–	A dash over a symbol indicates a mean value		

Qualification

I	Inspired
E	Expired
T_I or t_I	Inspiratory time
T_E or t_E	Expiratory time
A	Alveolar
T	Tidal
D	Dead space
V_D	Volume of dead space
VC	Vital capacity
FVC	Forced vital capacity
NiF or MiF	Negative or maximum inspiratory force

Symbols Regarding Blood

Q	Volume flow of blood, aka perfusion
S	Saturation
a	Arterial
v	Venous
$\bar{v}$	Mixed venous
c	Capillary (e.g., Vc = capillary bed volume in ml)
c'	Pulmonary end-capillary
vol %	A measurement used in blood analysis. vol % = g/100 ml of blood = g/dl. This is commonly used by respiratory care practitioners (RCPs) as the unit of measure for the oxygen content formula.

2

A Basic Review of the Anatomy and Physiology of the Cardio-Respiratory System

The subjects of anatomy and physiology can be complex; indeed, they can mirror politics and love regarding the twists and turns involved. Please remember that, as with this entire book, only selected information is presented in this section and that this information is simplified to serve as "triggers" for the reader to help him or her recall these topics during the examination. No one expects you to "play doctor," at least not until you take the RRT exams; therefore, the discussion provided will be basic, but relevant. You should have a good understanding of where things are (anatomy) and how they work (physiology) before reading this section, using the following information as a review.

EXTERNAL RESPIRATION

Oxygen (O_2) is moved into the alveolar sacs and carbon dioxide (CO_2) is removed to the atmosphere during external respiration. This is accomplished by breathing in and out. During external respiration, oxygen and carbon dioxide are exchanged across the alveolar–capillary membrane, between the alveoli and the hemoglobin (Hgb) in the red blood cells. The Hgb has Fe (iron molecules) that serve to attract the two gases. CO_2 diffuses across the membrane 19 times faster than O_2, assisting in this gas exchange at the alveolar level. In the lungs, CO_2 jumps off of the Hgb, across the alveolar–capillary membrane, and into the alveoli, making room for O_2 on the Hgb. A pressure gradient (basically a difference in the pressures of different areas) aids oxygen diffusion, with the pressures being higher in the alveoli.

The various therapies we provide, as respiratory care practitioners (RCPs), attempt to improve the efficiency of external respiration by clearing secretions, treating bronchospasms, or improving gas distribution and oxygenation in the lungs. Successful treatment of pulmonary diseases will result in the body's ability to maintain a proper acid–base balance and supply its tissues with enough oxygen to function properly.

Mechanical ventilation directly affects the body's ability to supply O_2 and eliminate CO_2 via the lungs. Mechanical ventilation at its initiation, attempts to take over the processes of mediating the acid–base balance and supplying oxygen to the blood for transport to the tissues. In short, mechanical ventilation takes over for external respiration.

INTERNAL RESPIRATION

The heart and the lungs work together to supply the body with O_2 and remove waste in the form of CO_2. The CO_2 is a waste product of internal respiration, or cellular respiration. Lactic acid is the end product of cellular respiration (metabolism); this is, through various means, broken down into what we will refer to as miscellaneous waste and carbonic acid.

A cell at rest will not produce as much lactic acid as a cell that is working; for example, when muscle cells are exercised they produce much more lactic acid than cells at rest. Lung disease reduces the body's ability to eliminate the waste efficiently, causing the waste to build up and destabilize the acid–base balance, potentially causing many problems ranging from fatigue to death.

CO_2, H^+ ions, and HCO_3^- are released into the blood from the carbonic acid. During cellular respiration, the O_2 is unloaded from the Hgb and used by the individual cells. The CO_2 is loaded onto the Hgb and released into the blood as a free gas for transport to the lungs, where disposal occurs. Elimination of the CO_2 from the body largely depends upon the lungs' ability to function properly (external respiration). Diseases such as emphysema and chronic bronchitis eventually lead to decreased lung function and as a result, patients with these diseases may retain an abnormally high amount of CO_2 in their blood at all times.

The cardio-respiratory system has two pumps, the thorax and the heart. The thorax pumps air into and out of the alveoli; the heart pumps blood into and out of the lungs, circulating it through the body after it is oxygenated. As the thorax expands, negative pressure is created in the space between the pleural membrane and the thoracic wall and diaphragm, the lungs expand and, as a result, more negative pressure is created. The negative pressure that is created in the lungs actually pulls the breath into the lungs.

When an adequate breath is taken, the lungs recoil and expel the breath. This recoil is generated by the elastic characteristics of the lung tissue, and relaxation of the muscles in the wall of thorax and the diaphragm. The elastic characteristics of the lungs can change as particular pathologies progress, making them stiffer. These changes in elasticity lead to changes in the lung tissue's ability to expand and snap back during ventilation, changing the compliance of the lung tissue.

Ideally, normal passive ventilation is a smooth process that involves little anatomically related resistance. The negative pressure generated in the thorax during this process also aids in venous blood return to the heart, whereas positive pressure breaths inhibit venous return; therefore, there is a great deal to be said for the virtues of passive, natural ventilation. The lungs and the heart work closely together; consequently, a problem in one eventually would have an adverse effect on the other.

CARDIAC OUTPUT

Some of the more frequent cardio-pulmonary problems stem from the heart's inability to balance its output with its input, causing a back pressure. When the back pressure is caused by increased resistance in the pulmonary vasculature (cor pulmonale) or by decreased right ventricular efficiency, right heart failure results, causing the fluid (blood) to back up in the veins throughout the body. This can cause a lot of pressure, sometimes forcing fluid out of the veins and into the extracellular space, resulting in pedal edema.

This problem can be severely compounded if the failure is systemic, or what is known as left heart failure. Under these circumstances, the back pressure may cause fluid to overflow into the alveoli as well as the rest of the body, filling the lungs with frothy pink secretions. This is called pulmonary edema and occurs when the patient experiences severe left heart failure.

The onset of left heart failure can be characterized as congestive heart failure (CHF). This can be noted by the RCP, upon auscultation, as rales (or crackles) being present in the lungs; rales are most obvious initially in the bases because of the affect gravity has on fluids. If untreated, this eventually will become pulmonary edema, a condition in which the lungs will eventually fill with fluid.

When the heart is unable to maintain a balance between the incoming blood volume and its own output, the previously mentioned situations will occur. More than one factor can be involved with the onset of such insufficiency, but in all cases immediate treatment is absolutely necessary.

Physiologic monitoring of patients who may be prone to the previously noted conditions can be accomplished in the critical care setting by using indwelling catheters that monitor central venous pressure, right and left ventricular pressures, and pulmonary artery and wedge pressure. These pressures, in turn, indicate the hemodynamic status of the heart and lungs and the operating efficiency of each particular component area. This information can be used to fine tune the cardio-pulmonary status of a patient before the operational failure can become acutely life threatening.

THE AIRWAYS

Having now droned on about the practical aspects of the cardio-respiratory system, let's focus our attention on a few pertinent facts regarding the use of our noses, along with some finer points regarding airways. Inspired gases that pass through our noses will, upon deposition in the lungs, be laden with 44 mg of water per each liter of air inspired; this number represents the amount of water in the air that reaches the alveoli and is called body humidity. When endotracheal or tracheostomy tubes are used as artificial airways, humidification becomes an issue of concern because the natural devices are bypassed. Additionally, the nose filters inspired air using various anatomical structures and this, too, becomes a concern when artificial airways are used.

Anatomically speaking, external respiration occurs only in the alveoli. Gas exchange *sometimes* occurs in the respiratory bronchioles. This generation of small airways directly precedes the alveoli. The airways contain no cartilaginous support and are composed entirely of smooth muscle tissue, or SMT. Airways above these generations do not participate in gas exchange; however, they do serve to transport, filter, heat, and humidify incoming gases.

In contrast to the smaller airways, the larger airways, specifically the trachea and mainstem bronchi, possess what is known as the mucocilliary escalator. This collection of ciliated cells moves secretions upward, to be expelled. The secretions are excreted from goblet cells and sub-mucosal glands that line the airways. These cells excrete the mucous, which we are all too familiar with, that traps minuscule particles that have not been filtered out by the nose.

Another anatomic feature to become familiar with is the carina. This is the point at which the mainstem bronchi split, or bifurcate, and present as a peak at the bottom of the trachea. The two things to remember are that (1) the ideal position for an endo tube is 2 cm above the carina and (2) the carina is innervated by the vagus nerve and when touched by anything, a strong cough response is triggered. This response becomes especially useful when a patient aspirates something and/or when suctioning is necessary. This reflex is called vagal stimulation or a vagal response.

CONTROL OF VENTILATION

All these functions are wonderful, but useless without control. The respiratory control center resides in the medulla, as do other autonomic functions. The central chemoreceptors, also located in the medulla, react most strongly to changes in the H^+ concentration (pH) and send signals to the medullary center to be processed; stimulation of these receptors (decreased pH) will result in decreased ventilation. There is another set of receptors in the carotid arteries in the neck. Known as the peripheral chemoreceptors, these receptors react most strongly to the amount of O_2 present in the blood, causing increased ventilation as the amount of O_2 decreases; or as O_2 increases, they signal the brain to decrease ventilation.

A further explanation of some fine points of terminology is now necessary. The following four prefixes will become important to our adventure: (1) a or an = without, (2) hyper = more than or higher than, (3) iso = same as, and (4) hypo = less than or below. Also remember the following suffixes: (1) emia = in the blood, (2) itis = inflammation, (3) oxia = general condition referring to O_2, (4) carbia = general condition referring to CO_2, (5) otomy = incision into, and (6) ectomy = removal of.

Having said that, note that the peripheral chemoreceptors are sensitive to O_2. With severe chronic obstructive pulmonary disease (COPD), we often find that the patient's central receptors are damaged beyond the point of functioning properly, and that under these circumstances the medulla relies almost entirely on the information supplied by the peripheral receptors. In this circumstance, the patient's ventilation is said to be controlled by hypoxic drive; that is, the medulla increases or decreases ventilation according to the amount of O_2 (P_{O_2}) in the blood, as per information received from the carotid receptors.

The more O_2 present (hyperoxemia), the less ventilation; the less O_2 present (hypoxemia), the more ventilation. In COPD, ventilation is at normal levels when the appropriate amount of O_2 is present in the blood. The danger in this situation is, if the peripheral chemoreceptors sense high amounts of O_2 present in the blood, the medulla may begin to decrease ventilation at inappropriate times, resulting in severe hypoventilation or respiratory arrest. It is for this reason that you never give more than 3 L/min of O_2 when a patient is suspected of being a CO_2 retainer.

In summary, the autonomic functions of the body, such as heart and lungs, are controlled by the medulla, where the respiratory control center is located. The respiratory center has two sets of sensors called chemoreceptors. One pair, the central chemoreceptors, is located in the medulla and responds to changes in pH. The second set, the peripheral chemoreceptors, is located at the bifurcation of each of the two carotid arteries and is sensitive to changes in P_{O_2}.

The heart and lungs are both pumps that move their fluids (yes, in the science of physics, gases are fluids, too) to coordinate the removal of waste in the form of CO_2 and secure an adequate O_2 supply for the tissues. A delicate balance is maintained in both systems and when one fails, the other will be directly affected. Understand these concepts and learn to use them in a deductive reasoning process to solve problems. Your test questions will be worded in ways that require you to think.

3

Hemodynamics Review

The following section is intended to be a brief, simple introduction into the subject of hemodynamics, not a complete review. You should focus on becoming familiar with normal values and having a basic understanding of the information provided by pulmonary artery catheters in terms of disease. The RCP should be aware of the changes that the patient experiences as a result of the treatment modalities that RCPs use as well.

The left ventricle is much more powerful than the right ventricle. The left ventricle's job is to perfuse the high pressure, high resistance peripheral circulation. While this is going on, the less powerful right ventricle is pumping blood (perfusing) to the low pressure, low resistance pulmonary vasculature with an identical blood volume. Remember, both volumes are the same—if they begin to vary, even slightly, right or left congestive heart failure will develop.

For example, let's assume each ventricle has an output of 70 ml/min with a heart rate (HR) of 100 = 7 L/min cardiac output. A decrease in output of 0.1 ml on the left would cause fluid to back up in the veins in the amount of 1200 ml for longer than an hour, forcing it into the interstitial spaces and lungs. If the patient had a pulmonary artery catheter in place, we would have observed a significant increase in pulmonary wedge pressure (PWP). The patient could have received treatment before the crisis had we known of the impending trouble.

If the right ventricle falls behind the left in output, the lungs will be safe, but alas, not the rest of the body. Additionally, while systemic pressure builds in the veins, the left ventricle is forced to work against gradually increasing pressures and its output will soon be affected.

Where does all this blood go? I'm glad you asked! The average person, let's say weighing ≈ 70 kg (150 lb), has between 5 and 6 L of blood circulating through his or her body. About 10% is in the lungs, 65% in the venous system, and about 25% in the arteries. Normal cardiac output is usually between 4–6 L/min. This is normal distribution at rest.

The pulmonary artery wedge pressure (PAWP) directly reflects the pressure changes inside the left ventricle. The PAWP is considered elevated if it increases over 15 mm Hg; it is considered low if it decreases below 5 mm Hg. An abnormally high PAWP (> 15 torr) signals the impending onset of pulmonary edema; low PAWP (< 5 torr) causes undesirable results such as myocardial infarction. Positive end expiratory pressure (PEEP) may affect the PAWP to the extent of increasing the PAWP 1 mm Hg (torr) for each 5 cm increase in PEEP.

The following are some other normal values associated with pulmonary artery (PA) catheters:

PA systolic	20–35 mm Hg
PA diastolic	5–15 mm Hg
PA mean	10–20 mm Hg
PAWP	5–15 mm Hg
CVP	5–15 mm Hg

Some specific problems reflected by these pressures may include the following:

- Pulmonary Hypertension. This can be caused by left ventricular dysfunction, increased pulmonary vascular resistance (PVR), or hypervolemia. Pulmonary hypertension is said to exist when PA pressures are > 35/15.
- Hypovolemia. This results in low pressures due to a lack of blood volume. Decreased blood volume may be the result of blood loss due to trauma, rupture of a great vessel like the aorta, or an extensive surgical procedure that involves a great deal of blood loss. Treatment could include giving blood and/or a protein–based volume expander like albumisol.

RCPS AND HEMODYNAMICS

Various treatment modalities and auxiliary airway maneuvers used by RCPs may affect the patient's hemodynamic status and it is within the RCP's scope of responsibility to be aware of the dangers and make recommendations accordingly. Specifically, some things to be aware of include the following:

1. High levels of PEEP or continuous positive airway pressure (CPAP) will cause a reduction in cardiac output in most patients; minimal levels will affect patients with a marginal cardiac status similarly. PEEP/CPAP should be used with caution in the cardiac patient under all circumstances.
2. Intermittent positive pressure breathing (IPPB) should be used with caution in patients who have a marginal cardiac status; high peak airway pressures cause "cardiac embarrassment," which leads to decreased cardiac output.
3. High peak airway pressures in patients being mechanically ventilated also will act to reduce cardiac output. If high peak pressures persist after the initial ventilator set up is complete and the patient has settled down and/or has been sedated, the RCP must determine the cause of the increased pressure and eliminate it promptly before serious cardiac side effects begin.
4. Modalities such as inspiratory holds, prolonged expiratory retards, and high levels of pressure support ventilation (PSV) also should be used with caution while treating the cardiac patient. In short, anything that will change the pressures in a patient's chest may affect his or her hemodynamic status to some degree, especially if that patient has a history of cardiac problems.

4

Hypoxemia

DEFINITION

It is important that we note some general considerations concerning hypoxemia, which is defined as decreased arterial oxygen tensions in the blood. Remember that the terms hypoxia and hypoxemia are not interchangeable. Hypoxia is a general term that describes an event or general condition dealing with low amounts of oxygen, like hypoxic encephalopathy or hypoxic drive. The term "hypoxemia" specifically indicates that the blood has low oxygen tensions, which in turn leads to a diminished oxygen supply to the rest of the body.

Remember that as RCPs, we work to ensure adequate ventilation and oxygenation in our patients. When considering hypoxemia and/or hypoxia, we are working to improve oxygenation by overcoming the various obstacles we may encounter.

CARDIOVASCULAR AND RESPIRATORY SYMPTOMS OF ACUTE HYPOXEMIA

Shortly after its onset, hypoxemia produces increased cardiovascular stress, which may include the following:

1. tachycardia,
2. arrhythmia (irregular heart rate), and
3. elevated systolic blood pressure.

Additionally, as the condition persists, hypoxemia causes an increase in the patient's work of breathing, the degree of which can be assessed by the degree of dyspnea the patient is experiencing.

PHYSIOLOGIC CAUSES

Physiologic causes leading to hypoxemia include the following:

1. Decreased alveolar oxygen (O_2) tensions ($\downarrow P_{A O_2}$). These can be caused by anything that prevents gas from reaching the alveoli or diffusing into the blood (shunt effect). Some examples would be mucous plugging, retained secretions, intubation of the right mainstem bronchus, bronchospasm, pneumothorax, hemothorax, or pyothorax. Treatment can range from supplemental oxygen in various concentrations to mechanical ventilation, depending on the condition's severity. The primary goal is to remove the obstruction to gas exchange and/or recruit alveoli into the process.
2. True intrapulmonary shunting. Blood from the right side of the heart enters the left without going to the lungs to pick up oxygen. This dilutes the amount of oxygen in the arterial blood entering the left side of the heart from the lungs. Two causes of this mixing are septal defects and valve regurgitation.
3. Any pathology that prevents efficient transport of oxygen across the alveolar capillary membrane, such as a thickening of that membrane. Pathologies usually associated with restrictive lung disease, such as Farmer's lung or asbestosis, may cause such membrane thickening.

OXYGEN THERAPY

We provide oxygen therapy to:

1. Correct hypoxemia and/or hypoxia (the general lack of oxygen),
2. Decrease work of breathing, and
3. Decrease myocardial work load.

CYANOSIS

We, as RCPs, usually associate cyanosis with a patient's lips and fingernail beds turning blue. Although this is true, by the time this condition becomes obvious, cyanosis is in its moderate to severe stages and your patient is already in the danger zone where oxygenation is concerned. Cyanosis also can be detected by analyzing the patient's arterial blood in an arterial blood gas (ABG) analyzer and carbon monoxide (CO)-oximeter. The average amount of available Hgb units is 15 g/dl; when five of these units or more are loaded with CO_2, CO, or if these units are missing all together (Hgb < 11 g/dl), cyanosis is considered to be present. Cyanosis is said to usually begin its onset when the Sa_{O_2} drops to 80% or less.

Clinical Signs of Cyanosis

Clinical signs include:

1. Dyspnea,
2. Lethargy,
3. Blue coloration of the nail beds and/or lips, and
4. General cardiovascular symptoms of hypoxia.

Cautions

1. You must know the Hgb.
2. The patient is dangerously hypoxic *before* nail beds and lips turn blue.

GENERAL NOTES ABOUT HYPOXEMIA

"Acute" means sudden or new, and "chronic" means long term.

1. Decreased Pa_{O_2} and Sa_{O_2} usually cause increased ventilation (hyperpnea: increased rate and/or volume).
2. Increased *hypoxia* can cause decreased ventilation due to central nervous system (CNS) depression, in some cases, due to insufficient cellular oxygen supply.

Symptoms

Symptoms include headache, confusion, and euphoria during early hypoxemia; depression, weakness, lethargy, drowsiness, and loss of coordination during a severe case; and unconsciousness during an extreme case of hypoxemia.

The following then may occur because the brain, heart, and kidneys require the most oxygen:

1. Increased blood flow to the brain,
2. Cardiac arrythmias,
3. Kidney failure, and
4. CO_2 removal may be impaired.

Chronic Hypoxemia

The word chronic indicates an ongoing condition that is usually left untreated because it goes undetected for years. Listed for your perusal are symptoms of some conditions that may develop because of this chronic lack of oxygen in the blood.

Symptoms

Symptoms include the following:
1. Persistent mental and physical fatigue, making it easy to become cyanotic;
2. Right–sided heart failure;
3. Pulmonary vasculature and airway constriction;
4. Lungs may stretch, over time, to increase surface area in an attempt to compensate for the lack of oxygen in the blood; and
5. Clubbing of nails may present.

Tissue Hypoxia

Tissue hypoxia is a general term used to describe various conditions that prevent the cells from getting the oxygen they require, but applies only to conditions that do not prevent the oxygen from getting into the alveoli initially. In other words, the oxygen gets into the lungs and blood adequately, but not into the cells. Hypoxemia does not exist.

Severe tissue hypoxia can lead to tissue infarctions, such as myocardial, brainstem, or renal infarctions. In these circumstances, there is an appropriate amount of oxygen bound to the Hgb, but particular areas of the body do not receive a sufficient amount of oxygen.

Hypoxemic Hypoxia

Causes of hypoxemic hypoxia include liquid in the alveoli, heart abnormalities, or thickened alveolar–capillary membranes. Some pathologies that may cause this condition are congestive heart failure, silicosis, farmer's lung, chronic bronchitis, bronchiectasis, pulmonary fibrosis, and near drowning.

Anemic Hypoxia

Anemic hypoxia causes a right shift on oxy-hemoglobin dissociation curve. When there is not enough Hgb, or it is loaded with CO (caused by carbon monoxide poisoning, like smoke inhalation causes), this prevents the requisite amount of oxygen from being carried by the blood to the body tissues.

Stagnant Hypoxia

In stagnant hypoxia (circulatory transport—aka venous stasis), the blood does not circulate properly throughout the body. There is enough Hgb and oxygen, they just are not circulated properly, so hypoxemia does not exist. This may be due to the shock of a trauma or cardiovascular disease and results in an inadequate supply of oxygen to the tissues.

Histotoxic Hypoxia

Histotoxic hypoxia is caused by cyanide or alcohol poisoning. There is adequate oxygen and perfusion, but the cells are blocked from using the oxygen, which means that hypoxemia does not exist. There is plenty of oxygen in the blood, but it simply cannot get into the cells. This results in general vasoconstriction, but vasodilation in the cerebral vasculature, kidneys, and heart, leading to eventual left–sided heart failure. Treatment includes oxygen therapy and pharmacologic therapy to remove the poisoning agent.

Our goal as RCPs is to treat hypoxia and/or hypoxemia with supplemental oxygen and, if necessary, mechanical ventilation. We attempt to ensure that there is an adequate supply of oxygen in the blood, ready for use by the body's cells at all times. This is part of our mission!

5

Pulmonary Pathology Review

We shall now briefly consider some of the diseases that may appear on your exam. This is not intended to provide complete details of pulmonary pathology, but to augment and reinforce the knowledge you already possess and give you enough information and triggers to recognize and react to descriptions of these conditions if they appear on your exam.

ASTHMA

In bronchial asthma, both restrictive and obstructive components may be present, but the pattern will be obstructive on a pulmonary function study (PFT). This is a condition that is caused by episodes of reversible bronchospasm, leading to airway obstruction. It is characterized by wheezing and dyspnea.

Asthma falls into two broad categories. *Extrinsic (allergic) asthma* is triggered by stimuli existing outside the body. Irritants such as dust or pollen may trigger attacks, as well as food allergies and infections like chronic bronchitis. Exercise can trigger this condition. Additionally, external factors like humidity, cold, or sudden changes in temperature and humidity may bring on an asthma attack. This condition usually first presents itself when a person is a child and is episodic in nature.

Intrinsic or nonallergic asthma may be triggered by emotional responses, stress, or external factors such as dramatic changes in temperature and air pollution levels. This condition usually presents itself as a person gets older and is considered to be a chronic form of asthma.

You will note some or all of the following upon assessment: decreased breath sounds, wheezing, rhonchi (as the attack progresses), increased use of accessory muscles, anxiety, nasal flaring, hypoxia, cyanosis, tachycardia, tachypnea, respiratory alkalosis leading to acidosis and hyperinflation, and resonance.

STATUS ASTHMATICUS

In severe status asthmaticus, you will notice that a respiratory alkalosis exists initially. You should become concerned if the ABG values move more toward normal without a corresponding decrease in severity of the symptoms. Should this happen, you should be prepared to intubate and ventilate because the patient will soon be in respiratory failure as the ABG values move through normal and into the range of respiratory acidosis.

Treatment of acute asthma attacks can be facilitated through the use of β_2 adrenergic bronchodilators such as Proventil or Alupent, IV aminophylline, and anticholinergic drugs (atropine and Robinul). Current conventional treatment of non-acute asthma often includes the use of inhaled anti-inflammatory agents like Beclovent or Azmacort and/or a mast cell inhibitor like cromolyn sodium (Intal) as prophylactic therapy; bronchodilators are used only when the situation becomes acute.

ADULT RESPIRATORY DISTRESS SYNDROME (ARDS)

ARDS, aka shock lung, oxygen (O_2) pneumonitis, white lung, et al., is an acute restrictive disease resulting in dyspnea, tachypnea, significantly decreased compliance, decreasing functional residual capacity (FRC), severe hypoxemia which can be refractory (unresponsive to oxygen therapy) in severe ARDS, and a widening A-a gradient as the disease worsens. The widening of the A-a gradient can be radical because patients often must be supported with high oxygen concentrations along with PEEP, but yet have arterial oxygen partial pressures (P_{O_2}s) only in the 40 to 60 torr range.

This disease is initiated by shock precipitated by severe or prolonged pulmonary trauma or hemorrhage. It is the pulmonary inflammatory response to the trauma that causes

ARDS. The onset can range from hours to days after the trauma, depending on its nature. Areas of patchy densities (large white areas on radiograph) forming large consolidations throughout both lungs can be noted on the radiograph. Treatment includes O_2 therapy, PEEP/CPAP, increasing FRC, treating atelectasis, chest physiotherapy (CPT) or mechanical ventilation if necessary. High levels of PEEP may be needed, along with high levels of F_{IO_2}, but use of O_2 should be minimized. The key here is to lower the O_2 before you lower the PEEP.

ATELECTASIS

Atelectasis is the incomplete expansion, nonaeration, and/or collapse of lung units. The RCP can detect the condition by noting tachycardia, dyspnea, changes in breath sounds, decreased or asymmetrical chest expansion, and, if extensive, a tracheal shift toward the atelectic lung. Atelectasis is a common complication postoperatively because many patients tend to splint their wounds after experiencing surgery. The tendency toward taking shallow breaths is strong when one considers that deep breathing causes pain and that coughing under these circumstances will give a new definition to the word pain. It is, therefore, incumbent upon us, the RCPs, to ensure that the patients use their incentive spirometers properly to prevent this condition. Atelectasis can lead to postoperative pneumonias or even ARDS in severe cases, so please understand that although it may not be of concern initially, atelectasis can become life-threatening if not treated promptly.

Treatment includes pulmonary toilet, re-expanding alveoli (incentive spirometry or IPPB), CPT, and/or O_2 therapy.

BRONCHITIS: ACUTE AND CHRONIC (BLUE BLOATER)

Acute bronchitis is an inflammation of the bronchial mucosa due to chemical irritation or bacterial infection.

Chronic bronchitis is a result of smoking, air pollution, or other chronic irritants. A chronic cough with continuous sputum production will be present. In severe cases, digital clubbing also may be present.

Treatment of bronchitis includes providing bronchial hygiene, O_2 therapy, bronchodilator therapy when an asthmatic component exists, and antibiotics. Please be aware that the terms bronchial hygiene and pulmonary toilet both refer to hydration of secretions through the administration of bland aerosols via pneumatic nebulizers (or ultrasonic nebulizers); this is done to facilitate liquification and expectoration of thick, viscous secretions and chest percussion and postural drainage where large quantities of secretions are present.

These terms are interchangeable and will pop up from time to time, but be aware that neither term refers to bronchodilator therapy.

BRONCHIECTASIS

Bronchiectasis is the permanent destruction of one or more bronchi because of the loss of elasticity. A productive cough will be present, and this cough may be chronic in advanced cases.

There are three types:

1. Saccular (cystic) bronchiectasis ends in sacs in the large bronchi.
2. Cylindrical bronchiectasis consists of an uneven widening of the 6th through 10th generation bronchi that end abruptly.
3. Varicose bronchiectasis affects generations 2 through 8 and has irregular areas of constriction with bulbous ends.

Treatment includes pulmonary toilet, bronchodilator therapy when indicated, and antibiotics.

EMPYEMA

In empyema, purulent fluid is found in the pleural cavity. Treatment requires the drainage tube to be surgically implanted.

EMPHYSEMA (PINK PUFFER)

This disease is characterized by the enlargement and permanent destruction of the air spaces beyond the terminal bronchioles.

There are two types. *Panlobular emphysema* involves the destruction of alveoli, alveolar ducts, and sacs. This type also can be caused by an a antitrypsin defect. *Centrilobular emphysema* causes the destruction of the respiratory bronchioles.

Emphysema's symptoms present themselves much like chronic bronchitis, but there is much less sputum production involved, if any. The chest X-ray (CXR) will show hyperinflation, and a barrel chest may be present along with digital clubbing, dyspnea, and hyperesonance due to trapped air in advanced cases.

Treatment includes O_2 therapy, bronchodilator therapy, pulmonary toilet, antibiotics, and steroids if needed.

FLAIL CHEST

Flail chest occurs when one part of the thoracic cage moves in the opposite direction of another during inspiration. This is caused by multiple rib fractures. This is a serious condition, because effective control of ventilation is lost. The respiratory pattern most often seen with a flail chest is called paradoxical respiration and describes how the rib cage moves inward on inspiration and outward on expiration, which is just the opposite of normal chest wall movement.

Treatment includes prompt stabilization of the chest wall and institution of mechanical ventilation. This treatment will allow the thoracic muscles to heal and the fractured ribs to set properly.

SMOKE INHALATION/CARBON MONOXIDE (CO) POISONING

Treat this condition with steroids and high F_{IO_2}s. The most obvious symptom of CO poisoning is that the patient will appear to have bright red, rosy cheeks and look very healthy; others are more subtle, such as severe headache, confusion, and lethargy. Remember that when you do an ABG, the P_{O_2}s will be analyzed as normal. After the patient's acid–base balance has been established, the arterial blood sample must be run through a CO-oximeter to check actual amount of CO that is attached to Hgb and measure the actual S_{aO_2}. Routine ABG analysis provides us only with a calculated S_{aO_2} (O_2 saturation); a CO-oximeter physically measures the amount of O_2 and CO bound to the hemoglobin. In cases of suspected smoke inhalation, it is critical that an arterial blood sample is analyzed in a CO-oximeter as well as an arterial blood gas analyzer.

CO has 200 to 250 times more affinity (attraction) for Hgb than O_2. This being the case, CO will be loaded onto Hgb before O_2 if both gases are present in equal quantities. The only way to force CO off of the Hgb is to deliver high concentrations of O_2 (as close to 100% as possible) to the patient; this is usually done via mechanical ventilation in moderate to severe cases of CO poisoning.

PULMONARY EMBOLISM

This is a complete or partial obstruction of the pulmonary artery blood flow to the lungs or one of its branches. This may cause severe hypoxemia because a great deal of dead space is created. The problem then is that the patient's ventilation is adequate, but there is no gas exchange taking place, leaving the blood unoxygenated, which results in severe hypoxemia. This pathology is treated symptomatically. PEEP and CPAP are useless because the problem isn't in the lungs.

PNEUMOTHORAX

This is the partial or total collapse of a lung. If severe, a chest tube must be inserted to evacuate the air from the thorax and re-expand the lung. The RCP should look for sudden onset of sharp pain, lack of breath sounds, sudden and severe dyspnea, and possible tracheal shift toward the lung opposite of the pneumothorax in severe cases; that is, if a severe pneumothorax exists on the right side, the patient's trachea will be pushed to the left. CXR will show black in the area of collapse.

Treat by administering O_2 and encourage incentive spirometry breathing (ISB) after re-expansion.

PNEUMONIA

Pneumonia is the inflammatory process in the air spaces of the lungs.

Lobar pneumonia often affects an entire lobe. *Bronchopneumonia* is an inflammation that affects airways and surrounding areas. *Interstitial pneumonia* is commonly called pneumonitis. Types of pneumonia are bacterial, viral, aspiration, pneumocystis carinii, and tuberculosis (TB) to name a few. Treatment depends on the type.

PLEURAL EFFUSION

Pleural effusion involves an excessive accumulation of fluid between the pleural membranes due to some type of pathology.

SLEEP APNEA

There are two types of sleep apnea—obstructive sleep apnea (OSA) and central sleep apnea (CSA).

OBSTRUCTIVE SLEEP APNEA

OSA is caused by an anatomic upper airway defect that causes the airway to obstruct during sleep. Symptoms include loud snoring, lack of energy during the day, headaches in the morning, and irritability. As a result of this physical obstruction, the patient actually will experience periods of apnea during which they may appear to struggle for breath. Treatment of OSA can be accomplished by instituting CPAP or bi–level positive airway pressure during the hours of sleep.

CENTRAL SLEEP APNEA

CSA occurs because of the failure of the respiratory control center in the medulla to send the signal to breathe to the respiratory muscles. This form of sleep apnea is usually caused by a central nervous system disorder, and this disorder must be treated to correct CSA. When observing the patient, you will note an absence of inspiratory effort and diaphragmatic movement. The patient will not appear to struggle for breath. Usual symptoms are possible mild snoring, mood changes, and daytime fatigue. Ventilatory support may be required to ensure proper ventilation, but in this case, the support may involve mechanical, time-cycled ventilation.

6

Pediatric Pulmonary Pathology Review

There are a few pathologies of note that the RCP may encounter exclusively in children. It would behoove us to become familiar with these because, you guessed it, they may show up on the test or, more importantly, in real life.

CROUP OR LARYNGOTRACHEO BRONCHITIS (LTB)

In this pathology, which affects children younger than 3 years, the offending organism is a virus, usually parainfluenza virus or respiratory syncytial virus (RSV).

Onset

Infection affects the subglottic area (below the vocal cords).

Symptoms

Symptoms include the following:
- Starts as a cold;
- Becomes worse at night;
- Develops a "barking cough;"
- White blood count (WBC) stays normal because infection is caused by a virus; and
- Fall, winter, and early spring are the prime times for onset of this condition.

Treatment

Symptomatic treatment includes the following:

- Cool mist or croup tent to reduce edema;
- Oral and intravenous (IV) hydration;
- Vaponefrin aerosols to reduce subglottic edema;
- Ribavirin aerosols (may be given for 8 or 12 hours duration in severe cases of RSV infection—this has many side effects and is no longer used as frequently as it once was);
- O_2 prn;
- Cough suppressant prn; and
- Endotracheal intubation (in the extreme case—this is done to ensure the airway will not be occluded by the swelling).

EPIGLOTTITIS

This condition usually strikes children 3 to 7 years old and is a bacterial infection usually caused by *Haemophilus* influenza B or strains of *Staphylococcus* or *Streptococcus*.

Onset

Onset is sudden with rapid progression to severe upper airway obstruction.

Signs and Symptoms

Symptoms include the following:
- Increasingly high temperature;
- Drooling is obvious because the patient cannot swallow the saliva;
- Muffled cough;
- Increasing anxiety;
- Increased WBC;
- The epiglottis is swollen and presents as "cherry red";
- Inspiratory stridor with general dyspnea;
- Very sore throat; and
- Fall, winter, and early spring are the prime times for onset of this condition.

Treatment

Treat infection with antibiotics. Treat fever. Insert artificial airway or endotracheal tube prn.

FOREIGN BODY ASPIRATION

Dangerous ages are younger than four years. Sixty-six percent of the time, the offending object is a seed or a peanut. The object is lodged in the right mainstem 70% of the time, the left mainstem 25% of the time, and lodges in the trachea 5% of the time causing respiratory arrest. Two percent of all obstructions are coughed out of the airway. Always evaluate a chronic cough! Peanuts break down into fatty acids, causing swelling and edema, possibly causing distal infections like pneumonia, abscesses, and bronchiectasis. Upon auscultation, the RCP may note a high pitched sound in the area of the obstruction. Treat with Heimlich maneuver, bronchodilators, CPT, or bronchoscopy prn.

BRONCHIOLITIS

This condition is serious if child is younger than two years. The offending organism commonly is a virus, usually RSV or adenovirus.

Onset

Onset is gradual.

Symptoms

Symptoms mirror those of a cold and include the following:

- Difficulty feeding;
- Edema, inflammation, and spasms of the airways;
- Increased residual volume;
- Obvious inspiratory and expiratory obstruction;
- Increased WOB;
- Respiratory acidosis; and
- Upper respiratory infection (URI) symptoms with wheezing and coughing (can be confused with asthma).

Treatment

Treatment includes the following:

- Ribavirin in severe cases;
- Careful hydration;
- Various types of bronchodilators;
- 25–35% O_2;
- CPT;
- Suction prn; and
- Insert airway or endo tube prn.

STATUS ASTHMATICUS IN CHILDREN

General signs and symptoms of this condition are the same as those of asthma. BS: ↓ T/O all fields, with diffuse wheezes.

Treatment

Treatment includes the following:

- O_2 prn, usually 30–40%;
- β_2 bronchodilators;
- Prophylactic antibiotics to prevent infection, which is more likely to occur because of a ↓ in the efficiency of the immune system's operation;
- Ensure proper hydration;
- Methylxanthine bronchodilators and/or steroid therapy; and
- Intubate and ventilate if the patient is on 70% O_2 and Pa_{O_2} < 60 torr, and/or Pa_{CO_2} > 45 torr.

INFANT RESPIRATORY DISTRESS SYNDROME (IRDS): NEWBORNS

Also known as hyaline membrane disease, IRDS is a condition commonly found in premature babies because they are born before their lungs are fully developed. In this condition, the infant's lungs are unable to exchange gases because there is a lack of alveolar surface tension. The signs and symptoms of IRDS are much like those of ARDS. The lungs will appear to be whited out on CXR; there also will be interstitial edema and fibrosis in the lung tissue. Static and dynamic compliance will be low, causing high ventilating pressures before Survanta or Exosurf are used. The child will require mechanical ventilation, possibly PEEP therapy, and treatment with bronchodilators and a surfactant substitute, such as Survanta or Exosurf.

Neonates with IRDS (or in general) are different from adults. They may require respiratory rates between 20 and 60. Peak airway pressures may range from 10 to 35 cmH_2O, PEEP up to 15 cmH_2O and F_{IO_2}s as high as 100%.

Extreme caution must be used when delivering high concentrations of oxygen to neonates because their fragile optic nerves can be easily damaged by high F_{IO_2}s. High concentrations of oxygen (over 40%) may cause a condition known as retrolental fibroplasia, which usually results in permanent blindness of the child. Be very careful whenever using O_2 with babies!

BRONCHOPULMONARY DYSPLASIA (BPD)

This condition is commonly caused by the long-term positive pressure ventilation of an infant, which leads to the abnormal development of the large airways and lungs. It is considered to be a form of chronic lung disease.

Generally, periods of ventilation longer than seven days, coupled with high peak pressures and F_{IO_2}s lead to the barotrauma that causes BPD. There are four stages, with atelectasis being an issue in all four stages and interstitial fibrosis in the last two stages; in stage four, actual emphysematous changes in the alveoli occur. The general symptoms are much the same as those of IRDS, including opacification on the CXR. Treatment includes (you guessed it) oxygen therapy, mechanical ventilation, careful maintenance of the patient's fluid balance, and aggressive pulmonary toilet.

So, I guess what I'm saying here is that after we get "premies" (newborns) over their IRDS, we have to re-ventilate to get them over the trauma we caused saving their young lives in the first place. That sounds a wee bit screwy, but that is the way it is.

7

The Major Gas Laws and Other Indispensable Academic Baggage

GAS LAWS IN ENGLISH

Why are gas laws so important? They tell us how gases react under certain circumstances. The word "law" indicates that when the conditions of the formula exist, the gas will *always* react in the outlined manner. This knowledge goes to the heart of what we do; this is the knowledge that we use to figure out why an alarm is going off or a patient's volume requires too much delivery pressure. Gas laws are one of the tools we use to solve problems with patients and equipment alike. Therefore, take the following advice:

1. Study your formulas!
2. Know that the units mm Hg and torr are the same thing, i.e., 30 mm Hg = 30 torr.
3. Know the following gas laws and what they mean. Be able to write the formulas, but above all, understand them!

Boyle's Law: Volume decreases as pressure increases, and vice versa, when temperature is constant.

Charles' Law: As temperature increases, volume increases and vice versa, when pressure is constant.

Gay-Lussac's Law: Volume is the constant. Pressure increases as the temperature increases.

Avogadro's Law: The greater the volume, the more molecules there are. Also, look up 6.02×10^{23}—this is the number of molecules in one mole of a given element or compound. This number is also called Avogadro's number.

Dalton's Law: Different gases in a mix all exert their own partial pressures, the sum of which constitutes the total pressure.

Poiseuille's Law: Leads to Venturi and Bernoulli principles.

Reynold's Number: Number is 2,000. If the number is < 2,000 = laminar flow; > 2000 = turbulent flow.

Bernoulli Principle: The greater the flow through a tube, the less the lateral wall pressure, facilitating air entrainment.

(Isn't this fun stuff? It's really not that hard—most people just make it that way.)

THE MAJOR GAS LAWS AND OTHER INDISPENSABLE ACADEMIC BAGGAGE

There are many laws governing the physical characteristics of fluids (gases are fluids, honestly), but we as RCPs need be concerned only with a few to understand the basics of respiratory care. These gas laws are presented here, hopefully in plain English, for the sake of academics and to complete your understanding of basic physics. The mathematical definitions of our gas law hit parade are presented here for your intellectual viewing pleasure and consideration.

Boyle's Law

Essentially, Boyle deduced that volume is reduced as pressure is increased and vice versa if other factors—in this case, temperature—remain constant. Consider this: as a piston decreases the volume in a cylinder, volume decreases as the gas compresses, causing the pressure it exerts on the cylinder to increase.

$V_1 P_1 = V_2 P_2$, when T remains constant.

Charles' Law

Charles says that changes in volume are directly proportionate to changes in temperature, on an absolute scale, with other factors—in this case, pressure—remaining constant. Simply put, as a gas is heated, it expands, displacing more volume; as a gas is cooled, the volume displaced decreases.

Pressure remains unchanged as this occurs; let's use 1 ATM (14.7 psi).

$$\frac{V_1}{T_1} = \frac{V_2}{T_2}$$

Gay–Lussac's Law

These gentlemen expressed nearly the same relationship as Charles, but using volume as a constant instead of pressure. Changes in pressure are directly proportionate to changes in temperature; that is, as pressure increases, temperature increases also and vice versa. This relationship is as follows:

$$\frac{P_1}{T_1} = \frac{P_2}{T_2}$$

Avogadro's Law

Avogadro's number = 6.02×10^{23}. Avogadro deduced that equal volumes of gases under identical conditions contain equal numbers of molecules, or that the number of molecules is directly proportionate to the volume of gas, all other factors remaining constant (pressure and temperature). This is simple: two separate 100 ml containers are full of O_2; if the temperature and pressure of these containers are the same, the number of molecules in the containers will be the same.

$$\frac{n_1}{V_1} = \frac{n_2}{V_2}$$

The previously described gas laws are the basics needed by every RCP to perform his or her duties. These are the tools we use to solve problems with equipment, administer treatments properly, and set up ventilators properly. Understanding the characteristics of gases under various conditions is pivotal to providing effective patient care.

Poiseuille's Law

Fluids flow *only* when acted upon by a force proportional to the pressure difference; that is, a force has to be exerted on a fluid to make it move and that force must overcome the resistance offered by the fluid and any factors that cause additional resistance. This law describes the relationship between a fluid and the tube it flows through. This information should be considered developmental because understanding the formula and the relationship will help you understand things like jet nebulizers and Venturi masks.

$$V = \frac{\Delta P \pi r^4 t}{8 L n}$$

Note that the density of a fluid is not a factor and that π and 8 are constants. V = flow, n = viscosity, L = length of tube, and DP = the pressure difference across the tube, to the fourth power of the radius (r) of the tube. Additionally, flow must be laminar; that is, Reynold's Number is < 2,000.

Once you sort through all of these factors and do the calculations, you are rewarded with the flow rate of the fluid in question. If all of the conditions of this law are met, this formula can be used to calculate or predict the flow rate of any fluid.

What does this all mean? As usual, I'm glad you asked. These gas laws prove helpful in several ways that may be obvious, at least for all except Poiseuille's Law, but let's clarify the issue to be certain.

Ideal Gas Law

The first three gas laws describe the relationships among volume, temperature, and pressure. In each of these laws, it is assumed that one of these three variables is constant, but all three affect the outcome. These three variables can be combined into one gas law, the Ideal Gas law.

$$\frac{P_1 V_1}{T_1} = \frac{P_2 V_2}{T_2}$$

All you need to do is set up your formula to solve for the variable in question, convert your temperature into Kelvin, and plug in the volume and pressures. Be aware that you must convert your volume and pressure measurements into the same units.

In the case of Poiseuille's Law, you must gather data concerning the characteristics of the tube and the fluid and then plug them into the formula. The information this law provides can be useful in determining the proper therapeutic mixture when administration of He_2/O_2 mixtures is being considered.

The prediction of flow is significant because the lower the density of a gas, the less possibility it has for turbulent flow; therefore, there is less possibility for an effective cough. An effective cough requires turbulent flow. Additionally, the use of less dense gases increases the volume of gas delivered.

When thinking of *flow*, remember that flow is the relationship between the linear movement of volume and time; flow = V/T or volume/time. Hence, the expressions liters per minute, gallons per hour, yada, yada, yada. Velocity = distance/time, like miles/hour—don't confuse flow and velocity. Basically, remember that flow is always a given volume measurement per unit time; flow is never only 6 L, it is always 6 L/min. When describing volume, you use only a measurement of volume, e.g., 6 L; when one discusses flow, one must always include the measurement of whatever is moving and the unit of time it takes that amount of stuff to move. If no unit of time is indicated, flow does not exist!

Relative Humidity

Relative humidity (RH) evaluates exactly what the term indicates. This is a comparison between what the possible humidity of a gas sample could be in contrast to what it actually is at a given temperature. This is the same relative humidity that we hear about every day on the TV weather report that compares the air's potential water carrying capacity to the amount it actually holds at that time.

Keep the following fact in the back of your mind: the warmer the gas is, the more water it will hold. The cooler the gas, the less water it will hold.

$$RH = \frac{content}{capacity} \times 100 = \% RH$$

$$e.g., RH = \frac{22 \text{ mg/L}}{44 \text{ mg/L}} \times 100 = 50\% RH$$

Percent relative humidity illustrates the relationship between how much humidity exists versus how much there could be in a given gas sample at the given temperature.

Body Humidity

The concept of body humidity (BH) works on the assumption that water vapor pressure (P_{H_2O}) equals 47 torr at 37°C (body temperature). This is a constant! Water vapor pressure is always 47 torr at body temperature and air always carries 44 mg/L (44 mg of water/liter of gas) at that temperature. Possible humidity = 44 mg/L.

$$BH = \frac{actual\ humidity}{possible\ humidity} @ 3°C$$

Body Humidity Deficit

The concept of body humidity deficit (BHD) becomes relevant when we work with patients who are intubated or have a tracheostomy tube in place. Under those circumstances, the patient's natural humidification mechanisms (which provide 100% BH) are bypassed, resulting in less humidification taking place on inspiration. The RCP is therefore responsible for providing enough supplemental humidity to make up the difference. BHD is the difference between what the body needs (possible) and the amount of humidity that actually exists in the inspired gas.

Room air usually will have a temperature that is less than 37°C (98.6°F), so it will be carrying much less water than gas heated to 37°C. This difference is the BHD.

BHD = possible water content (mg/L) – actual gas content.

Basically, the previous equation tells us the amount of water we must add to the inspired gas to reach the desired 100% body humidity.

Air Capacity (Know These!)

At 37°C, water vapor pressure = 47 torr [at sea level or 1 ATM (1 atmosphere = 14.7 psi)], and water carrying capacity of air at 37°C = 44 mg/L of gas.

*Remember to subtract the water vapor pressure (P_{H_2O}) of 47 torr from your alveolar-air equation.

These are the tools you will use to determine whether to add additional humidity, and if so, how much you will be required to add. You may not routinely go to these lengths in the clinical setting, but as an RCP, you are expected to know the particulars regarding every aspect of providing supplemental oxygen, supplemental humidification, auxiliary airway maneuvers, and mechanical ventilation safely and effectively. Trust me, the day will come when you will use this information in the clinical setting.

8

Acid–Base Balance

Welcome to the five-cent tour of acid–base balance. Please understand that volumes have been devoted to this subject. However, we are not here to explore the secrets of biochemistry; we have a test to prepare for, so let's begin with some basic definitions.

We study the arterial blood to evaluate how the heart and lungs are performing. If we were to study venous blood from an arm or leg, we would see only what has transpired in that limb, nothing else.

DEFINITIONS

ACID: a substance capable of donating H^+ (hydrogen ions).
e.g.: H_2CO_3 (carbonic acid) $\longrightarrow H^+ + HCO_3^-$
BASE: a substance capable of accepting H^+.
e.g.: $OH^- + H^+ \longrightarrow H_2O$
$HCO_3^- + H^+ \longrightarrow H_2CO_3$

Hydrogen ions are what we care about!
pH: only measurement that allows us to gauge the body's acidity or lack thereof. pH scale goes from acid (1) to base (14), with 7.40 being the neutral pH for the human body.
Acidemia: an acid condition of the blood, pH < 7.35.
Alkalemia: an alkaline condition of the blood, pH > 7.45.
Acidosis: the process causing acidemia.
Alkalosis: the process causing, you guessed it, alkalemia.
P_{CO_2}: known as the respiratory parameter because it is influenced *only* by respiratory factors.
Normal P_{CO_2} = normal ventilation
High P_{CO_2} = HYPOventilation
Low P_{CO_2} = HYPERventilation

As the pH moves down, the blood becomes more acidic as the P_{CO_2} rises. This is called *respiratory acidosis*. CO_2 is the acid-producing compound in the blood. pH will rise as the P_{CO_2} falls because there is less acid in the blood. Where does the CO_2 go? It is exhaled! Conversely, a low P_{CO_2} and high pH results in *respiratory alkalosis*.

PATHOLOGY

Now that we have defined respiratory acidosis and alkalosis, we shall consider some of their causes.

Respiratory Acidosis (High P_{CO_2} Due to Hypoventilation):

Causes of this condition include the following:

1. Obstructive lung disease;
2. Oversedation and other causes of reduced function of the respiratory center, even with normal lungs, (i.e., head trauma, drugs, alcohol, etc. (You do, of course, remember the respiratory center is in the medulla); and
3. Anything that might cause hypoventilation. (An example would be Pickwickian syndrome or OSA).

Respiratory Alkalosis (Low P_{CO_2} Due to Hyperventilation)

Causes of this condition include the following:

1. Hypoxia—hunger for oxygen causes increased respiratory effort;
2. Nervousness and anxiety;
3. Pulmonary embolus, fibrosis, etc.;
4. Pregnancy; and
5. Other causes of hyperventilation like frequent emesis.

NON-RESPIRATORY PARAMETERS

HCO₃⁻ and Base Excess

These are influenced only by *metabolic* causes, not by respiratory causes. The metabolic process, as far as we are concerned, is anything non-respiratory that affects acid–base status such as diabetes or uremia. When metabolic problems arise, they, too, can cause an increase or loss of acid. Base excess is just an acidity indicator that has been arbitrarily fixed at 0, normal being considered +2 to –2.

METABOLIC ACIDOSIS

When acids accumulate, the body loses bicarbonate, causing a drop in HCO_3^- levels, below normal, and base excess values become negative. Therefore, decreased pH and decreased HCO_3^- with a normal P_{CO_2} indicate a metabolic acidosis (non-respiratory acidosis).

Causes

Causes of metabolic acidosis include the following:
- diabetic ketoacidosis; poisoning with salicylates, methyl alcohol, or ethylene glycol; lactic acidosis; renal failure; and diarrhea.

METABOLIC ALKALOSIS

Conversely, a loss of acid triggers an increase in HCO_3^-. When pH and HCO_3^- rise while the P_{CO_2} remains normal, we have a metabolic alkalosis (non-respiratory alkalosis). Base excess creeps into the + range.

Causes of metabolic alkalosis include the following:

- diuretic therapy, corticosteroid therapy, Cushing's disease, acid loss from upper GI tract via vomiting, and nasogastric (NG) tube.

PARAMETER REGULATION

Respiratory parameter (P_{CO_2}) is regulated by the lungs; therefore, both gas and acid are regulated here.

Non-respiratory parameter (HCO_3^-) is regulated, for the most part, by the kidneys; therefore, solution and base are regulated here.

COMPENSATION

Abnormal pH is returned toward normal by altering the component not affected, i.e., if the P_{CO_2} is high, the HCO_3^- is retained to compensate.

CORRECTION

Abnormal pH is returned toward normal by altering the component primarily affected, i.e., if the P_{CO_2} is high, the P_{CO_2} is lowered, correcting the abnormality. For example, it could be lowered by hyperventilation.

NORMAL VALUES

pH: 7.35 – 7.45; < 7.35 = acidosis, > 7.45 = alkalosis
P_{CO_2}: 35 – 45 torr; < 35 = alkalosis, > 45 = acidosis
P_{O_2}: 80 – 100 torr; < 40 torr = severe hypoxemia
    40 – 60 = moderate hypoxemia
    60 – 80 = mild hypoxemia
HCO_3^-: 22 – 26 mE/l
BE: – 2 – +2
S_{aO_2}: > 95 %

As people age, their physiology changes somewhat and what was once normal changes as well. Because we are discussing normal values, let's see what happens to normal values for P_{aO_2} as people age. The following table illustrates the normal P_{aO_2}s for various age groups. If your patient is older than 60 years, remember that their normal P_{aO_2} is < 80 torr and supplemental oxygen may not be necessary.

Age	Age–Specific P_{aO_2} Normal Value
60 to 70 years	70 torr
70 to 80 years	60 torr
80 to 90 years	50 torr

Please be aware that a blood gas with a normal pH and another abnormal value usually reflects a chronic condition, whereas a blood gas with abnormal pH and another abnormal value usually reflects an acute situation.

HCO_3^- is the buffer that counterbalances acid, thereby regulating the acidity of the blood.

We will take this section fairly slow, because ABG interpretation is an RCP's primary diagnostic tool—one which, happily, confuses just about everyone else, including many doctors. The formulas we will encounter serve to broaden our ability to see where no one else can and visualize what may be happening, allowing us to make the appropriate changes to the patient's therapy. Hang in there, it really does all come together after you get through this.

HENDERSON-HASSELBALCH EQUATION

This is a device that allows us to mathematically compute the pH, based on the HCO_3^-, dissolved blood CO_2, and carbonic acid. In the following explanation, it is important to remember that small "p" stands for the negative log of a number. The official equation is as follows:

$$pH = pK + \log \frac{[HCO_3^-]}{[\text{dissolved } CO_2 \text{ gas and } H_2CO_3]}$$

However, the normal expression is written as:

$$pH = pK + \log \frac{[HCO_3^-]}{[H_2CO_3]}$$

It is understood in this simplified version, that most of the H_2CO_3 is in the form of dissolved CO_2 gas. In clinical practice, we measure the pressure exerted by dissolved CO_2 gas, allowing us to, yet once more, rewrite the equation as (capital "P" stands for the pressure of the dissolved gas):

$$pH = pK + \log \frac{[HCO_3]}{[P_{CO_2} \text{ in mm Hg or torr}]}$$

Dissolved gases are measured in mEq/L you say, and indeed, you are correct. Now we must convert mm Hg to mEq/L by multiplying mm Hg × 0.03. Speaking of revelations, pK is a constant, a number that someone arrived at, which is now unquestionably substituted for pK; the number is pK = 6.10. So now our equation is as follows:

$$pH = pK + \log \frac{[HCO_3]}{[0.03 \times P_{CO_2}]}$$

This is the practical version. Here's an example in operation:

$$pH = 6.10 + \log \frac{[24 \text{ mEq/L}]}{[0.03 \times 40 \text{ mm Hg}]}$$

$$pH = 6.10 + \log \frac{24 \text{ mEq/L}}{1.2 \text{ mEq/L}}$$

Because the 24/1.2 = 20, we now find the log of 20:

pH = 6.10 + log 20
(the log of 20 is 1.30), so:
pH = 6.10 + 1.30
pH = 7.40

And there you have it, the secrets of the H-H equation, revealed for all to see.

To use the H-H equation:

1. You need to know the patient's bicarb and P_{CO_2}.
2. Next, convert the P_{CO_2} into mEq/L, now CO_2 content, by multiplying it by 0.03.
3. Divide it into the bicarb.
4. Next, find the log of that number (from a table) and add it to 6.10.
5. The result is the pH.

MISCELLANEOUS CONSIDERATIONS

In chemistry, an *ion* is a substance that has an electrical charge. It is *not* a molecule; it *is* only one of the components molecules are made of. Ions have positive and negative charges, allowing them to combine using principles familiar to us as electro-magnetism.

In our discussions, we have considered two ions, H^+ and HCO_3^-. These easily combine with each other because of their opposite charges. A molecule of hydrogen, for example, would be composed of two H^+ ions, making it H_2.

Just for the sake of mention, there are four buffer systems that are in operation. They are:

1. Bicarb,
2. Hgb,
3. Phosphate (P_{O4}), and
4. Serum protein.

As you know, we are primarily concerned with bicarb, but Hgb does come into play when studying the oxi-hemoglobin dissociation curve, as Hgb affinity for O_2 increases as pH increases, causing the curve to shift left. Conversely, the curve shifts right as pH decreases, causing decreased Hgb affinity for O_2.

BLOOD GAS ANALYSIS

The following provides a few facts about older ABG analyzers you may need to know.

Applicable Gas Laws

Gramm's, Henry's, and Dalton's laws are applicable gas laws.

Electrodes and What They Measure

pH Electrode (Sanz Electrode)

Know about the 4M KCL (potassium chloride) salt bridge, the Ag/AgCl reference electrode, and the fact that the electrode measures $[H^+]$ (hydrogen ion concentration).

P_{CO_2} Electrode (Severinghaus Electrode)

This is actually a pH electrode and measures pH. It is called a Severinghaus electrode, named after its inventor.

P_{O_2} Electrode (Clark Electrode)

Commonly called a Clark electrode, the P_{O_2} electrode consists of a platinum cathode and an Ag/AgCl anode. It actually measures P_{O_2}. You will see the Clark electrode used again in polarographic O_2 analyzers.

HCO₃⁻ and Sao₂

These are calculated values, which are derived by the machine, based upon the previously mentioned data. The only way to get a *measured* Sa_{O_2} is to run the blood sample through a CO-oximeter, which will provide you with the amount (%) of O_2 on the Hgb along with the CO and Hgb.

BLOOD GAS INTERPRETATION NOTES AND CAVEATS

Suspected Carbon Monoxide Poisoning/Smoke Inhalation

If you are questioned about the status of firemen who have come to the ER and have *normal ABGs*, remember that Pa_{O_2} will be analyzed as normal with CO poisoning, giving you a normal Sa_{O_2}. You must run the sample through a CO-oximeter to get the CO level and true Sa_{O_2}. CO has a higher affinity for Hgb than does O_2; the ABGs will show high P_{O_2}s with CO poisoning, and the calculated Sa_{O_2} will be 100%. Treatment for CO poisoning is to administer 100% O_2 via mask or ventilator, depending on the patient's needs.

High P_{CO_2}s

With vent patients, these are treated by increasing the $\dot{V}_E$ (usually you increase the rate, sometimes the $\dot{V}_T$). This causes CO_2 to be blown off, just like hyperventilation.

Low P_{CO_2}s

Patients on vents are treated by decreasing the $\dot{V}_E$, usually the rate, allowing CO_2 to build up.

pH

In both cases, the pH will change, too. Increased $\dot{V}_E$ = Increased pH; Decreased $\dot{V}_E$ = Decreased pH. Your goal, always, is to get the pH in the normal range—that will be the *patient's* normal, even if the P_{CO_2} is still high. Normal pH = Compensation! So, your goal is to get the pH between 7.35 and 7.45. Watch the pH, that's your primary indicator!

9

A Review of the Oxi-Hemoglobin Dissociation Curve and O_2 Transport Considerations

Before we become involved in this topic, let's take a moment to list the factors that cause shifts in the curve, thereby causing a change in the Hgb's affinity for O_2. Use the curve in Figure 9–1 for a graphic representation of this section.

CURVE SHIFTED LEFT, CAUSING INCREASED AFFINITY

Causes of this are

1. Decreased Pa_{CO_2};
2. Decreased $[H^+]$ - (increased pH);
3. Decreased body temperature;
4. Decreased 2,3-DPG;
5. Increased carbon monoxide (CO)—changes curve shape; and
6. Presence of fetal or met Hgb—also changes shape of the curve.

CURVE SHIFTED RIGHT, CAUSING DECREASED AFFINITY

Causes of this are

1. Increased Pa_{CO_2};
2. Increased $[H+]$ - (decreased pH);
3. Increased body temperature; and
4. Increased 2,3-DPG.

Now that we have listed what affects the Hgb's affinity for O_2 and what happens to the curve, let's consider the impact of each factor.

Hgb

One molecule of Hgb has four Fe^{++} (Fe = iron, Fe^{++} = ferrous iron) and can therefore carry four O_2 molecules (O_2 has a $--$ charge) per molecule of Hgb. When Hgb is bound with O_2, it is called oxi-hemoglobin. When Hgb is unbound, having neither CO or O_2, it is known as reduced Hgb. CO_2 bonds with globin molecules, not heme, leading to the Bore effect, which is that when CO_2 content increases, the heme molecules' affinity for O_2 decreases. Conversely, as the Pa_{O_2} increases, CO_2's affinity for Hgb is decreased; this condition is known as the Haldane effect. CO_2 has 200 to 300 times more affinity for Hgb than does O_2 and diffuses across the alveolar–capillary membrane 19 times faster than does O_2. Met Hgb doesn't carry O_2, is abnormal, and is Fe^{+++} (ferric). Normal Hgb = $\geq$ 12 gm/dl; anemia exists at $\leq$ 10 gm/dl, while polycythemia = >17 gm/dl.

2,3-DPG

The whole name is 2,3-diphosphoglycerate; it's an enzyme that enhances the dissociation of O_2 from Hgb by competing with O_2 for the iron-binding site. Lowered levels of 2,3-DPG will, therefore, produce increased Hgb affinity for O_2, which has the effect of shifting the curve to the left; higher levels will shift the curve right.

Pa_{CO_2}

As Pa_{O_2} increases, CO_2's affinity for Hgb is decreased, and vice versa. CO_2 is a waste product produced by the tis-

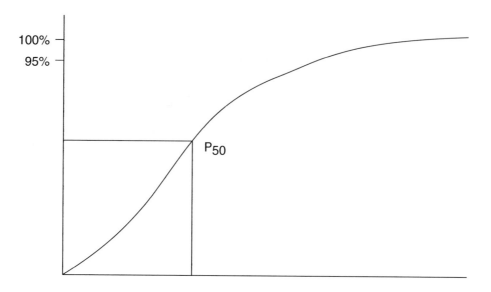

Figure 9–1. Oxi-hemoglobin Dissociation Curve

---

sues. It is carried by red blood cells (RBCs) in a dissolved state in the blood. Twenty percent is carried bound to Hgb, known as carbamino-hemoglobin.

P_{50}

The Pao_2 at which a patient's Hgb is 50% saturated; normal is PaO_2 = 27 torr = 50% Sao_2. Increased affinity = decreased P_{50}.

HCO_3^- Mechanism

$HCO_3^- + H_2O = H_2CO_3 \longrightarrow H^+ + HCO_3$ which is carried in the RBCs as HCO_3^- and H_2CO_3 in the plasma. If HCO_3^- is used, that is, goes out of the RBC, it is replaced by Cl^-. This is known as the chloride shift.

KNOW THE FACTORS

Know the factors that shift the curve left and right. Don't worry about the "whys," just that it happens and under what circumstances because the *test* won't dwell on the details of chemistry. Be able to look at an ABG result and know which way the curve shifts based on the pH, i.e., 7.51; P_{CO_2}, 32; P_{O_2}, 60; HCO_3, 28; and Sa_{O_2}, 96%. Note that with a pH of 7.40 and P_{O_2} of 60, the S_aO_2 should be 90%; but, with the increased affinity that Hgb has for O_2 in an alkaline environment, a *left shift* in the curve occurs so that the Hgb is really 96% saturated.

Conversely, if your results are 7.30, 62, 60, 22, 85%, you should recognize that the curve has *shifted right* because of increased acidity and the Hgb now has less affinity for O_2.

10

Pathogenic Organisms and Respiratory Care

Pathogenic organisms, or disease-causing organisms, are a constant threat to patients with respiratory disease or those patients who are compromised because of tracheostomy tubes, the need for mechanical ventilation, or a variety of other conditions, some of which require surgical intervention. The goal here is to provide thumbnail sketches of some of the more common organisms we encounter in the clinical environment. All microorganisms are potentially dangerous if introduced into a patient's lower respiratory tract. Here we shall limit our exploration of this topic to a few of the more common pathogenic organisms and the various techniques RCPs can use to exterminate them.

First, if the RCP suspects that an infection exists, he or she must determine that this is, in fact, true. The RCP must then determine precisely what organism is causing the infection, where the infection is, and what medications, specifically antibiotics, can be used to combat the infection.

DIAGNOSTIC TOOLS, TECHNIQUES, AND INDICATORS OF PULMONARY INFECTION

We have several diagnostic tools available that can help us isolate the offending pathogen, determine the extent of the infection, and develop a course of treatment. They are

1. Auscultation: This can reveal any areas in the lungs that may have excessive secretions or are decreased, indicating atelectasis or pneumonia.
2. Body Temperature: An increase may be indicative of an infection somewhere in the body.
3. Productive Cough: If the product is colored other than white and/or has an odor, this could indicate a pulmonary infection. Refer to section on sputum characteristics.
4. Increase or change in pulmonary secretions, over the patient's norm, may indicate an infection.
5. Increased heart and respiratory rates may indicate an infection or atelectasis.
6. Laboratory Testing:
   a. Complete blood count (CBC): The WBC may be indicative of a developing infection (> 10,000).
   b. Sputum Culture (C&S): By obtaining a sputum culture, we can isolate, analyze, and grow a colony of the particular offending organism. From this culture, we can do several tests to isolate the organism and determine its sensitivity to various antibiotics. They are included in the following:
      1. Gram Stain [Gram (+) and (–), or purple and pink, respectively];
      2. Culture (grows colony to use in sensitivity tests);
      3. Sensitivity (to assorted antibiotics);
      4. Acid–fast bacillus stain (AFB) (reveals the presence of *Mycobacterium tuberculosis*).
   c. CXR: This may reveal the precise location, nature, and extent of a pulmonary infection.

SOME THOUGHTS REGARDING THE TREATMENT OF RESPIRATORY INFECTIONS

Aggressive pulmonary toilet in conjunction with antibiotic therapy is indicated for most pulmonary infections. The traditional routes of administration for antibiotics are orally (PO), intramuscularly (IM), or intravenously (IV); but antibiotics also can be aerosolized. This option enables us to apply the medication directly to the affected area while minimizing any systemic side effects of the drug, but is also less effective than the other routes. Because there are different types of pulmonary infections, treatment depends upon the nature of the particular infection.

The treatment of respiratory infections varies depending upon the specific nature of the pathology. Aerosol therapy (AT), IPPB, CPT, and postural drainage (PD) are modalities that can be useful, even dramatically effective, depending on the nature of the disease. In addition to deciding on the proper treatment modalities, the RCP must take other steps to maximize the potential for successful treatment of the infection.

Some considerations, in addition to those mentioned previously, that may be useful in the treatment of respiratory infections are

1. Adequate humidification of the broncho-pulmonary tree via cold steam, Babbington, or ultrasonic nebulizers is useful in treating infiltrates and consolidated areas of the lungs.
2. Aerosolized antibiotics are given via small volume nebulizers (SVNs).
3. Administer mucolytics via SVN or direct instillation, PRN for copious secretions.
4. Frequently hyperinflate tubed or trached patients via manual resuscitator bag of ventilator sighs between scheduled treatments, followed by suctioning.
5. Incentive spirometry q1 – q2° is used to re-inflate the alveoli.
6. CPT and PD using positions that focus specifically on the affected area(s) of the lung.
7. Ensure proper patient hydration via oral fluid intake, if feasible.
8. Attempt to ensure adequate patient hydration via IVs, "G," "J"' or NG tubes if the oral route is impractical.
9. Use proper infection control techniques when handling equipment to prevent nosocomial infections (hospital acquired infections). Change equipment qod.
10. Use universal and/or appropriate infectious disease precautions to prevent nosocomial infections in other patients, staff, or yourself.
11. Special care should be taken with immunosuppressed patients.
12. The most common infections in a hospital are nosocomial infections. Proper hand washing is the single most effective way to prevent these infections.

Please be aware that bacteria are becoming harder to kill, especially those found in the clinical setting, so hit them hard, fast, and be careful in the process. Take no prisoners!

THE SECRETS OF SPUTUM AND SOME ORGANISMS THAT MAY LURK WITHIN

Specific insight can be gained from observing the particular characteristics of the sputum produced by your patient. Allow me to provide you with some highlights regarding this emotionally stimulating and exciting subject.

TYPES, CHARACTERISTICS, AND DISEASE

Mucoid: Sputum may appear clear and thin to frothy in consistency and may be seen with asthma, cystic fibrosis, mycoplasma pneumonia, pulmonary edema, TB, and viral pneumonia.

Frothy Pink or Pink: This type of sputum is commonly observed with well progressed pulmonary edema.

Blood Streaked: This may be seen with pneumococcal or staphylococcal pneumonias.

Prune Juice: This presents with an offensive odor and dark brown color, and may be mucopurulent in its general characteristics. This may appear with pneumococcal or Klebsiella pneumonias.

GROSS BLOOD

Hemoptysis: (The definition is "to cough up blood.") Bright red, frothy blood accompanies this and is usually seen with cancer, trauma, bronchiectasis, and TB.

Currant Jelly: Blood clots appear, which are darker than frank blood. This is commonly seen with Klebsiella and cancer.

Rust Color: Sputum is mucopurulent with a tinge of red and may appear with bronchiectasis, cancer, and pneumococcal pneumonia.

Purulent: Secretions are thick, yellow, and viscid with an offensive odor due to pus being a component. They usually appear with an abscess, chronic bronchitis, cystic fibrosis, various bacterial pneumonias, and TB.

Mucopurulent: Secretions are yellow to green and have the characteristics of both mucoid and purulent secretions. They appear in cystic fibrosis, chronic bronchitis, pseudomonas pneumonia, and, at times, TB.

Of course, more can be said about the intimate details of sputum, but it is this sort of thumbnail information that will be presented in an exam. If you are familiar with the type, characteristics, and related diseases regarding sputum, you will be able to properly evaluate the questions you encounter.

In terms of the real world, it is always important to observe and note the characteristics of the sputum produced, specifically the color, amount, and consistency. Sputum often will give advanced warning of the impending onset of a potentially serious, infectious pathology, the effect of which may be minimized with prompt treatment. The essentials of treatment of these pathologies center on the use of antibiotics and aggressive pulmonary toilet, such as AT ISB, and CPT with postural drainage in conjunction with humidity and oxygen therapies.

To round out your knowledge regarding patient assessment, read the next section on breath sounds and chest examination in general. These topics are always used in conjunction with the topics of basic vital signs, temperature, blood pressure, pulse, and respiratory rate. That information, along with the RCP's chest/lung evaluation, will help complete the picture when the possibility of a pulmonary pathology exists.

11

Algebra, Respiratory Care, and You

We all hate it, but there it is—that indispensable tool that we need to carry out our duty to humanity. First we shall look at calculating cylinder duration, then move on to physiologic formulas. I am aware that you have heard all of this before, but you will run across these formulas on the exam, so we will review them again.

CYLINDER DURATION

You need to remember only two tank factors, "E" and "H." These are the sizes we commonly use.

E cylinder tank factor = 0.28, but 0.3 will work.
H cylinder tank factor = 3.14, but 3.0 will work.
Just remember 0.3 and 3.0!!

$$\frac{\text{Duration}}{\text{(Time)}} = \frac{\text{gauge pressure (psi)} \times \text{Tank Factor}}{\text{Tank's Flow Rate}} = \text{Time in min}$$

Example: How long will an E cylinder with 1800 psi last while running at 8 L/min?

$$T = \frac{1800 \text{ psi} \times 0.28}{8 \text{ L/min}} = \frac{504}{8} = 63 \text{ min (answers are in min)}$$

Example: How long will an H cylinder with 1600 psi last running at 6 L/min?

$$T = \frac{1600 \text{ psi} \times 3.14}{6 \text{ L/min}} = \frac{5024}{6} = \frac{837.33 \text{ min}}{60 \text{ min/hour}} = 13.96 \text{ hours}$$

At least one of these will be on your exam.

ALVEOLAR AIR EQUATION

Remember that P_B = barometric pressure in torr; if none is given, use 760 torr. P_{H_2O} = water vapor pressure which is 47 torr.

Example: What is alveolar P_{O_2} when Pa_{CO_2} = 40 torr and FI_{O_2} = .21?

$$\begin{aligned}
P_{AO_2} &= (P_B - P_{H_2O}) FI_{O_2} - [1.25 \times Pa_{CO_2}] \\
&= (760 \text{ torr} - 47) .21 - [1.25 \times 40 \text{ torr}] \\
&= (713) .21 - [50] \\
&= 149.73 - 50 \\
&= 99.73 \text{ torr or } 100 \text{ torr}
\end{aligned}$$

O_2 CONTENT FORMULA

This is the formula used to calculate the O_2 content of arterial or venous blood. If you subtract venous content from arterial content, you get an idea of what the patient's O_2 consumption may be. Content is measured in volumes %.

Example: Hgb = 15 g, Pa_{O_2} = 80 torr, Sa_{O_2} = 98%

$$\begin{aligned}
Ca_{O_2} &= 0.003 (Pa_{O_2}) + (1.34 \times \text{Hgb} \times Sa_{O_2}) \\
&= (0.003 \times 80 \text{ torr}) + (1.34 \times 15 \times 0.98) \\
&= 0.24 + 19.70 \\
&= 19.94 \text{ vol \% or } 20 \text{ vol \% (normal value)}
\end{aligned}$$

Example: Hgb = 15, Pv_{O_2} = 50 torr, Sv_{O_2} = 75% (same patient)

$$\begin{aligned}
Cv_{O_2} &= (0.003 \times 50 \text{ torr}) + (1.34 \times 15 \times .75) \\
&= 0.15 + 15.08 \\
&= 15.23 \text{ vol \% or } 15.0 \text{ vol \% (normal value)}
\end{aligned}$$

A–V DIFFERENCE

The logical follow up to the last two calculations is to calculate the arterial–venous content difference, which will tell us how much O_2 has been consumed by the patient.

$$\begin{aligned}
C(a-v)O_2 &= Ca_{O_2} - Cv_{O_2} \\
&= 20 \text{ vol \%} - 15 \text{ vol \%} = 5 \text{ vol \% (normal value)}
\end{aligned}$$

 A-a GRADIENT

This is the gradient that exists between alveolar and arterial P_{O_2}s.

Example: P_{AO_2} = 100 torr, P_{aO_2} = 90 torr

$D(A-a)O_2 = P_{AO_2} - P_{aO_2}$
= 100 torr − 90 torr
= 10 torr (< 10 torr on room air = normal value)
(< 100 is normal on 100%)

A/A RATIO

a/A Ratio = P_{aO_2} / P_{AO_2}
= 80 torr / 100 torr = 0.8 (0.8 = respiratory quotient) at any F_iO_2

These formulas should be committed to memory, especially the alveolar air equation, content formulas, and A-V difference. It is likely that these will show up on your exam.

< 0.6
V/Q mismatch responds to O_2 therapy

< 0.15
Refractory hypoxemia

anything between .6 – .15 will respond to O_2

$$FiO_2 \text{ needed} = \frac{(PaO_2 \div a/A \text{ ratio}) + PaCO_2}{P_B - 47}$$

% Shunt — Tells the % of how much blood is being shunted by cardiac output

$$\frac{Qs}{Qt} = \frac{CcO_2 - CaO_2}{CcO_2 - C\bar{v}O_2}$$

$\frac{A-aDO_2}{20 \text{ vol \%}}$ = % Shunt
↑ normal of O_2 content
if not given use 20

Anything ↑ 30% requires aggressive cardiac
↳ ECMO

20-30% — means vent. failure

12

Examining the Chest and Assessing the Patient's Respiratory Status

Many times physicians rely on the staff who are "on the scene" to supply them with invaluable information regarding a patient's status. To do this effectively, the RCPs, as specialists, must be thorough in their patient evaluations. All of the facts must be considered in this evaluation, both objective and subjective.

The evaluation of the chest encompasses both objective, or observed, evaluation and subjective, or opinionated, evaluation. The most efficient way to form an overall conclusion is to begin with those facts that can be observed. These include the color of sputum, a patient's breathing pattern, vital signs, lab and radiograph results, and factors regarding observed characteristics of the chest. Once this information is gathered, the RCP can percuss and auscultate the chest to accumulate more data upon which to base a conclusion. Auscultation and percussion are a bit more subjective than direct observation and, therefore, should be done after the objective data are gathered. Let's consider the chest examination procedure. There are four general areas—inspection, palpitation, percussion, and auscultation.

INSPECTION

Face

Check the patient's expression. Does it appear stressed or relaxed? Check for nasal flaring; if present, dyspnea is likely. Check if the patient has pursed lip breathing, an additional sign of dyspnea.

Body Position

Check posture and weight. Obesity can be a hint that OSA may be a factor and in itself may cause dyspnea. Poor posture also may promote dyspnea; any upward pressure on the diaphragm may cause dyspnea because the excursion of this muscle can be inhibited.

Neck

Check the position of the trachea from midline. A shift in tracheal position may indicate a pneumothorax or severe atelectasis or consolidation. Check distention of the jugular veins, which could signal cardiopulmonary stress or impending or current heart failure.

Shape of Chest

Check for deformities such as the following: pectus carinatum (pigeon chest), pectus excavatum (funnel chest), barrel chest, kyphoscoliosis, or any remarkable musculature or scars. Check for symmetry during respiration. If chest appears asymmetric, various conditions may exist such as pneumothorax, flail chest, and splinting due to pain. Asymmetric expansion due to major consolidation is also possible.

Breathing Pattern

Check the excursion of the chest and abdomen. Check for use of accessory muscles and sternal retractions. Check breathing rate; is tachypnea or bradypnea present? Check the inspiratory:expiratory (I:E) ratio (normal is 1 to 1.5:2). Finally, check the rhythm; look for normal, regular breathing (eupnea) as opposed to Cheyne–Stokes, Biot's, or other irregular breathing patterns (Figure 12–1). Normal diaphragmatic excursion is 1 to 3 cm. Diaphragmatic excursion greater than 3 cm may indicate hyperventilation and less than 1 cm may indicate hypoventilation.

The RCP should note the type of breathing pattern exhibited by the patient during the evaluation. The RCP should be

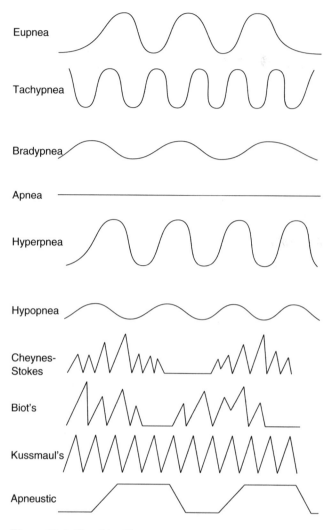

Figure 12–1 Breathing Patterns

familiar enough with the various breathing patterns to use routinely to describe a patient's status. The three terms listed in the following are more states of breathing than patterns. Please refer to Figure 12–1 for graphic depictions of the various patterns.

Eupnea: Normal breathing—12 to 18 breaths/min at normal tidal volumes.

Orthopnea: A patient's need to sit upright to breathe. Dyspnea increases as the patient's head is lowered.

Dyspnea: General difficulty in breathing.

Skin and Digits

Check the color of the skin overall and mucous membranes in particular for signs of cyanosis; mucous membranes are a healthy pink color in the normal circumstance. Check the nail beds, by squeezing, for proper capillary refill and normal pink color. Check the fingers for signs of clubbing and/or tremors.

Palpitation

This is the fine art of using your sense of touch to evaluate the chest. Check the position of the trachea relative to midline. Check chest and diaphragm excursion ($\approx$ 3 cm). Check for tenderness. Check for skin turgor, diaphoresis, and sub Q emphysema. Check tactile and vocal fremitis—have patient repeat "99" in a normal voice; these vibrations will be transmitted to the RCP's hand as it rests on the chest wall. A decrease in vibrations indicates the presence of air, fluid, or tissue. An increase in vibrations indicates consolidation.

Percussion

These will be presented as note, an example, and the pathology to which it relates. Resonance = normal lungs. Dull (normally heard over the heart and liver) = consolidation, atelectasis, tissue, or fluid, such as pleural effusion or pulmonary edema. Flat (large muscle-like thigh) = severe atelectasis, pleural effusion, or pneumonectomy. Hyperresonance (abdomen) = acute asthma, emphysema, or pneumothorax. Tympany (large gastric bubble) = large pneumothorax.

Auscultation

This is the one you all have been waiting for—breath sounds. Before we talk about the sounds, let's review some of the more commonly used nomenclature. The common terms are

- BS = breath sounds;
- BBS = bilateral breath sounds;
- CTA = clear to auscultation;
- Rales = crackles; and
- Rhonchi = rumbles (coarse wheezes).

Normal Breath Sounds (By Type and Description)

Vesicular BS are the normal sounds heard over most areas of the lungs, having a 3:1 I:E ratio. Bronchovesicular BS, the sounds heard over the carina, have a 1:1 I:E ratio. These are heard in the larger airways. Bronchial BS, the sounds heard over the manubrium, have a 2:3 I:E ratio. Tracheal BS are the normal sounds heard over the trachea.

Abnormal Breath Sounds

A to E Egophony

While listening to the patient's chest, have the patient say the letter "E." The normal sound you should hear is the letter

"A." If the sound is the letter "E," the fluid is in that area of the lung, because fluid transmits sound far better than air.

Complete Absence of BS in an Area

This is a large pneumothorax, a serious consolidation, or a hemothorax.

Decreased BS

These can be expected in cases of restrictive or obstructive disease. Additionally, BS may be decreased in areas of a pneumothorax, fluid accumulation, and increased tissue density, such as occurs with fibrosis or cancer. Obesity also may cause decreased or diminished breath sounds because of adipose tissue density.

Increased BS

That's right, I said increased, which may occur in cases of consolidation, like pneumonia, atelectasis, and fibrosis. These types of pathologies increase sound transmission. Increased BS usually progresses from vesicular to bronchial as the condition's severity progresses.

Wheezes

These are distinctive, high pitched sounds made as air passes through spasmodic small airways, having an almost musical quality. These can occur during the inspiratory and/or expiratory phases and usually are caused by bronchospasm. The wheeze is a common characteristic of asthma, chronic obstructive pulmonary disease (COPD), and other diseases that have reactive small airways associated with them.

Rales (Crackles)

These are commonly associated with atelectasis, pulmonary edema, congestive heart failure, COPD, pneumonias, and/or any pathology causing an accumulation of fluid in the lungs. Rales are best illustrated by the sound Velcro makes as it separates, reflecting the airways popping open on inspiration.

Rhonchi (Rumbles)

These are usually noted when accumulated fluid is present in larger airways. The rumbling nature of the sound also can be described as a low pitched, coarse wheeze generated as air passes over the secretions during *inspiration* and/or *expiration*. Rhonchi may begin to appear as a consolidation begins to break up or as a severe case of bronchospasm begins to relax, releasing trapped secretions. Rhonchi frequently clear with coughing because the secretions are expelled during a cough. Some pathologies associated with rhonchi are asthma, COPD, pulmonary edema, bronchitis, pneumonias, and cancer.

Part II: Oxygen Therapy

- Flow Regulators and Flowmeters
- Oxygen Delivery Systems
- Aerosol Generators and Humidity
- Equipment Cleaning and Sterilization Review
- Government Regulations and Bulk Oxygen Systems

13

Flow Regulators and Flowmeters

FLOW REGULATORS

Flow regulation devices come in a variety of forms to allow us to do different jobs. These devices can be indexed to cylinders, quick-connect outlets, or free-standing equipment. A regulator is a combination of pressure reduction and regulation device, while indicating and controlling flow rate. A flowmeter is just that—a flow-indicating and controlling device that is attached to a regulated pressure source. Regulators have two components with different functions. Flow meters serve one function.

Regulators have (1) pressure-reducing valve(s) and (2) a flowmeter. The reducing valve(s) reduces pressure from a higher pressure gas source to 50 psi, whereas the flowmeter controls and indicates gas flow after the pressure has been reduced to 50 psi. The more reducing valves, called stages, a regulator has, the more control over pressure it allows. Reducing valves are available in two types (1) preset (Figure 13–1) and (2) adjustable (Figure 13–2).

Single stage regulators reduce pressure from 2,250 psi to 50 psi in one step. Two stage regulators go from 2,250 psi, to ~ 700 psi, to 50 psi.

Multi-stage regulators reduce pressure in various multiples. In medicine, all regulators for standard respiratory therapy (RT) equipment end with a pressure of 50–55 psi.

Standardized Connections

Various gas sources use different standardized connecting devices to attach regulators and flowmeters.

- DISS: Diameter Index Safety System is used primarily on low pressure devices.
- PISS: Pin Index Safety System is used to ensure that the appropriate regulators are used on high pressure cylinders of size "E" and smaller.
- ASSS: American Standard Safety System ensures proper regulation of high pressure of gases from "H," "K," and "M" cylinders.

Additionally, there is a plethora of quick-connect devices that simply snap together or plug into the wall outlets found in many institutions. Don't worry too much about the specific names or what each one looks like; worry about name recognition and what I am about to tell you. If you are asked what to do if you unplug a Shrader QC device from the wall and high pressure gas rushes from the wall outlet, you must know that the correct answer is to reinsert the adapter back into the outlet from which you removed it. Do *not* call maintenance, hide under a bed, or anything else. PUT IT BACK WHERE YOU GOT IT!

Know the PISS pin combinations for O_2, CO_2, and medical air. Know that all regulators have an ambient (room pressure) side with an equalization port (simply a hole) and a high pressure side. If that diaphragm ruptures, high pressure gas will escape from the equalization port. Another little tip is that, before you put the regulator on the tank, you should crack the valve on the tank for a split second to blow out the dust and then attach the regulator.

FLOWMETERS

The topic of flowmeters will appear on any comprehensive respiratory test and will require the testee to have a good working knowledge of the equipment, just as is the case with regulators. Keep in mind that you will be tested by the entry-level exam, which is technical in nature.

So, a flowmeter's function is to control and indicate gas flow. You will be tested on the following three primary types of flowmeters:

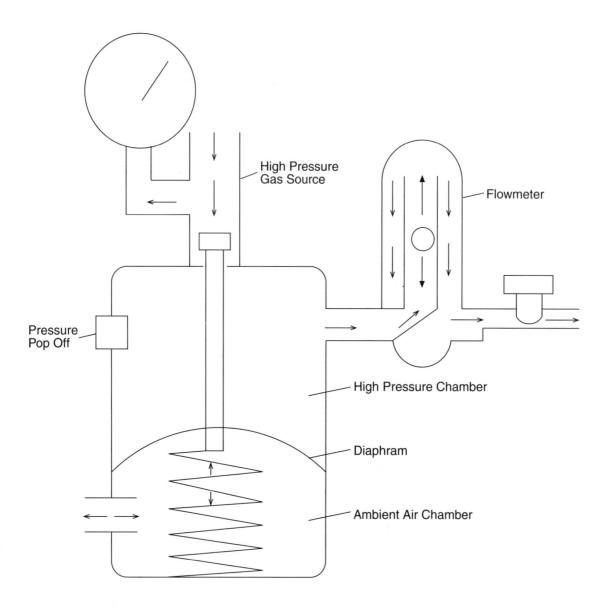

Figure 13–1 Preset Regulator

1. Pressure compensated flowmeter (Figure 13–3).
2. Uncompensated flowmeter (Figure 13–4; both pressure compensated and uncompensated flowmeters are known as Thorpe tubes); and
3. Bourdon gauge, which is mechanically the same as a tank pressure gauge (Figure 13–5).

The pressure compensated and uncompensated Thorpe tubes have a *variable orifice*, whereas the Bourdon gauge

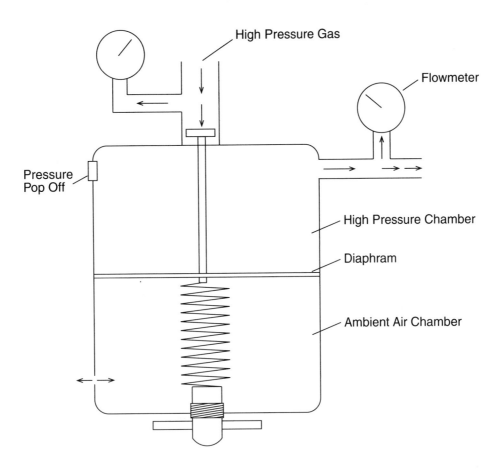

Figure 13–2 Adjustable Regulator

has a *fixed orifice* (Figure 13–5) through which the gas flows. What does this mean? Well, it means that as you turn the flow control (knob) on a Thorpe tube (compensated or not), the size of the hole that the gas comes out of changes. On the Bourdon gauge, the size of this hole always remains the same. This is one of those facts that someday may help you solve a problem, so you should store it in your data bank.

Thorpe Tubes: Facts You Must Remember!

The compensated types are calibrated for a specific gas, O_2, He_2, etc. at 760 torr (usually this is sea level). A compensated flowmeter will say it is calibrated to 50 psi; uncompensated will not be calibrated to 50 psi and therefore will have no label to this effect. You must use an oxygen flowmeter

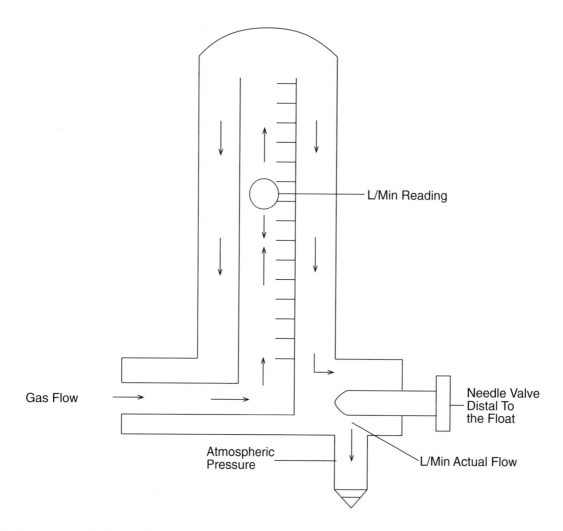

Figure 13–3 Compensated Thorpe Tube

with oxygen, and air with air, etc. Both have a variable orifice.

Uncompensated Flowmeter

The needle valve (flow control) comes before, or upstream, of the calibrated meter. If any back pressure is applied to the gas flow, the gauge will read low, resulting in a higher gas flow to the patient than what is indicated on the meter.

Compensated Flowmeter

The needle valve is located after (downstream) the calibrated meter, causing the meter to read accurately when back pressure is applied.

If the flowmeter you have in your hand is unmarked regarding its pressure compensation status, here's how you figure it out.

1. Take the flowmeter to a 50 psi outlet.
2. Plug it in.

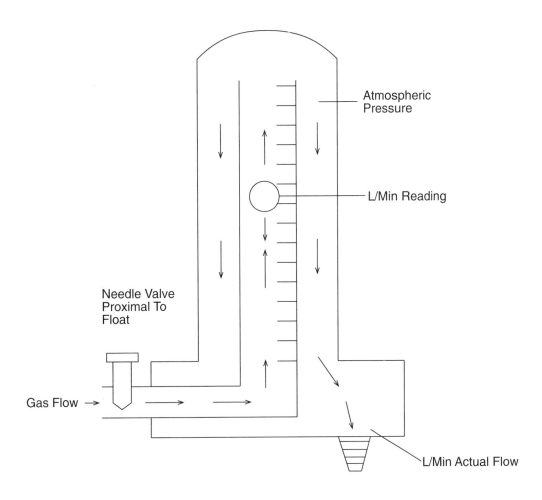

Figure 13–4 Uncompensated Thorpe Tube

3. If the flowmeter is compensated, the ball will jump slightly when you plug the device into the outlet and return to "0."
4. If the flowmeter is *uncompensated, the ball will not jump at all*.

If this test is not possible, you must take the flowmeter apart to discern the location of the needle valve.

Bourdon Gauge

This gauge is, in reality, a pressure gauge on which the calibration reflects flow in relation to the pressure the gauge senses. This type of gauge will still indicate flow when the flow is totally obstructed, because pressure still exists at the gauge's sensor. When back pressure is applied, these devices will read high, with the actual flow to the patient being lower

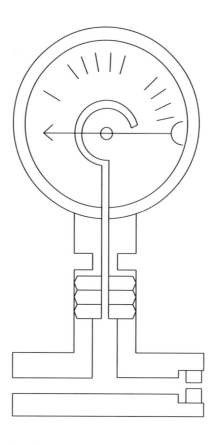

Figure 13–5 Bourdon Gauge

than that indicated by the gauge; therefore, this gauge *is not* back pressure compensated. Unlike Thorpe tubes, Bourdon gauges are not position-dependent for accurate readings and are better during transporting of patients because they can indicate flow, even when turned upside down. If you turn a Thorpe tube upside down, the ball will fall to the top of the gauge. Many "E" cylinder regulators use the Bourdon gauge to indicate flow; if possible, use one of these when accompanying a patient who is being transported.

Know the difference between compensated and uncompensated Thorpe tubes, and be able to identify diagrams of all flowmeters.

14

Oxygen Delivery Systems

Oxygen delivery systems vary widely in type and effect. There are two basic classes of delivery systems used in medicine today. The first consists of *low flow devices*. These devices vary in their performances because they supply the patient with supplemental oxygen, which is mixed with room air as the patient inspires. The actual F_{IO_2} the patient receives varies, because a fixed amount of O_2 combines with varying amounts of room air as the patient's minute volume changes. The second class consists of *high flow devices*. These devices provide patients with their total inspiratory gas requirements, premixed with the appropriate amounts of oxygen and room air. These are important definitions to remember. In a nutshell, a low flow system provides variable, supplemental F_{IO_2}s, whereas high flow systems provide a constant F_{IO_2} at flow rates high enough to meet the patient's inspiratory demands.

Some other useful terms are F_{IO_2}, which means fraction of inspired oxygen, with room air F_{IO_2} being 0.21; P_{AO_2}, which means partial pressure of alveolar oxygen; and P_{aO_2} which indicates the partial pressure of oxygen in the arterial blood. The big "A" indicates alveolar, whereas the small "a" indicates arterial. *These symbols are not interchangeable!*

LOW FLOW DEVICES

Let's discuss low flow devices. Low flow oxygen devices increase the patient's inspired F_{IO_2} by facilitating the entrainment of O_2. The naso and oropharynx are used as physiologic reservoirs from which the oxygen is entrained into the inspiratory gas stream, and thus inspired.

Nasal Cannulae

There are two major advantages to using this type of device. One is patient comfort and the other is the easy delivery of low F_{IO_2}s.

A few points to remember about nasal cannulae follow:

1. Deliver flow rates of < 1 up to a maximum of 6 L/min.
2. F_{IO_2}s range from ≈ .24 to .44. This varies as the patient's minute volume increases (↓ F_{IO_2} at a constant flow rate) or decreases (↑ F_{IO_2} at a constant flow rate).
3. Humidify a nasal cannula at 4 liters per minute (lpm) and up to maximize patient comfort. The dry gas may dry the mucous membranes of the nasal passages.
4. Nasal cannulas are contraindicated with nasal polyps and nasal drainage.

Simple Mask

Simple masks are used to deliver mid-range F_{IO_2}s relatively effectively. The F_{IO_2}s delivered by simple masks depend on the patient's inspiratory demands, just like a nasal cannula.

Some points of interest follow:

1. Use a simple mask with flow rates of 6–10 L/min.
2. F_{IO_2}s can range between ≈.40 and .60.
3. Never use a simple mask with flow rates under 6 L/min, because CO_2 will not be flushed from mask and may be rebreathed by the patient.
4. The holes in the sides of the mask allow air entrainment and should not be blocked under any circumstances.*
5. All masks can cause pressure necrosis at the site of the seal.*
6. A nasal cannula is needed during the patient's meals to facilitate eating.*
7. Any masks can trap secretions.*

---

*applies to all masks.

Partial Rebreather Mask

These masks are designed to deliver mid to high-range F_{IO_2}s.

1. Use with flow rates of 8–15 L/min.
2. F_{IO_2}s range from ≈ 0.5 to 0.7, or even 0.8, depending on the patient's inspiratory demand.
3. Set the flow rate high enough to keep bag inflated at least one third full.

Non-Rebreather Mask

This is the big boy, sorry, the big person on the block. When you need to deliver as much oxygen as you can, in a hurry, this is the mask to reach for first.

Use flow rates of ≥ 12L/min up to the flush setting to keep bag inflated and achieve F_{IO_2}s of 0.8 to 1.0.

Use the following rule of thumb for O_2 concentrations (know when to switch devices!):

Nasal cannula: 24%–40% Use with lower $\dot{V}_E$.
Simple mask: 40%–60% Use with low to moderate $\dot{V}_E$.
Partial rebreather: 50%–80% Use with low to moderate $\dot{V}_E$.
Non-rebreather: 80%–100% Use with low to high $\dot{V}_E$.

Nasal cannulas are variable devices at best, as we have noted, but here is a rule of thumb for O_2 concentrations. The following approximate concentrations apply when used on patients with average or slightly increased $\dot{V}_E$s: 1 lpm = 24%, 2 lpm = 28%, 3 lpm = 32%, 4 lpm = 36%, 5 lpm = 40%, and 6 lpm = 44%.

One last note on low flow devices—do not use a bubble humidifier with O_2 delivery systems running at flow rates higher than 6 or 8 lpm, because these higher flow rates will cause the humidifier's 4 psi pop-off to activate. These humidifiers provide little additional humidity to oxygen at lower flow rates, but should be used when running a nasal cannula at 4 lpm or more to increase patient comfort and prevent mucosal dehydration.

REMEMBER THE FOLLOWING WHEN DEALING WITH ANY TYPE OF HUMIDITY

- Water pressure in the lungs = 47 torr
- Water content = 44 mg/L
- Relative Humidity = a % of absolute or how much humidity there is versus how much there could be (content/capacity)
- Body humidity—goal is 37°C at 47 torr, expressed as actual/possible at 37°C
- Body humidity deficit = possible-actual humidity
- Water is measured in two ways: (1) mm Hg or torr (pressure) or (2) mg/L (content)

HIGH FLOW DEVICES

High flow systems, as stated, provide a premixed gas source with a constant F_{IO_2} at flow rates that meet or exceed the patient's inspiratory demand. High flow systems use a venturi to entrain the necessary amount of room air into an oxygen stream, providing the desired, preset F_{IO_2}. Here's how it works. We hook a venti mask or cold steam nebulizer to a 100% O_2 source and set the flow meter, for example, to 10 L/min. We now set the venturi collar on either device to 40%.

These two actions cause the following events:

1. O_2 flows through the "jet" at 10 L/min.
2. Air is pulled into the gas stream from the room through the "entrainment ports" and mixed with the O_2.
3. At the 40% setting, three parts room air is mixed with one part 100% O_2 to yield the desired 40% F_{IO_2}. Placing air first, this gives us an air to oxygen "entrainment ratio" of 3:1.
4. The total flow at the patient is 40 L/min of gas containing 40% oxygen.

Here is a list of some commonly used F_{IO_2}s and their corresponding air:oxygen entrainment ratios.

F_{IO_2}	Entrainment Ratio/Air:Oxygen
24%	25:1
28%	10:1
30%	8:1
35%	5:1
40%	3:1
50%	1.7:1
60%	1:1
80%	1:3
100%	0:1

Once you have this information, you can use it to find the total flow of the system. Add the numbers in the ratio together and multiply them by the flow rate the flowmeter is set on. Example: What is the total flow of a 40% cold steam running at 10 L/min? We know from our handy chart that the entrainment ratio is 3:1 to get 40%. 3 + 1 = 4; 4 × 10 L/min = 40 L/min total flow.

Let's consider some of the high flow delivery devices available to us, along with supplemental humidification devices. These are off-the-shelf systems.

Venti Masks

These are high flow devices that are composed of a mask, a 6-inch length of wide-bore tubing, and a venturi. The venturi is the device that has the jet and entrainment ports incorporated into it and, therefore, mixes the gas. As the gases are mixed, flow increases dramatically through the wide-bore tubing, providing a flow to the patient higher than what he or she is breathing. Because we can control the exact F_{IO_2} and the flow is > than the patient's $\dot{V}_E$, we are assured of the F_{IO_2} we are delivering to the patient. We can be sure that a chronic CO_2 retainer is receiving only 24%! Humidification devices cannot be used with venti masks because they cause back pressure. Because of flow limitations, venti masks go from only 24% to 50%.

Cold Steam Nebulizers

F_{IO_2} ranges from 28 to 100%. These devices operate on the same principle as outlined previously, but provide particulate humidity in addition to precise F_{IO_2}s. This humidity is provided courtesy of Bernoulli (Figure 14–1), whose principle says water can be pulled through a capillary tube, broken into particles, and suspended in the gas stream for delivery to the patient. This is the preferred device for tubed patients, replacing the humidity lost because of a tracheostomy or endotracheal tube. To obtain adequate flows, use two nebulizers in tandem for F_{IO_2}s over 50%. You will have a complete indoctrination on the function of cold steam nebulizers in the following sections, but be aware that they are a high flow O_2 delivery system.

SOME THOUGHTS

Now, we're starting to get really serious, but before we get into the hairy stuff, let me take a moment to fill you in on a few more tidbits regarding the information we already have covered. You must condition yourself to use whatever information the exam question provides you with, combine it with your own knowledge, and solve the problem. In other words, be clever. You possess certain facts. Use those facts to work through the questions. None of this stuff is imported from Mars! Every one of you has used your head in clinical, don't forget. I know all of you have solved countless problems successfully and can do so on an exam.

For example, if you are asked about back pressure affecting the flow reading on a device with a fixed orifice, you know only a Bourdon gauge has such an orifice; therefore, it is not back pressure compensated because it senses back pressure, not actual flow. Take the data you are given and make it work in your favor. Always start with what you know is true. Having said this, let me just ease my own mind by adding a few more fun facts to the mix.

AIR ENTRAINMENT CONSIDERATIONS

The F_{IO_2} of any device that entrains air is affected by a number of things, such as the following:.

1. Any obstruction downstream of the entrainment ports will increase the F_{IO_2}. Why? Because an obstruction causes total flow through the tubing to decrease; if flow decreases, air entrainment decreases as well. If air entrainment decreases, less room air will mix with the oxygen, causing less dilution of the oxygen. This results in the patient getting less total flow, but what they do receive is of a higher oxygen concentration due to less air entrainment. What can cause this? Water in the tubing! Remember, water in the tubing (or anything like that) causes the patient to receive an increased F_{IO_2}.
2. Any obstruction of the entrainment ports also will cause an increased F_{IO_2} to be delivered to the patient. Things like bed sheets and blankets have been known to be laid on top of venti masks, causing the same effect as described in item 1.
3. Remember, when adding your entrainment ratios to your gas source flow rate, 1:3 for example, all components are equal. If a nebulizer is running at 10 lpm, then 30 lpm is being entrained, for a total of 40 lpm. With all entrainment devices, as total flow decreases because of downstream obstruction, F_{IO_2} increases!

HUMIDITY FUN FACT

An exam question that might plague you concerns another little physics fact that water evaporation in a bubble humidifier causes its water temperature to drop. As cold gas passes through the water, taking some of it along with it, the water temperature is reduced because of molecular loss.

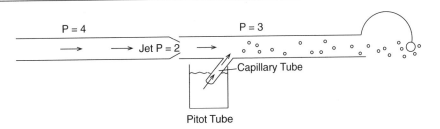

Figure 14–1 Bernoulli Principle

15

Aerosol Generators and Humidity

THINGS YOU SHOULD REMEMBER

Remember that nebulizers produce particles, and humidifiers produce molecular humidity.

Ultrasonic Nebulizers (USN)

USN is the accepted abbreviation for ultrasonic nebulizers (Figure 15–1) and, in this case, is not a reference to United States Navy or sailors. They are electrically powered nebulizers that use a piezoelectric crystal (ceramic element) to set up vibrations. When a device is said to have piezoelectric properties, it means that when an electrical current is passed through the crystal, the crystal changes shape. The shape changes (expansion and contraction) cause vibration.

These vibrations are passed through a liquid-filled (with water) chamber (couplant chamber) for amplification and are focused on the diaphragm that forms the bottom of the medicine cup, where the vibrations break the solution down into small particles. These particles (90% of them) are between 0.5 μm and 3.0 μm, which is considered to be the ideal therapeutic particle size range by most sources. Particle size is controlled by the transducer, which is preset to 1.35 megacycles.

Mist control is accomplished in two ways. Mist production, or mist density, is controlled by amplitude, which is controlled by a dial that is simply calibrated from 1 to 10 on most industrial units. The output of mist from the medicine cup is controlled by a blower, or fan, which may or may not have variable speed settings. The fan simply pushes the mist out of the medicine cup and has no part in actual mist production. If supplemental oxygen is required, it must be bled into the gas stream.

If the USN fails to make a proper mist, do the following:

1. Make sure the unit is plugged into a wall outlet, that all the connections are tight, and that the controls are set properly.
2. Check the fluid level in the med cup.
3. Check the fluid level of the couplant chamber. To do this, you must remove the med cup by unlatching it and lifting it off the unit. The water you visualize is the couplant.

To set your device properly, turn the control until you can *barely see a mist* coming out of the tube. An output of 1 to 3 ml/min is adequate to achieve a therapeutic effect. Easily seen, dense mists are inappropriate and dangerous. Maximum USN output can be 6 ml/min, and a dense USN treatment can easily cause bronchospasm, possibly severe enough to cause death. No kidding, an ultrasonic neb can make a thick London fog look like a clear, sunny day, so be careful.

Solo and Hydrosphere

These are pneumatically powered (gas-powered) devices that produce desirable aerosols that are therapeutically effective, producing particles in the therapeutic range ≈ 60% of the time. These devices run off a constant pneumatic power source, but their flow can be controlled by controlling air entrainment, much like cold steam nebulizers. Air entrainment, although possible, is only crudely accomplished by these nebulizers and should not be relied upon to deliver accurate F_{IO_2}s. These devices use the Babbington principle of operation (Figure 15–2), which shoots a gas jet though an opening in a water-coated glass sphere. Water entrainment is facilitated through the use of the Bernoulli principle.

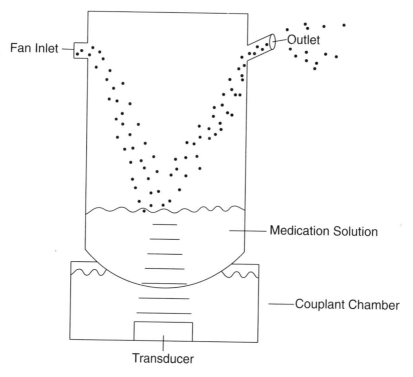

Figure 15–1 Ultrasonic Nebulizer

Once again, be careful not to generate a dense mist, because this may be dangerous. Remember the word Babbington, because these aerosol generators are commonly referred to as such; if you see "Babbington," this type of nebulizer is what they mean!

These devices, as well as USNs, are indicated in the treatment of thick, viscous secretions, like those associated with bronchiectasis and acute bronchitis, or can be used to induce sputum specimens.

Cold Steam Nebulizers (Jet Nebulizers)

These are pneumatically driven and use the Bernoulli principle as operational justification. These devices are commonly used to provide supplemental humidity and O_2, whereas the other aerosol generators have difficulty providing accurate F_{IO_2}s (Figure 15–3). These devices serve well in the role of providing additional humidity and supplemental oxygen when a patient is tubed or trached. Cold steam nebulizers produce particles in the therapeutic range ≈ 40% to 50% of the time. Particles in the 5 to 10 μm range usually rain out in the nose, whereas those ≤ 1.0 μm in diameter make it to the alveoli; once there, those particles < 0.3 μm are usually exhaled.

Cold steam nebulizers are also indicated for the first 24 hours after extubation to help prevent subglottic edema, specifically laryngeal edema. The mist will help prevent potentially dangerous edema and laryngospasm, whereas the supplemental oxygen will counter hypoxemia.

Some Notes on Particulate Humidity

All of the previously mentioned devices produce water particles (particulate humidity). There are several drawbacks to particulate (aerosolized) humidity, such as the following:

1. Particles in a dense mist can cause irritation and may lead to bronchospasm.
2. Microorganisms can hitch a ride on these particles allowing them to turn up in some of the most inconvenient places, like the lower airways or even the alveoli. I am sure that we can all agree that this is an unqualified bad thing. For this reason, it is imperative that we, as RCPs, are absolutely sure that only sterile solutions are used in any nebulizer and that the entire system is cleaned and changed according to strict infection control policy, which usually requires a complete system change every 48 hours.
3. Over-hydration may occur and cause dried secretions to swell. This may, in extreme cases, lead to mucous plugging on a grand scale and could be life threatening.

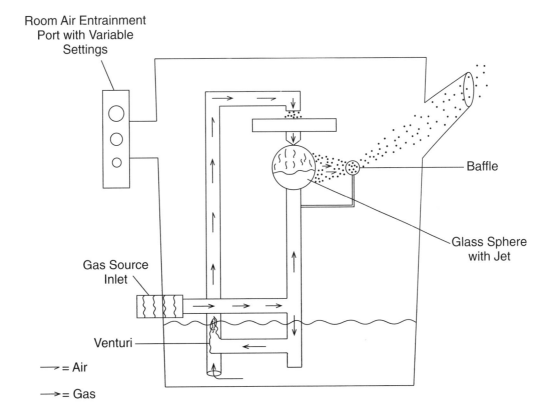

Figure 15–2 Babbington Nebulizer

4. At higher oxygen concentrations, too little humidity may be delivered to the patient and plugging may occur because of the dried secretions. When using a cold steam nebulizer that is not designed to deliver high mist output at high oxygen concentrations, it is advisable to set up a double system to ensure adequate humidity and oxygen.
5. Retention of the particles is an issue—only the optimum sized particles will stay in the lungs; the small particles will be exhaled, therapeutic sized particles will be retained, and larger particles will rain out before they reach the alveoli.
6. Particle clearance is facilitated through (a) exhalation and (b) biologic mechanisms like the muco-ciliary escalator and macrophages.
7. Aerosol particles are unstable; therefore, they are difficult to keep suspended in gas streams. The typical solution used in bland aerosols is sterile water; however, half strength (0.45%) and normal (0.9%) saline may be used as well.

Molecular Humidity

This is the type of humidity that is found in the air we breath and is produced by cascade or wick-type humidifiers. Both of these devices heat the gas as it passes through them, enhancing the humidification process. Microorganisms cannot hitch rides because they are larger than the water molecules; they can grow in the water that accumulates in the tubing, making infection control procedures necessary.

These humidifiers usually are used on ventilators to provide the requisite humidity but may be used as stand-alone units or in conjunction with a CPAP unit. A cascade can provide 100% body humidity, at any flow rates you may need to use, in the passover mode (with the diffuser basket removed) and is, therefore, considered to be indicated when humidification is a primary concern in the treatment of the patient.

Body Versus Relative Humidity

Yes, I am acutely aware that this topic already has been mentioned several times, but for the sake of driving home

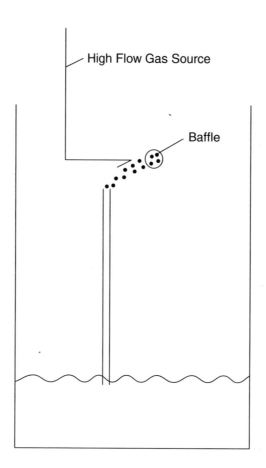

Figure 15–3 Jet Nebulizer

various points, this sort of repetition is commonplace in this book. Adequate humidification of the airways is essential because when dry gas is humidified, the mucous membranes in the large airways surrender less water to the gas passing through them. Minimizing this water loss prevents the following three undesirable side effects: (1) crusting of the mucous membranes, (2) water loss to exhaled gas, which can lead to (3) mucous plugging and possibly atelectasis.

As RCPs, our concern is to compensate for any humidity deficit. We can accomplish this by adding a simple bubble humidifier to a nasal cannula running at 4 L/min or more and by ensuring that an intubated or trached patient is provided with the proper amount of supplemental humidity.

The normal relative humidity found in room air usually ranges between 30–70% (depending on the air temperature); we must, therefore, heat all inspired gas to between 32°–37°C to gain the required 80–100% relative humidity necessary to properly humidify the airways and alveoli.

Factors in Humidification

The three major factors that affect the efficiency of humidifiers are as follows:

1. The more gas surface area that is brought in contact with the water, the more humidity the gas absorbs.
2. The longer the gas is in contact with the water, the more humidity the gas will absorb.
3. The greater the temperature of the gas and the water, the greater the capacity of the gas to carry water.

The following are four primary types of humidifiers in use today that produce molecular humidity:

1. Bubble or bubble diffusion humidifiers
   a. Provide increased patient comfort at low flow rates.
   b. May be used on low flow devices and venti masks up to ≤ 8 L/min.

c. Increase gas surface area by passing gas through a diffusion basket or diffusion stone.
2. Passover humidifiers (Figure 15–4)
   a. Gas passes over the surface of the water.
   b. Humidification chamber can be heated to increase the capacity of the gas to carry water.
3. Cascade humidifiers (Figure 15–5)
   a. Can provide 100% body humidity.
   b. Can be heated.
   c. Can be used in bubble diffusion or passover modes.
   d. Can be used with very high flow rates.
   e. Commonly used on ventilators and CPAP systems.
4. Wick humidifiers
   a. Can provide 100% body humidity
   b. Can be heated.
   c. Can be used on ventilators or CPAP systems.

In recent years, significant improvements in heat and humidity exchangers have led to a decreased use of molecular humidification devices, but they are still used when copious secretions are an issue and are still testable.

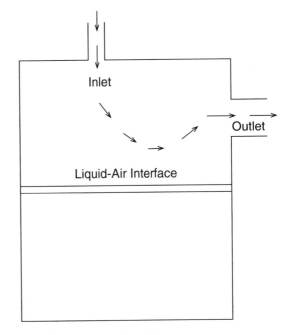

Figure 15–4 Passover Humidifier

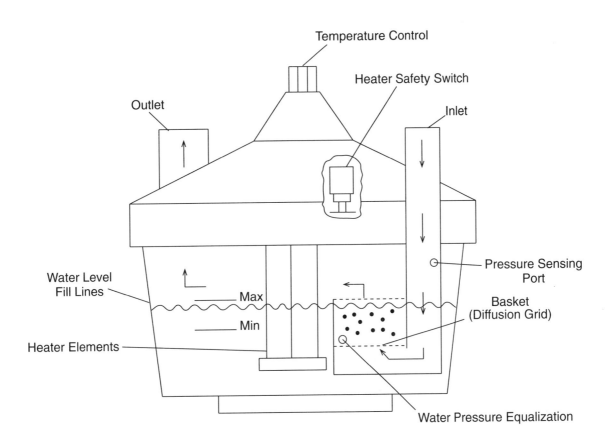

Figure 15–5 Cascade Humidifier

16

Equipment Cleaning and Sterilization Review

This seems, on the surface, to be a topic that we, as RCPs, do not need to be concerned about because most departments have staff who take care of these details; however, the National Board of Respiratory Care (NBRC) is going to expect you to have basic knowledge in this area. You no doubt will have received information on this fascinating subject in school, but there are a few points that warrant repeating.

The following points are intended to reinforce key factors involved in the proper cleaning and sterilization of reusable equipment. The practice of sterilizing and reusing disposable equipment is not considered in this discussion because this practice can compromise patient safety. Depending on the specific process, there are four possible variables that will have an impact on the effectiveness of a sterilization procedure. These are temperature, humidity, pressure, and time.

You should be familiar with the basics of the major methods of sterilization in use today. These are pressurized steam autoclave, dry heat, pasteurization, ethylene oxide (ETO), and glutaraldehyde.

Know the following:

1. With the exception of pasteurization, they all kill spores.
2. If water is added to ETO, the result is that the poison ethylene glycol (antifreeze) is produced.
3. Humidity is water vapor, and is therefore dangerous if added to ETO; it combines with the gas to form antifreeze.
4. It is difficult to kill the spore *Bacillus sterothermophilus*; it is for this reason that this organism's spores are used as a control to ensure proper sterilization.
5. Familiarize yourself with the various types of packaging.
6. Air bubbles and protein matter in or on equipment will render any sterilization procedure ineffective.
7. Understand that different methods destroy cells in various ways.

The major effects the different sterilization methods have on bacteria are as follows:

1. Denaturation of cellular protein;
2. Coagulation of cellular protein;
3. Changes in bacteria cell surface tension, which leads to cell wall rupture;
4. Cell lysis; and
5. Interference with metabolic pathways.

Another germane topic is that of universal precautions, and isolation and reverse isolation procedures. Refamiliarize yourself with these techniques to be sure you understand their indications and rationale, as well as the consequences of improper application of these procedures.

With the evolution of methacillin-resistant *Staphylococcus aureus* (MRSA), universal precautions are necessary for all heath care providers, and, on a more lethal note, the existence of vancomycin-resistant *Enterobacter* (VRE) makes following proper isolation procedures a matter of life and death for both you and your patients. These measures help prevent the spread of these and all pathogenic organisms. Failure to follow proper procedures may not only result in an increase in nosocomial infections, but will facilitate the infection of persons outside of the facility as well. Sloppy practice of infection control procedures will put your family and loved ones at risk as well as yourself. Be familiar with the indications for isolation procedures, as well as some of the organisms that generate their need, so you have an idea of what will happen to you and your patients if you get sloppy. Additionally, be able to recognize why and when these precautions should be taken. Conversely, be familiar with reverse isolation procedures, along with the hows and whys behind them.

17

Government Regulations and Bulk Oxygen Systems

Our goal here is to gain some insight into the various bulk oxygen systems we shall encounter and some of the government regulations that govern the use of these systems. Much of this is common sense, some is not. We shall learn what the coded markings on cylinders mean and what lox (liquid oxygen) systems are composed of. We will keep it simple, but remember, you may be asked about these topics, especially cylinder markings.

Regulating agencies of concern to us are the Department of Transportation (DOT), which is a federal agency that oversees the construction and shipment of gas cylinders. Another federal agency of concern is the Food and Drug Administration (FDA), an agency of the Department of Health and Human Services (HHS). The FDA regulates the purity of medical gases and drugs.

Recommending bodies are groups that make recommendations to the government regarding regulations that concern their areas of expertise. Recommending bodies are as follows:

- Compressed Gas Association (CGA) comprises individuals in the compressed gas industry.
- National Fire Protection Association (NFPA) is involved with setting standards to prevent fire and explosions. This includes setting standards for the storage of flammable and oxidizing gases. This association is concerned with the use of flames around O_2.
- Occupational Safety and Health Agency (OSHA) sets standards for safety in the workplace and is a federal agency.

There are more recommending bodies, but these are the biggies.

CYLINDER MARKINGS

High pressure, compressed gas, or liquid cylinders are made of seamless steel and are stamped Type 3A or 3AA, which are the DOT specs for these cylinders (TANK WILL BE STAMPED Interstate Commerce Commission "ICC" IF MANUFACTURED BEFORE 1967). Markings that are found on the shoulders of tanks, in order of appearance, are as follows:

Front Markings

DOT 3AA 2015: 2015 = Service pressure.
54321 = Serial number.
TGIF = Ownership mark.
"H," or "K," or "E," etc. = manufacturer's mark indicating cylinder size.

Rear Markings

8 H 82 = Date of original hydrostatic test. E.E. 17.5 = Elastic expansion of 17.5 cc at 3360 psi.
CR.MO. = Chrome molybdenum steel used.
SPUN = Spinning process used to manufacture tank.

A star beside the hydrostatic test date indicates tank may be overfilled safely by 10%. Subsequent hydrostatic test dates will be listed chronologically.

An RCP is most likely to encounter "D," "E," "G," "H," and "K" tanks. All tanks are color-coded to ensure proper use of the gas within. Green is O_2, gray is CO_2, brown is He, yellow is air. A combination of colors indicates a mixture of gases.

Large cylinders are frequently connected in a series (typically six or more) to form what is called a cascade. These systems may be used as short-term backups for liquid systems.

Many hospitals have piped in O_2, which comes from a liquid reservoir outside the building. These systems are composed of a network of plumbing that carries 50 psi gas into the facility, which is divided into zones. These systems have control panels to monitor pressure and control valves in each zone. It is these zone valves that allow the gas to be shut off in the case of an emergency. Know where these valves live!

Part III: Treatments and Medications

- Respiratory Pharmacology
- Intermittent Positive Pressure Ventilation and Human Physiology
- The Secrets of IPPB
- Incentive Spirometry Breathing
- Aerosol Therapy with Small Volume Nebulizers
- CPT and Postural Drainage
- Cuffed Endotracheal and Tracheostomy Tubes and Airway Suctioning
- Oxygen Analyzers

18

Respiratory Pharmacology

REVIEW OF THE NERVOUS SYSTEM

Because a complete discussion of pharmacology is beyond the scope of this context, I shall attempt to classify some of the more commonly used respiratory medications by their operational characteristics and their appropriate routes of administration.

First, a classic thumbnail sketch of the nervous system is presented. The two primary branches of the nervous system are central (CNS) and the peripheral. The peripheral nervous system splits into two more branches—the somatic efferent and the autonomic nervous system, the latter of which is of concern in this discussion.

Sympathetic Nervous System

The autonomic nervous system is divided into two main branches, both of which are relevant to RCPs. The first of these, the sympathetic (adrenergic), is responsible for energy expenditure and is stimulated by norepinephrine. The sympathetic nervous system contains two more divisions of concern to us—alpha and beta. These divisions are composed of receptor sites that, when stimulated, effect a particular physiologic response.

Alpha receptors are stimulated by phenylephrine, causing vasoconstriction, a response that is blocked by administering phentolamine. An alpha response is desirable when treating children who have croup or epiglottitis, or adults with upper airway inspiratory stridor. The administration of racemic epinephrine (the chemical mirror image of epinephrine) produces vasoconstriction (alpha response), thereby reducing the localized edema that causes these problems while effecting mild bronchodilation (beta response).

The beta receptors are the biggies where RCPs are concerned. They're our favorites because they are our strongest allies against the dreaded bronchospasm. Of course you know that where we are concerned, the beta receptor splits into two branches, beta 1 and beta 2. The stimulator for both of the beta receptors is isoproterenol; the blocker is propranolol. The $ß_1$ receptors, when stimulated, initiate a cardiac response that increases the heart rate. $ß_2$ receptors provide the bronchodilator response. The ideal situation is to find a $ß_2$ stimulant that does not cause a $ß_1$ response too. Until albuterol was approved by the FDA, everything we had at our disposal caused at least a mild cardiac response; now we have a powerful bronchodilator with almost no $ß_1$ side effects, hence it's the drug of choice. Other $ß_2$ specific drugs we use include the following: Alupent (metaproterenol), Isuprel (isoproterenol), Proventil and Ventolin (albuterol), Serevent, Bronkosol (isoetharine), and Brethine (terbutaline sulfate).

Parasympathetic Nervous System

The parasympathetic (cholinergic) branch of the autonomic nervous system is the energy-conserving branch of the nervous system. Its stimulator is acetylcholine (ACH) and the blocker is atropine sulfate. RCPs administer atropine sulfate or Atrovent to facilitate bronchodilation through this route by blocking acetylcholine. Another drug that provides us with atropine-like bronchodilation is Robinul (glycopyrrolate).

Neuromuscular blocking agents are drugs commonly used in the intensive care unit (ICU) setting to control patients who fight the vent, causing mechanical ventilation to fail. These agents, such as Pavulon and curare, paralyze the patients but do not sedate them. A sedative, such as morphine or diazepam, *must* be given in conjunction with these drugs to relieve the patient's mental agitation.

Mucolytic agents, such as Mucomyst or Mucosil, are drugs that break down the disulfide bonds in sputum. The generic name is acetylcysteine. It is important for the RCP to remember that a patient allergy to sulfa drugs or eggs is a contraindication for using this drug; additionally, care must be taken to deliver this drug in conjunction with, or immediately after a dose of a beta-specific bronchodilator because it may cause bronchospasm.

Steroids, such as Vanceril, Azmacort, and Decadron are useful in preventing an inflammatory response that can be associated with asthma, pneumonitis, and sarcoidosis. They are contraindicated in patients with acute pulmonary infection and status asthmaticus. These medications are administered via metered dose inhaler (MDI) as a rule, but other steroids may be aerosolized.

Cromolyn sodium is a mast cell stabilizer, that is, it moderates the inflammatory response to airway irritation. It is of no value in an acute situation.

Methyl xanthines are bronchodilators that are administered orally or via IV. To be therapeutic, a plasma level of this drug must be constantly maintained and carefully monitored. An average normal is 10–20 µg/ml. Drugs in this group include theophylline, aminophylline, theobromide, and Theo-Dur. These drugs may be given in addition to other bronchodilator therapy that may include beta adrenergic drugs and atropine or its derivatives.

These drugs are covered more thoroughly in the Physician's Desk Reference (PDR), but these are the main groups that you will be responsible for on your exam. Other medications, such as morphine, various antibiotics, Lasix, and more have been given via small volume nebulizer (SVN), but it is unlikely these options will appear on your exam.

For exam purposes, as well as for clinical application, you must be aware of which combinations of drugs can be used effectively. For example, Proventil, Atrovent, and methylxanthine together are appropriate therapy and approach the problem of bronchospasm via three different pathways. To gain more details about these medications, please refer to the following, where current drugs are outlined.

"HOT" DRUGS CURRENTLY USED IN RESPIRATORY CARE

Let's take a moment to review the current, conventional wisdom regarding respiratory pharmacology. I am not going to provide all of the chemical details that a text does; rather, I will outline the drug, the indications for its use, and the clinical conditions under which it can be helpful to the patient.

Beta Agonists

These are used to reverse acute bronchospasm with an almost instantaneous onset of action.

This group includes the drugs we are all familiar with, the β_2-specific bronchodilators. The drugs in this group include Isuprel, Bronkosol, Alupent, Proventil, and Ventolin. All of these drugs elicit a fairly strong β_2 response, the response that we wish to see when trying to reverse bronchospasm. The caveat is that there is usually at least a moderate β_1 response (cardiac stimulation) associated with these drugs.

Studies have shown that the most effective bronchodilators with the least amount (minimal) of cardiac side effects, tremors, or nervousness are Proventil and Ventolin (both are brand names of albuterol sulfate). Albuterol is not right for everyone, but it works most of the time. Typical doses of albuterol are 0.25 ml–0.5 ml in 2.5–3.0 ml of normal saline solution (NSS; 0.9% saline solution) q4°; 0.5 ml is the more acceptable and therapeutic dose. Albuterol has minimal cardiac side effects, but actually can cause bronchospasm in 15% of the patients, so there is a trade off. If your patient complains of increased tightness or has more wheezes after an albuterol treatment, a change to Alupent (metaproterenol sulfate) should be considered.

Alupent or Metaprel (metaproterenol sulfate) is every bit as effective, possibly slightly more so, than albuterol; however, it has a moderate cardiac effect while frequently causing tremors and anxiety. Alupent works well on tough bronchospasm, but its side effects can make the drug difficult for many patients to tolerate comfortably. If albuterol is not doing an acceptable job at reversing bronchospasm, a switch to Alupent should be considered; however, careful consideration should be given to the possible side effects versus potential benefits derived from the drug's use. The maximum adult dose of Alupent is 0.3 ml in 2.5–3.0 ml NSS q4°. If this dose proves too high, reduce the dose to 0.2 ml or even 0.1 ml.

The bottom line when choosing between these two drugs is to try the albuterol first; if that doesn't work well or causes problems, use 0.3 ml of Alupent. If the patient has trouble tolerating the side effects of Alupent, try reducing the dose to 0.2 ml.

Generally, these drugs reach maximum effectiveness (peak) in 1 to 2 hours, becoming ineffective 4 to 5 hours after administration. The literature accompanying albuterol states that it is effective up to 6 hours after it is given, but this varies. The zone of decreased effectiveness can be minimized by using one of the longer acting atropine derivatives, which begin to peak at 1 to 2 hours and do not become ineffective (theoretically) until after the next dose of β_2 bronchodilator can be given. Albuterol and Alupent are the two current drugs of choice when battling bronchospasm and can be used in conjunction with the atropine derivatives that act upon the parasympathetic system. Additionally, these two groups can be used with methylxanthines to provide a three-pronged attack on bronchospasms. This approach also covers the peaks and troughs of the other drugs.

Other, older drugs in this group are not used anymore because of high cardiac side effects or low effectiveness of bronchodilation. Isuprel, for example, has a strong bronchodilation effect, but also has a strong cardiac effect. Bronkosol has little cardiac side effect, but has only a moderate β_2 effect.

Anticholinergic Drugs

The anticholinergic effect on the parasympathetic nervous system is produced by the administration of atropine sulfate or its derivatives. Anticholinergic drugs work by inhibiting the enzyme cholinesterase, which causes bronchoconstriction. The inhibition of cholinesterase promotes bronchodialation.

The drugs that can accomplish this are atropine sulfate, Atrovent (ipratropium bromide, an atropine derivative), and Robinul (glycopyrrolate). All of these drugs produce blockage to the release of cholinesterase, thereby blocking bronchospasm induction.

These drugs have a slower onset and longer duration than their beta agonist counterparts and, therefore, can be used to enhance bronchodilation during a longer period. This enhancement can be accomplished because the effectiveness of an atropine derivative increases while the effectiveness of the β_2 bronchodilator is beginning to decrease. Atropine and its derivatives commonly peak in effectiveness at 2 to 3 hours, gradually decreasing to an ineffective level at 6 to 8 hours. They also work through a different neuropathway, which means they are independent of the actions of other medications. This group of drugs is of little use in an acute situation because they have a slower (10 to 30 minute) onset than the fast–acting beta agonists.

Racemic Epinephrine

This drug is commonly used to treat children with croup. It has a moderate alpha effect (α), which causes vasoconstriction, facilitating the reduction of swelling in the upper airway. It also exerts a mild β_1 effect and a moderate β_2 effect.

This is the drug of choice for the treatment of children with croup. It relieves the edema and facilitates bronchodilation with little cardiac side effect. Commonly seen brand names of this drug are Vaponefrin, microNefrin, "S-2," and Asthmanefrin. These solutions usually come in 2.25% concentrations, the average dose being from 0.25–0.5 ml with 1.0 ml being the maximum dose to be diluted in 3–4 ml normal saline solution (NSS).

Adrenocorticoids and Glucocorticoids

The latest conventional wisdom in the treatment of asthma and other conditions causing reactive airways is to minimize the use of β_2 drugs. Studies have found that patients with reactive airway disorders can be maintained by using these anti-inflammatory agents routinely or in conjunction with an anticholinesterase. In this scenario, β_2-specific drugs are used only with the acute onset of bronchospasm.

Some brand names of this group are Azmacort, AeroBid, Beclovent, and Vanceril. These are metered-dose inhalers, and dosage can range from two to six puffs bid to two to four puffs qid. It is important to instruct the patient to rinse his or her mouth after the use of these drugs, because these drugs upset the normal oral flora, causing a Candida albicans (thrush) infection.

Some Thoughts on Serevent

This is a β_2 adrenergic drug, but it is intended as a maintenance drug in the treatment of asthma. It is slower acting than most β_2 drugs. The literature specifically states that Serevent is of little use in acute situations. Recommended doses are two puffs BID (q 12°). There has been considerable controversy surrounding this drug because several deaths have been linked to it. In each case, it was determined that an overdose of Serevent had occurred because the patient had tried to treat acute bronchospasm inappropriately. So, be aware that Serevent is a maintenance drug only, and not to be used with acute onset.

APPENDIX 18–A

RESPIRATORY MEDICATION QUICK STATISTICS

Generic Name	Brand Name	Dose	Common Side Effects
Beta-adrenergic agonists; Indications: Bronchospasm; Forms: Solution, MDI*			
Albuterol Sulfate	Proventil, Ventolin	0.25–0.5 ml, q4–6°	A,B,C,D,E,F,G,H(8%),I,J,K,Q**
Metaproterenol Sulfate	Alupent, Metaprel	0.2–0.3 ml, q4–6°	A (<1%),B,C,D,E,F,G,H,I,J,N
Bitolterol Mesylate	Tornalate	2 puffs, q4–6°	A,B,C,D,Q
Isoetharine HCL	Bronkosol	0.5–1.0 ml, q4–6°	A,B,C,D,E,F,G,L,M,N,O,P,Q**
Terbutaline Sulfate	Brethine, Bricanyl	2 puffs, q4–6°	A,B,C,D,E,F,G,L,O,P
Beta-adrenergic agonists, available in MDI form only.			
Pirbuterol	Maxair	2 puffs, q4–6°	A,B,C,D,E,F,Q**
Salmeterol Xinafoate	Serevent	2 puffs, q12°	A,C,D,E,F,G,H
Anticholinergic (Parasympathetic) Agents in Aerosol and MDI Forms			
Atropine Sulfate		0.5–1.5 mg, q4–6°	A,B,C,D,G,I,O,P,R,U
Ipratropium Bromide	Atrovent	unit dose of 0.5 mg in 2.5ml NSS or 2 puffs, q4–6°	A,B,C,D,E,F,G,H,I,O,P,R,S,T,U
Glycopyrrolate	Robinul	1–3 mg, q8°	A,B,C,D,E,F,I,R,S,T,U
Mast Cell Stabilizers			
Cromolyn Sodium	Intal	20 mg, (2 ml) qid	F,H**,I,J,K,N,T,U,X
Mucolytic Agents			
Acetylcysteine Solution (10%)	Mucomyst, Mucosil	1–5 ml, q4–8°	F,H**,V,W
Steroids			
Flunisolide	AeroBid	2 puffs, bid (q12°)	C,F,G,X,Y,Z,AA,BB,CC
Triamcinolone Acetonide	Azmacort	2–4 puffs, bid (q12°)	Y,Z,AA,CC
Beclomethasone Diproprionate	Beclovent, Vanceril	2 puffs, q4–12°	X,AA,CC,DD

73

A = TACHYCARDIA
B = HYPERTENSION
C = PALPITATIONS
D = NERVOUSNESS
E = TREMOR
F = NAUSEA AND VOMITING
G = HEADACHE
H = BRONCHOSPASM
I = HOARSENESS
J = OROPHARYNGEAL EDEMA
K = RASH
L = INSOMNIA
M = WEAKNESS
N = DIZZINESS
O = RESTLESSNESS
P = EXCITABILITY
Q = PARADOXICAL BRONCHO-SPASM (in 15% of patients)
R = DRYNESS OF MUCOUS MEMBRANES
S = EYE PAIN
T = URINARY RETENTION
U = DYSPNEA
V = FEVER, CLAMMINESS, CHEST TIGHTNESS, DROWSINESS
W = BRONCHORRHEA AND RHINORRHEA
X = JOINT PAIN AND/OR SWELLING
Y = ACUTE PULMONARY INFECTIONS
Z = EOSINOPHILIA
AA = ORAL CANDIDA/ASPERGILLUS INFECTIONS
BB = ADRENAL SUPPRESSION
CC = SORE THROAT
DD = DEPRESSION
 * = Fatalities have been reported from excessive use of sympathomimetic aerosols.
** = Fatalities have been reported from this side effect.

19

Intermittent Positive Pressure Ventilation and Human Physiology

Intermittent positive pressure breathing (IPPB) is commonly described as the therapeutic application of inspiratory positive pressure to the airways. The most important factor in the effective delivery of an IPPB treatment is that it is administered by a competent RCP.

The six primary positive physiologic effects of IPPB are discussed in the chapter on IPPB but for the purpose of our discussion here, it is important to remember that to have the optimum effect, IPPB must increase alveolar distending pressures so that the difference between alveolar and pleural pressure also increases. An increase in this pressure difference, then, facilitates the existence of a large volume of gas in the airways. The other physiologic effects occur because of this gas volume. Much of the information covered in this section is true of continuous mechanical ventilation as well.

WORK OF BREATHING (WOB)

Mechanical support of ventilation is, in part, the process of providing auxiliary ventilatory power, which then allows the patient's ventilatory muscles to rest. It follows that, when a patient's WOB increases, we may be able to use IPPB as a tool to take on some of the patient's workload, providing a rest for the patient's muscles. Additionally, mechanical support may result in patient tolerance of more beneficial ventilatory patterns that certain patients cannot tolerate during spontaneous breathing.

An example could be that Mss Bonaparte has a respiratory rate (RR) of 38 and a very shallow V_T. Along comes an RCP, with Bird in hand, who hooks him up and doubles his V_T, decreasing the patient's rate to 26 and thereby normalizing the I:E ratio. Try it out.

CLINICAL GOALS OF IPPB

The RCP wishes to use IPPB to provide Mssr Bonaparte with a sufficiently larger V_T and a more physiologically advantageous I:E ratio than he can manage on his own.

A disease that limits the depth of an individual's breath can be manipulated with IPPB so that an increase in volume of up to three or four times the patient's normal occurs. Without this substantial increase in V_T, the IPPB is ineffective.

Effective application of IPPB to Mssr Bonaparte has some additional effects as well. We have mentioned mechanical bronchodilation as an effect but in diseased lungs, this effect is dramatically enhanced if the treatment is properly applied.

It appears that with IPPB in these same diseased lungs, there is increased ventilation of the alveolar pores of Kohn. It follows that a properly administered IPPB would increase collateral ventilation through its effects on those lungs.

Improving and Promoting the Cough Mechanism

Bronchial hygiene depends upon the effectiveness of the patient's cough. Essential components of an effective cough include the ability of the patient to take a deep breath (vital capacity) and the optimal distribution of this breath into the small airways, powered by slow inspiratory flow rates and ending with a short inspiratory pause. If an acutely ill patient is unable to produce a VC of 10–15 ml/kg, then IPPB may be indicated to improve that patient's ability to cough. The benefit of the IPPB must be questioned if the treatment delivers < 100% of the patient's predicted VC.

Ventilation Distribution and Medication Delivery

IPPB can be used to improve ventilation in those patients with a ventilation/perfusion mismatch (V/Q mismatch). Utilization of IPPB decreases the incidence of postoperative atelectasis and pneumonia as well as re-expands atelectatic alveoli. Expansion of atelectatic alveoli is effective only with the use of large V_{TS}, slowly inspired and with the application of an inspiratory hold at the cycle's end. With this goal in mind, treatments should be given no further apart than q3°. To "blow off" CO_2, treatment frequency should be q1°–q2°.

Medications may be delivered with IPPB if a patient is unable to take deep breaths, or even adequate breaths. However, there is no advantage to using IPPB solely for the purpose of medication delivery if the patient is able to inspire adequately because of other, more effective passive methods of delivery. Compared to these yet to be defined methods of delivery, IPPB is considerably less effective, providing, at best, 10%–20% particle deposition. Because of impact, 5%–10% of the medication is lost in the mouth and is swallowed. The physical characteristics of the positive pressure breath increase the amounts of medication that is lost, rendering passive inspiration superior to IPPB for this purpose.

Hazards of IPPB

Hazards include the following:

1. Excessive ventilation → alveolar hyperventilation;
2. Excessive oxygenation—dangerous to CO_2 retainers;
3. Impedance of venous return to heart → drop in cardiac output (CO) → dyspnea and tachycardia;*
4. Increased intercranial pressure due to venous drainage being decreased;
5. Barotrauma—carefully evaluate any chest pain with IPPB [This is due to increased mean airway pressures (MAP) generated by IPPB];
6. Hemoptysis;
7. Increased airway resistance—may precipitate bronchospasm;
8. Nosocomial infection (infection acquired by the patient in the hospital);
9. Gastric distention (patient's swallowing of air due to poor cooperation); and
10. Psychological dependence.

If IPPB decreases venous return, guess what incentive spirometry breathing (ISB) does? That's right, because of decreased intrathoracic pressure, ISB increases venous return.

---

*Venous return decreases because of increased intrathoracic pressure. This may cause a decrease in CO. This effect may be minimized by using proper I:E ratios (with long expiratory times) and slow (low) respiratory rates.

The Secrets of IPPB

IPPB is a form of therapy that was once widely used to deliver aerosolized medications and provide lung expansion via the use of a positive pressure breath. It has, however, now become relegated to a more specialized role, having been replaced by aerosol therapy via small volume nebulizers as the primary method of medication delivery. IPPB is unique in its effects and is therefore effective when used in specific situations, such as providing deep breaths to patients who are unable to do so on their own because of spinal cord/brain injuries and assisting the patient with COPD in blowing off CO_2. The key to an effective IPPB is a knowledgeable RCP. We have discussed the physiologic effects of IPPB in a previous section, so we shall concentrate on the technical aspects of IPPB in this section.

DESIRABLE PHYSIOLOGIC EFFECTS OF IPPB

1. Increases V_T;
2. Decreases work of breathing (WOB);
3. Can improve the I:E ratio (normal = 1:2; be sure you allow enough expiratory time to prevent air trapping);
4. Improves medication delivery (if your patient can't take deep breaths);
5. Improves cough; and
6. Increases mean airway pressure (MAP), therefore causing mechanical bronchodilation.

ELASTANCE, COMPLIANCE, FLOW, AND RESISTANCE

Lung expansion is influenced by two factors, elastance and compliance. Of the two, compliance is of the most concern. Compliance decreases as lungs stiffen and increases as lungs become more elastic. It reflects the relationship between changes in volume per changes in pressure. Lung compliance can be calculated as follows:

$$\text{Compliance} = \frac{\Delta \text{ Volume (ml)}^*}{\Delta \text{ Pressure (cmH}_2\text{O)}}$$

* Please be aware that volume units of measure differ between institutions, but the NBRC seems to like ml. In any case, all you have to do is move the decimal point.

Another important concept is flow (volume/min), defined as a change in pressure/resistance. Essentially, this means that as resistance increases, flow decreases. Conversely, resistance decreases as flow increases; therefore, if flow remains constant, resistance to that flow increases as the lungs become more full.

MEAN AIRWAY PRESSURE

This is a reflection of the pressure, peak, and minimum that is constantly exerted on the alveolar sacs and airways. It is expressed as follows:

$$\text{MAP} = \frac{\text{Maximum Pressure} - \text{Minimum Pressure}}{2}$$

Sensitivity

This refers to the setting that regulates the effort the patient must expend to trigger the machine breath. The usual setting used for sensitivity, with both IPPB and ventilators, is -2 cmH$_2$O.

Pressure Control

When you set the pressure on an IPPB machine, you are setting the V_T you wish to deliver to the patient. The higher the set pressure, the more gas the machine will push into the patient's lungs and vice versa.

Remember that V_T is the volume involved in a normal breath, whereas VC (vital capacity) is a deep breath that is forced in and out. So what, you ask? Well, IPPB can be used to increase V_T or augment VC, causing CO_2 to be "blown off" and the lungs to be expanded properly to mechanically treat atelectasis. Because of these characteristics, IPPB is useful in the treatment of the patient who has suffered neurological damage or who has COPD.

Flow Rate Control

This controls the speed at which the gas flows into the patient's lungs. Faster flow rates reduce the inspiratory time, whereas slower flow rates prolong the inspiratory time.

Pressure-Time Relationships

The RCP must ensure that adequate time is allowed for the expiratory phase to prevent air trapping and auto PEEP. Time can be manipulated by using several devices, but the pressure and flow controls are the major tools we use to manipulate this relationship. They are as follows:

1. Insipiratory hold;
2. Expiratory retard, which slows expiration, causing an increase in "E" time;
3. Increasing MAP by either method or increasing peak airway pressure or "time @ pressure";
4. Increasing frequency (rate) decreases "E" time, and decreasing frequency increases "E" time;
5. Increasing flow rate decreases "I" time and increases "E" time, whereas decreasing flow rate increases "I" time and decreases "E" time; and
6. Increasing pressure (while flow remains constant) increases "I" time and decreases "E" time, whereas decreasing pressure decreases "I" time and increases "E" time.

You must be able to understand and use pressure-time relationships. You may think at this point in your career that you always will have time to work this stuff out but believe me, your job will be much easier and you will feel so much more at ease if you just take the time to learn this now.

THE BIRD MARK 7

Let's hone our knowledge of the Bird Mark (MK) 7, because this is the machine the NBRC likes, by covering a few facts that may pop up on the exam. The Bird MK 7 is a pressure-cycled, pressure-limited machine and, therefore, acts like all other machines of that type; what I'm saying is that this is good general information on pressure vents, too.

You should be familiar with Bird IPPB units and their controls and be able to explain their functions. To begin with, you set the pressure limit (big control on left of machine), which determines the volume of the breath. The volume will change if compliance changes, the patient's position changes, secretions accumulate, etc. The machine will always deliver the preset pressure. Next, we could set the flow control (large numbered dial on the front—by the way, the numbers are just a reference, they do not indicate flow!) that does exactly what any other flow control does, controls T_I and T_E, that being to increase or decrease the inspiratory and/or expiratory times. Next, we have to set the sensitivity control (big control on right), which sets the amount of patient effort required to trigger the vent, minus two (–2) cmH_2O being standard.

These are the major controls, but there are two other controls on the MK 7 that we haven't touched upon formally; these are the apnea control and the air mix. First, let's talk venturis. The Bird air mix control is an "on" or "off" control. When the air mix control plunger is pulled out, the literature says the machine will deliver between 40–60% O_2; when it is pushed in, the venturi entrainment ports are closed, causing 100% O_2 to be delivered to the patient. Because air entrainment is terminated in the 100% ("in") position, the flow rate provided by the MK 7 will decrease by ≈ 75% (using the 3:1 air to O_2 mix for 40%), a dramatic and noticeable decrease. In light of this, if you are asked what happens to the flow rate of a Bird MK 7 when the air mix control is in the 100% (or "in") position, the answer is that the flow rate supplied by the machine decreases. When the air mix control is in the 40–60% (or "out") position, the machine provides much higher flow rates. The air mix control's effect on flow is what makes the numbers on the flow dial useless. Know this, not only because it may come up on the exam, but because it applies to venturi characteristics.

The other control worth mentioning is the apnea control, which is nothing more than an expiratory timer to be used when the patient is not capable of spontaneous ventilation. Setting this control is a matter of trial and error. Because there is no calibration provided, the RCP must simply continue to turn this control until the desired rate is achieved. Be aware that this setting is delicate and that changes in the patient's condition or position may change the rate. You must, therefore, check the machine often when using it as a ventilator. It is doubtful that you will be asked about this control on the exam, but there it is, just in case.

Additional things to be aware of when giving IPPB therapy are that you may need to use a Bennett seal, otherwise known as a flange, on the mouthpiece. With nose clips, you may need this device to get a good seal if the patient is unable to properly seal the mouthpiece with his or her lips. The flange is always your first option after the straight mouthpiece.

If under extreme circumstances, the flange mouthpiece fails to do the job, you may have to use a mask. The effectiveness of an IPPB delivered via mask is questionable, but if you must use a mask, be sure it covers the nose and mouth and that you do not occlude the patient's airway with the patient's tongue. Watch out for aspiration. Mask treatments are, as stated, the least effective way to deliver IPPB; furthermore, there are serious contraindications for mask therapy, so don't be too quick "on the trigger." If you do use a mask, be careful! Aspiration is a real possibility.

Be familiar with pressure-time relationships and the manipulation thereof because they will reappear when we discuss mechanical ventilation. All are important, but manipulation of pressure, flow rate, and frequency (respiratory rate) are the most important! Know how each affects the other. Know how they affect insipiratory and expiratory times. In short, know how to get the most out of your IPPB therapy. Know that NEEP (negative end expiratory pressure) sucks the air out of the lungs after exhalation, causing bad things like airway collapse and atelectasis.

INDICATIONS FOR IPPB

1. To increase the V_T of patients postoperatively;
2. To increase the V_T of patients with COPD, causing CO_2 to be blown off, therefore keeping them off ventilators;
3. To augment the V_T and VC of patients with neuromuscular damage [i.e., amyotrophic lateral sclerosis (ALS), spinal cord injury, etc.], preventing pathologies like atelectasis, etc.; and
4. To augment the patient's ventilation while they wean from the ventilator.

Be sure to use IPPB instead of ISB if a patient cannot reach 75% of their predicted VC.

Incentive Spirometry Breathing

Incentive spirometry breathing (ISB) is the most effective way to prevent or treat postoperative atelectasis caused by secretions blocking communicating air passages between alveoli or hypoventilation. The following are ISB buzzwords you need to know:

1. Sustained maximal inhalation (SMI), that is, after the patient has taken the deep breath, effort should be made to continue to inhale, even though no volume increase occurs.
2. Inspiratory capacity (IC) is the capacity measured by ISB. The patient takes as deep a breath as possible from a resting start, that is, they do not forcibly exhale before the deep breath.
3. Atelectasis can set in as soon as 1 hour after deep breathing.
4. Ideal frequency for ISB is q1° to q2°w/a. These days, as hospitals try to aggressively control costs, there may not be adequate staff to do ISB with patients every 1 to 2 hours; if this is the case, try this approach: You should instruct your patients to do the exercise (ISB) 10 times every hour or two, after you've explained why the exercise is so important, and tell them that someone from RT will visit four times a day to check on their progress. This approach to ISB is becoming common practice of medical surgical units, but not in the intensive care setting.

On an exam, ISB should always be your first answer for a question asking about postoperative prophylactic therapy.

22

Aerosol Therapy with Small Volume Nebulizers

Aerosol therapy is the primary method used by RCPs to deliver aerosolized medications, spanning from the routine bronchodilators to more exotic drugs, such as mucolytics, steroids, antibiotics, and even alcohol and morphine. Introducing these drugs directly into the airways of the lungs has several advantages. First, the medication is applied directly to the tissues upon which it is meant to act, thereby reducing the likelihood of stimulating an overall systemic response to the various drugs, while facilitating a more effective response to the medications.

Small volume nebulizer (SVN) therapy came into its own in the mid 70s, nudging IPPB out as the primary therapy for medication delivery. Studies had shown at that point that SVN, or as we call it AT, therapy facilitated a significant increase in particle deposition, as much as 30%–40% in the most optimistic studies, thereby maximizing the medication's effect on the smooth muscle tissue of the tracheo-bronchial tree. The switch to AT was made for this reason.

It has been theorized that the cause of the improved particle deposition can be attributed to the fact that, unlike IPPB, passive inspiration facilitates laminar air flows, leading to more even distribution and deeper penetration of the inspired V_T within the lungs. This, coupled with the fact that passive ventilation reverses the pressure gradients encountered in IPPB therapy—allowing the particles of medication to be sucked into the lungs naturally, rather than pushed under pressure—causes the particles to reach and linger in the desired areas a little longer. This then, allows the medication to impact, or rain out onto, the desired anatomy to a much greater extent than had been previously possible. IPPB therapy's positive pressure causes particle deposition to occur higher in the tracheobronchial tree, rendering a large proportion of the particles ineffective. Fifty percent of the particles generated by small volume nebulizers are in the 0.5 to 5.0 µm diameter range.

AEROSOL THERAPY TREATMENT

On the test, the first thing you indicate you do before beginning any task is *wash your hands*! Then the physician can begin. The physician's order should specify what medication and diluents are to be used, along with the type and frequency of the treatments.

Usually, RCPs deliver a bronchodilator via AT. This must be diluted, usually with normal saline solution, because if a small amount of bronchodilator, usually < 1.0 ml, was placed into the SVN it would last only for one or two breaths. It is therefore necessary to add a diluent to maximize the amount of medication inspired by the patient during an average of 10–15 min, running the SVN at 6 to 8 L/min.

It is undesirable for the patient to suffer the side effect of hyperventilation while taking the treatment, yet good particle deposition is desired. To facilitate optimum penetration and deposition, the patient should be instructed to take normal breaths, while taking a deep breath only every fourth or fifth breath and to hold that deep breath for 1 to 2 sec before exhaling. This will ensure patient comfort while maximizing the treatment's desired effects.

Aerosol treatments last as long as the prescribed medication lasts. Once this is nebulized, the treatment is finished. The RCP should evaluate the patient both before and after each treatment to gauge the effectiveness of the treatment. The patient's heart rate should be checked before, during, and after each treatment to ensure no unacceptable β_1 (cardiac) side effects arise. If the patient's heart rate increases more than 20 beats per minute (bpm) during the course of the therapy, the RCP should terminate the treatment immediately. Additionally, if the patient's heart rate is > 120 bpm before the treatment, the therapy should not be given until the physician is consulted. Heart rate should be charted both before and after treatment.

To properly assess the effectiveness of a treatment, the RCP should auscultate the patient before and after treatment. This will allow the RCP to make recommendations regarding any required changes in therapy, while monitoring the patient's response to the therapy. Additionally, this information provides all clinical practitioners with the information necessary to effectively evaluate and treat the patient.

Any cough, productive or not, should be noted as well. Should the cough be productive, appropriate notations should be made regarding the color, odor, and consistency of the expectorated secretions. A subjective response also should be solicited from the patient, like the answer to "how do you feel?"

After noting the heart rate, breath sounds, cough, and secretions before and after treatment, the RCP should note, specifically, what medications and diluents were used in the treatment, along with the dosages. Remember to note the date and time, too.

After completing all tasks described previously, the RCPs must, once again, *wash their hands*!

Remember to check allergies, CXR, and laboratory test results before performing the therapy.

23

CPT and Postural Drainage

The goal of these therapies is to remove accumulated secretions from the various segments of the lungs. Many times, doctors will order the specific positions in which they wish RCPs to place the patient to facilitate drainage but more often they will leave that detail up to the RCP.

The most important factor regarding the proper positioning of the patient is to carefully consider the anatomy of the segment to be drained and to place the patient in a position that will allow that area to be drained efficiently. Be aware that when a physician orders the patient to be placed in the left lateral decubitus, the physician means that the patient is to be placed on his or her left side (left side down, right side up); the reverse is true for right lateral decubitus. Having said this, let's look into the particulars of chest percussion.

GOALS OF CHEST PERCUSSION

The following are the goals of chest percussion:

1. To prevent the accumulation of secretions in the lungs and airways;
2. To increase mobilization of secretions;
3. To improve the efficiency of ventilation; and
4. To maximize gas distribution.

PERCUSSION DO'S

1. Only percuss over the rib cage.
2. Percuss directly on the skin.
3. Percuss with a smooth, even rhythm.
4. Be sure you're making a popping sound when you percuss.
5. Percuss each area 3–5 min.
6. Percuss lower lobes while patient is in Trendelenburg position, unless contraindicated.
7. Have the patient take slow, deep breaths while being percussed.
8. Have the patient extend arms above his or her head to separate the ribs, enhancing the effect of the percussion waves.

PERCUSSION DON'TS

1. Don't percuss over the abdomen.
2. Don't percuss over the liver.
3. Don't percuss over the floating ribs; the kidneys are behind them.
4. Don't percuss over the spine.
5. Don't percuss over the sternum.
6. Don't percuss over incisions.
7. Don't percuss directly over chest tubes.
8. Don't percuss aggressively over the heart.
9. Don't percuss over a gown or towel.
10. Don't percuss over the female breast tissue or bony areas.

SOME CONTRAINDICATIONS OF PERCUSSION

Be advised, the following contraindications are not hard and fast rules:

1. Flail chest or fractured ribs;
2. Conditions that may cause a hemorrhage;
3. Metastatic bone cancer or brittle bones in general;
4. When percussion would cause more pain, increasing muscle splinting;
5. When subcutaneous emphysema is present in the neck or thorax;
6. Gross obesity (percussion is rendered ineffective by the many layers of fat—the shock waves fail to reach the air space of the lungs);

7. Pulmonary emboli (the concern here is the source of the embolism and the chance that percussion may cause another to be generated);
8. Spinal fusion;
9. Fresh burns;
10. Resectable lung tumors (percussion may cause them to spread before surgery); and
11. Empyema.

POSTURAL DRAINAGE

Percussion and drainage go hand in hand, but there are a few caveats you should be aware of before standing your patient on his or her head.

Do's

1. Use the drainage position whenever possible.
2. Drain each area treated for 20–30 min.
3. Encourage deep breathing while patient is in Trendelenburg position or during drainage.
4. Instruct patient to cough only when you instruct them to do so, that is, after the treatment (bad things can happen if a patient coughs in Trendelenburg position).
5. Give bronchodilator before treatment.

Don'ts

1. Drain patients with NG tubes.
2. Drain patients who have head trauma.
3. Drain patients after cardiac surgery.
4. Cough patients frequently while they are in Trendelenburg position.
5. Reposition patients after spinal fusion.
6. Drain patients who have empyemas.

Be aware that the Trendelenburg position can stress the cardiovascular system and cause an increase in intracranial pressure.

CLINICAL INDICATIONS FOR PERCUSSION AND DRAINAGE

Clinical indications are the following:

1. Bronchiectasis;
2. Cystic fibrosis;
3. COPD;
4. Acute atelectasis;
5. Pneumonia;
6. Lung abscess;
7. Bed-ridden patients; and
8. Postoperative patients.

Like everything else in this life, we must evaluate every situation based on its own circumstances but by using the previous guidelines, you will have some specific parameters by which to make a judgment. Each situation is unique. Retained secretions can cause serious clinical problems and may even cause life-threatening illness.

In some cases, the problem becomes one of choosing lesser evils. Sometimes the side effects may be minor when compared to the problems secretions can cause. As RCPs, we must evaluate each situation on its own merits and communicate our opinions to the physician so that a decision can be made regarding the course of treatment necessary.

SOME THOUGHTS REGARDING DRAINAGE POSITIONS

Generally, when you wish to drain a particular segment of the lungs, you should consider the effect gravity will have on the secretions. To do this, you must be aware of the anatomy of that area.

Apical segments should be drained with the patient sitting and his or her arms laid across a table about chest high and leaning slightly forward. The lower lobes of both sides are drained most efficiently with the patient lying on either the right or left side, in Trendelenburg position, whereas the right middle lobe is usually drained with the patient in the right lateral decubitus. In each case, the primary factor in efficient drainage is the path taken by the airways to the larger airways leading to the mainstem bronchi.

The various positions required to drain particular areas is a burden that is placed on you, the RCP candidate. The key to the process is to know your pulmonary anatomy. In this way, you will be able to determine if the anterior or posterior segments of a lobe are being drained and which lobe is affected by the procedure.

CPT AND POSTURAL DRAINAGE NOTES

Know the indications and contraindications. The standard length of time for actual percussion is 3–5 min, for drainage at least 20 min. Be aware of the fact that when doctors write orders for (R) or (L) lateral decubitus, they intend the side indicated to be the down side, that is, the side the patient is lying on. For example, (L) lateral decubitus means that you lay the patient on his or her *left* side. Remember that we don't percuss over the heart, spine, or soft organs like the liver and spleen.

If you are asked what position to use to drain a particular lobe, think about how you would fill that area with fluid, then put the patient in the opposite position to drain the area. For example, if a patient aspirates while lying on the back, you drain the patient by laying him or her on the stomach and elevating the hips. Get it? Stuff, like aspirate or endo tubes, is more likely to go into the right lung because the angle of the right mainstem bronchus is less than that of the left and is larger in diameter.

Additionally, instruct your patient *not to cough* unless you, the RCP, specifically instruct him or her to do so. Remember that! It may come up on the test. Definitely know what and when to drain!

24

Cuffed Endotracheal and Tracheostomy Tubes and Airway Suctioning

THOUGHTS ON TUBE SIZE

All too often, patients are doomed to fail before weaning ever begins. The reason is simple—the patient has been saddled with much too small of an airway to facilitate reasonably adequate, independent ventilation. The size and type of airway are vital to the effectiveness of our weaning efforts. It is our responsibility to ensure that we provide the patient with an airway through which an adequate amount of air can be moved easily, allowing the patient to sustain him- or herself, continuously without mechanical assistance. It is essential that the proper size endotracheal or tracheostomy tube be inserted from the beginning, because up-sizing the tube later can be difficult, if not impossible. Tube sizes, such as #8, refer to the inside diameter of the tube in millimeters.

For average-size adults, a reasonable size tube should have an inside diameter (ID) of 8 or 9 mm. In petite individuals, a 6 or 7-mm tube may be marginally acceptable but on the whole, undesirable. For the average to large adult, these sizes are unacceptable, without exception. Size 10 (10-mm) tubes may be necessary in large-framed individuals. Size 10 tubes are rarely used, but are often indicated. An average size pediatric tube is 4–5 mm but this depends on the size and age of the child. The rule of thumb for pediatrics is to use a tube that equals the patient's little finger in diameter. Both tracheostomy and endotracheal tubes are sized by the same standard, that is, an ID measurement in millimeters.

ENDOTRACHEAL TUBES VERSUS TRACHEOSTOMY TUBES

Of the two routes available for endotracheal intubation, it is generally considered desirable to perform nasotracheal intubation if the tube will be used only for the short term. Nasotracheal intubation is considered superior for short-term airway maintenance because the tube is easier to stabilize, is easier to work with, allows the patient to eat and drink, and is less prone to accidental extubation. The drawbacks include higher incidence of sinusitis, great potential for tissue necrosis of the mucous membranes in the nasopharynx, and increased incidence of middle ear infections. Nasal endotracheal tubes should be re-taped every 24 to 48 hours.

Oral tubes, however, are much less stable, have less potential for the various infections, and eliminate the chance of tissue damage to the nasopharynx. Drawbacks include the following: they prevent the patient from taking any meaningful oral nutrition; they must be switched from one side of the mouth to the other every 24 hours and re-taped to prevent tissue necrosis; and they may cause the patient to gag whenever the tube is moved, even slightly.

In either case, there are significant drawbacks to endotracheal intubation in general and careful attention should be given to the care of the tube and the surrounding tissue. Although less of a concern for the RCP, close attention should be payed to the nutritional status of the patient, because a malnourished patient will not wean easily from the vent, if at all. So keep a proverbial weather eye on the nutritional status; it will make your patient's recovery easier, not to mention your job.

A transition from endotracheal tube to tracheostomy tube should be considered if it appears that the patient will require more than 7 to 10 days to wean from the ventilator. The reasons for this include allowing the patient to eat normally, itself an important consideration; reducing the possibility of infection and tissue necrosis in the naso and oropharynx; reducing the possibility of damage to the vocal cords; improving patient communication; and reducing tracheal wall damage caused by high pressure endotube cuffs, to name a few.

CUFF CHARACTERISTICS

Cuff pressure is another consideration when a patient requires mechanical ventilation. Most endotracheal tubes use a low volume, high pressure cuff, whereas the majority of tracheostomy tubes use a high volume, low pressure cuff (Figure 24–1). In both cases, the goal is to establish a patent airway, using the cuff to create a seal. For short-term use, the endotracheal tube is the ideal choice because of its less invasive nature but by using high pressure cuffs, these tubes can cause tissue and structural damage to the trachea. Low volume, high pressure cuffs contact less tracheal surface area, but subject that same surface to higher pressures. High pressures are more likely to cause tracheal stenosis, tissue necrosis, and a host of other complications.

Use of the high volume, low pressure cuff, as is the case with tracheostomy tubes, spreads the same amount of pressure over a greater surface area and greatly reduces the occurrence of the undesirable side effects already mentioned. This approach dramatically reduces the pressure at any given point of contact, reducing the chance of tracheal mucosal and/or structural damage while maintaining a tight seal. When long-term ventilation becomes a necessity, it is crucial to have a tube in place with a high volume, low pressure cuff.

TYPES OF TRACHEOSTOMY TUBES

DIC Versus Non–DIC

Tracheostomy tubes vary in styles, with some serving more specialized functions but there are essentially two types of cuffed tubes—those without inner cannulas and those that have removable and/or disposable inner cannulas. A tube having a disposable inner cannula (DIC) facilitates the maintenance of a clear, patent lumen during the long term. By allowing us to remove and clean the inner cannula periodically and then replacing it, airway patency can be ensured during extended periods. With periodic cleaning, we can ensure that dried secretions or other obstructions do not cause the lumen of the tube to be artificially narrowed, causing ventilation to be impaired. Endotracheal tubes do not have inner cannulas at all and like those tracheostomy tubes without a DIC, do not allow us this degree of security and are ideally used in short-term situations. Policies vary between institutions, but most will replace an endotracheal tube with a tracheostomy tube if it appears that the patient will require mechanical ventilation for periods exceeding 7 to 10 days.

Fenestrated and Cuffless Tracheostomy Tubes

Fenestrated tubes are specially designed tracheostomy tubes that come in both cuffed and cuffless styles. Fenestrated tubes are different because they have a series of slits, usually three or four, molded into the curve of the outer cannula. These tracheostomy tubes act like all others, facilitating ventilation and suctioning with their inner cannulas in place. When patients begin to wean and become strong enough to speak for short periods, the cuffs can be deflated and the inner cannulas are removed, allowing air to pass through the slits as well as around the deflated cuff. The fenestrations (slits) drastically decrease airway resistance. As mentioned, both cuffed and cuffless stainless steel Jackson tracheostomy tubes are available with these fenestrations.

Cuffless tracheostomy tubes are available in both plastic and stainless steel. Cuffless tubes are used to ease the transition from cuffed tracheostomy tubes to nothing, in terms of artificial airways. The major reasons to use these tubes is to (1) provide access to the airway in the event suctioning is required, and (2) to allow us to plug the tracheostomy tube to build the patient's endurance until he or she is strong enough to tolerate total decannulation. This plug allows the patient to speak normally and breathe through the natural airway, thus eliminating the need for supplemental humidity. The majority of the cuffless stainless steel tubes encountered are of the Jackson type, and these have both inner and outer cannulas and are available in fenestrated styles.

Troubleshooting Tubes

It is the RCP's responsibility to ensure the patency of the entire airway, tube included, and the RCP must be aware of any changes that may indicate a potential problem with the tube.

Low Residual Volume, High Pressure Cuff

High Residual Volume, Low Pressure Cuff

Figure 24–1 Cuff Types

With both endotracheal and tracheostomy tubes, if it becomes difficult to pass a suction catheter through the tube and/or the peak airway pressure is seen to rise, serious consideration should be given to replacing the tube if it does not have a DIC. Before you change the tube, check for cuff herniation and obtain a chest radiograph to check tube placement. The cuff may be "herniated," that is, overlapping and therefore occluding the opening of the tube. This may be a result of excessive cuff pressure. To check for cuff herniation, completely deflate the cuff and then reinflate it to the proper pressure. If the problem is not resolved, consider changing the tube. If a CXR shows bad tube placement, withdraw or advance the tube accordingly. In the case of a tube with a DIC, the cannula should be removed, cleaned, and replaced. If the problem persists, the ideal solution is to replace the tube.

CUFF PRESSURE

Endotracheal and tracheostomy tube cuffs should be inflated using a pressure manometer. This device allows us to effectively inflate a cuff, while ensuring that excessive pressure is not exerted on the tracheal mucosa. Tracheal mucosal capillary pressures range between ~ 20–30 cmH$_2$O; therefore, by keeping our cuff pressures in this range, or lower if possible, we prevent stenosis and minimize the possibility of tissue necrosis.

If a manometer is not available, the minimal leak technique (MLT) should be used. The MLT simply involves the RCP listening to the patient's neck at the site of the cuff. Air is withdrawn from the cuff until a leak is heard through the stethoscope; air is then gradually injected into the cuff until only a small, momentary leak is heard at end inspiration/peak pressure. This is the point at which the cuff is left inflated. Using the MLT in conjunction with a pressure manometer is ideal, especially if higher than 30 cmH$_2$O is required to maintain a seal that facilitates proper ventilation. Never shoot an indiscriminate amount of air into a cuff. Bad things can happen! You may rupture the cuff immediately or if you leave the air in, you may cause tracheal stenosis or tissue necrosis, so always be sure your cuff pressures are properly regulated before leaving the bedside.

SOME NOTES ON INTUBATION

To intubate a patient with an endotracheal tube, you will need the following tools:

1. Laryngoscope;
2. Magill forceps;
3. A 10 cc syringe;
4. Water-soluble lubricant;
5. Local anesthetic, such as Cetacaine; and
6. Endotracheal tube.

There are two types of laryngoscope blades that we commonly find in the clinical environment—the Miller blade, which is a straight blade, and the Macintosh, which is a curved blade. These blades range in size from 0 to 4 and all have a small light bulb that illuminates the patient's laryngopharynx so we can see what we are trying to do. The power source for these lights is two batteries located in the handle of the scope. All of this equipment is commonly found on crash carts and should be checked regularly. Ideal endotracheal tube position is 2 cm above the carina. After intubation, auscultate immediately; then, you must get a CXR to check for proper tube position. If the tube is in too far, it may have slipped into the right mainstem bronchus; if so, you will have little or no breath sounds on the left.

SOME NOTES ON SUCTIONING

We have all done this but for the record, we must touch upon a few fine points to ensure consistency for your exam. Remember that suctioning is a vital, but traumatic, invasive procedure; so, always be sure that it is absolutely necessary before you do it.

SUCTIONING PRESSURES

The following suctioning pressures are negative:

1. Adults: –80 to –120 mm Hg (some sources say –110 to –140)
2. Pediatric patients: –60 to –80 mm Hg (or –100 to –120 mm Hg)
3. Infants: –40 to –60 mm Hg (or –60 to –100 mm Hg)

These values are guidelines. If you are asked about suctioning pressures on the exam, you have some ranges to work with. Mostly, the focus should be on adult care and the range I found published more often is the one listed first.

TYPES OF CATHETERS

1. Straight catheters. This is the common type we see in suction kits. These catheters have thumb ports that allow us to control the application of suction. Closed systems (i.e., Ballards and Portex) fall into this category.
2. Coude's catheters. These have a curved end, allowing the RCP to maneuver the device into the desired mainstem bronchus.
3. Closed suction systems. Once again, these are systems of the Ballard type that are intended to be left inline for periods of up to 24 hours. The manufacturers recommend that these systems are changed at 24-hour intervals. The advantage is that these systems do not require the circuit to be opened to room air each

time the patient needs suctioning, reducing the chances of infection and maintaining relatively consistent ventilation and oxygenation.

AIRWAY TO CATHETER SIZE RATIO

1. Suction catheters should not be greater than one half of the ID of an endotracheal or tracheostomy tube.
2. Conversion from millimeters to French gauge: The ID of the tracheostomy or endotracheal tube × 3 = French gauge so (ID/2) × 3 = French gauge size catheter you should use. This gives you the maximum French size catheter you should use.

THE PROCEDURE

1. Oxygenate before and after with high F_{IO_2}s. This will help prevent various cardiac arrythmias, especially PVCs and bradycardia. Use 100% O_2!
2. Fifteen sec is the maximum time the suction catheter should be left in the trachea each time the catheter is inserted.
3. Apply suction intermittently as you withdraw the catheter. Five sec is the maximum time for suction application, intermittently.
4. Hyperinflate the patient before and after, either with sighs (on vent) or bag valve mask (BVM). This helps prevent atelectasis, etc.
5. Check all alarms if your patient is on a ventilator after you have finished. Be sure they are all turned back on!

It is a good idea to flush the suction catheter after completing the procedure with NSS. This will clean the lumen of the tube, flushing any pathogens to the suction canister and ensuring the patient will not be re-contaminated by them. For your exam, you should understand the conversion from millimeters to French sizes and be able to use this practically.

Suctioning is an invasive, potentially traumatic procedure that also causes vagal (vagus nerve) stimulation. This being the case, be as gentle as possible and remember to preoxygenate. Let's look at hypoxia, a common side effect of suctioning.

SIGNS OF HYPOXIA

Signs include the following:

1. Various cardiac arrythmias such as parosysmal atrial tachycardia (PVCs), PATs, etc;
2. Tachycardia or bradycardia (the most common to watch for); and
3. Increasing patient restlessness and/or severe shortness of breath.

MISCELLANEOUS

1. Check breath sounds, before and after treatment. Check before to establish the need for suctioning and after to assess the effectiveness of the procedure. This is also a check to see if a pneumothorax has occurred, if the endotracheal tube has slipped, or any other undesirable side effect has occurred during the procedure.
2. Chart what you have done, observed, and yielded as a product, including color, consistency, odor, and amount. Note any NSS or Mucomyst instillation and its effect. Include comments on the patient's cough reflex and tolerance of the procedure, as well.
3. Be acutely aware of the fact that because you are bypassing the upper airways (when suctioning via endotracheal or tracheostomy tubes), there is a significant risk that you may introduce pathogenic microorganisms while suctioning. To minimize this risk, follow sterile procedures to the letter. If the sterile gloves or catheter touch *anything* not sterile, scrap them and get new sterile equipment.
4. When performing nasotracheal suctioning, with or without a nasopharyngeal airway, use a water-soluble, sterile lubricant. Additionally, when you stimulate a cough, advance the catheter quickly into the trachea. (When you feel the catheter impact on the epiglottis, instruct the patient to cough.) Having the patient cough opens the airway, thus allowing you to advance the catheter.
5. Protect yourself whenever you are exposed to potentially dangerous organisms—you never know what lurks in a person's sputum. You may be exposing yourself to an exotic strain of TB or MRSA, so always wear a mask and eye protection when suctioning a patient without a closed system like the Ballard or Portex catheters.
6. In the case of thick or purulent secretions, it may become necessary to "thin" them for them to move up the catheter. This can be accomplished by simply instilling 1–5 ml of NSS into the tracheostomy or endotracheal tube, waiting a few seconds, and then suctioning the saline and thinned mucous out of the airway. This may be repeated several times if needed, but if it becomes necessary to repeat this procedure more than three times in one suctioning session, it is advisable to consider using Mucomyst.

It becomes dangerous and difficult for the patient to tolerate repeated assaults with a suction catheter and it is our responsibility as RCPs to minimize the patient's risk and discomfort when possible. Mucomyst is a drug that breaks down sputum so that it becomes thin and more manageable, but it has its drawbacks. Mucomyst can cause severe bronchospasm and should be used carefully in patients prone to this; this problem is minimized if we use it directly after a bronchodilator treatment has been given.

Having said that, the usual procedure is the same as for any patient you are preparing to suction. Before you are ready to insert the catheter, instill 2–5 ml of 10% Mucomyst give the patient a few deep breaths with a BVM device and then suction the patient. Use only one dose of Mucomyst during a given procedure and do not exceed the prescribed dose written in the physician's orders. Mucomyst may unleash a flood of secretions that could overwhelm the patient, so don't run away after you're through observe your patient for a few minutes and be sure to auscultate.

A proper order for a mucolytic agent will include the name of the drug, the dose, the strength of the drug (Mucomyst comes in 10% and 20% strengths), the frequency, and the conditions under which it should be used. An example of a proper order would be: instill 4 cc of 10% Mucomyst after AT, q8º prn for exceptionally thick secretions.

This is the short version of my wisdom on suctioning. The most important things to keep in mind are that you don't suction unless it is clearly indicated and when you do, follow sterile procedures to the letter!

25

Oxygen Analyzers

You all have heard of oxygen analyzers; they're those gismos that we use to ensure that our patients are receiving the proper F_{IO_2}. Did you know that there are five different types? Oh yes, and we must care deeply about all of them. We shall look at this list of five while considering the virtues of each type. We will arrange the pertinent facts regarding analyzers in a manner that will allow us to quickly recall those facts. Keep in mind that *blue crystals* are dry, whereas *pink crystals* are wet.

PHYSICAL ANALYZERS

These use Pauling's principle, which says that O_2's paramagnetic property causes glass dumbbells filled with N_2 to be repelled. The following are facts pertaining to physical analyzers:

1. The mm Hg (torr) scale is always accurate, regardless of altitude.
2. They are responsive to the number of O_2 molecules. Readout is calibrated in mm Hg, so P_{O_2} is reflected on readout, along with O_2%.
3. They take a static sample.
4. Gaseous H_2O affects accuracy.
5. They use blue crystals to absorb moisture—change them when they become pink.
6. The Beckmann D2 is a fragile, brand name example.
7. They are safe in any atmosphere and consume no O_2.

ELECTRIC ANALYZERS

These use a Wheatstone bridge or thermal conductivity. These work on O_2's ability to disperse heat and measure it as an increase in current. The following are facts pertaining to electric analyzers:

1. They consume O_2 to sample gas.
2. They are unsafe with flammable gases because of the electrical charge.
3. The amount of increase in electrical current is due to increased cooling from O_2.
4. P_{O_2} is reflected on readout.
5. Brand names are MIRA and OEM.
6. Drying crystals: OEM is blue → pink; MIRA is pink → blue. Blue dehydrates gas sample, whereas pink hydrates it perfectly.

CHEMICAL (SCHOLANDER) ANALYZERS

These are never used clinically. These analyzers read out the true F_{IO_2} (O_2%) and use chemical absorbers in the analysis process. These units are not portable!

MASS SPECTROMETER

Gases are ionized, separated, and measured. These are highly accurate devices, but alas, are not very portable.

ELECTRO-CHEMICAL ANALYZERS

These are the ones we are all familiar with. There are two types. They are as follows:

1. Galvanic fuel cell (make their own power, but have slower response time); and
2. Clark (polargraphic) electrode (uses batteries for power to polarize electrodes).

Calibration is usually done with three screws for both types and is accomplished by room air CAL, 100% CAL, and "0" set.

Clark electrodes, which are the most common, do the following:

1. They are fast to respond.
2. They work continuously in any position.
3. They are affected by P_{H_2O}.
4. They read high with PEEP.
5. They use a KCL solution to generate a chemical reaction.
6. They measure P_{O_2} and read out F_{IO_2}.
7. They consume O_2.

Some examples are Bio Marine (galvanic fuel cell), Hudson, Teledyne, and IL (Clark).

Both types are affected by P_{H_2O} and consume O_2.

The type you are most likely to encounter is the Clark electrode electro-chemical analyzer. The others, although important in their specific applications, are of little use to the RCP because we require a fast response and a high degree of portability in our analyzers.

Part IV: Mechanical Ventilation or the Art of Respiratory Therapy

- Ventilator Classification
- The Modes of Ventilation
- Ventilator Alarms
- Basic Ventilator Controls
- Indications, Effects, and Complications of Mechanical Ventilation
- Implementation of Mechanical Ventilation and Ventilator Checks
- The Ventilator Set-up and Fine Tuning the Vent to the Patient
- Troubleshooting Tips
- Weaning the Patient from the Ventilator
- Pulmonary Function Testing

This is the part you have been waiting for! You have, no doubt, asked yourselves the questions: Why must I know all this physics and chemistry? Why do I have to know how gas reacts under various conditions and all this nonsense to grind out breathing treatments? Nay, you have but peeked through the door, one that is about to be opened wide so all can be revealed. The answer to these questions is: you must know these scientific tidbits to perform the most important part of your mission—the management of patients supported by mechanical ventilators. In the ICU environment, all other health care professionals look to the RCP to properly advise and manage patients suffering from respiratory failure.

The reason our profession is so specialized is because of the complexity of the pathologies we treat and the technical sophistication of the equipment we use in that treatment. By any technical standards, our front line ventilators use the latest microprocessor technology and precision machinery but to effectively bring technology into the fight against disease, there must be a trained practitioner bridging the gap between the patient and the technology. Technology is useless unless someone knows how to maximize its effectiveness.

Ventilators, hereafter referred to as vents, are only machines. They cannot assess and react to the sometimes fast-changing circumstances that accompany many pathologies; they are useless without someone to set them properly; and they cannot be set properly without a well-trained clinician to assess the overall situation.

So, now we begin in earnest. We shall begin by discussing the various types of vents, moving into the more complex realm of clinical assessment and therapeutic application after we have gained an understanding of the equipment and treatment modalities available.

26

Ventilator Classification

The following are parameters used to define any given vent. Familiarization with these will enable you to understand test questions that require problem-solving skills because problems unique to one type of vent are not necessarily applicable to another. Be especially aware of the differences between pressure and volume vents!

1. Pressure—Positive *or* negative. A positive pressure vent is any machine that "gives" the patient a breath. A negative pressure vent is like the old "iron lung" or the modern cuirass or poncho vents.
2. Power—source of physical power that energizes the driving mechanism. The following are three options:
   a. Electric;
   b. Pneumatic; and
   c. Electric/pneumatic.
3. Driving mechanism—the mechanical force that produces the flow of gas necessary to deliver a V_T. The following are three options:
   a. Pneumatic;
   b. Piston; and
   c. Bellows.
4. Number of circuits—the paths the gas flow follows inside the machine. They are
   a. Single; and
   b. Double.
5. Cycling parameter—the physical parameter that, when reached, results in termination of inspiration. The following are four options:
   a. Volume (Bird 6400);
   b. Pressure (IPPB);
   c. Time; and
   d. Flow.
6. Limit—physical parameters that cannot be exceeded but are not cycling parameters. Examples would be high and low pressure limits.
7. Flow pattern—four basic options include the following:
   a. Square wave;
   b. Sine wave;
   c. Accelerating; and
   d. Decelerating.
8. Internal resistance is as follows:
   a. High;
   b. Medium; and
   c. Low.

This reflects the ability of the driving mechanism to maintain the programmed flow pattern in the face of increasing back pressure.

9. Auxiliary airway maneuvers are as follows:
   a. Sigh (usually 1.5–$2 \times V_T$);
   b. Inflation hold (inspiratory plateau);
   c. Expiratory retard; and
   d. PEEP/CPAP.

On the exam, a ventilator may be described as an electrically powered, volume-cycled, pressure-limited machine. This tells you that once the desired volume is achieved, the inspiratory cycle is terminated, unless more pressure is required to deliver the V_T than is allowed by the pressure limit set by the RCP. An example of a time cycle is a vent on which the RCP sets an inspiratory time (in seconds, say 0.5), and once this time is expired, inspiration is terminated.

Electrical/pneumatic-powered, time-cycled, pressure-limited vents are used in the NICU and Pedi-ICU environments almost exclusively, whereas electric volume-cycled, pressure-limited vents are found in the adult ICU setting. Keep this in mind if the exam asks you to choose the appropriate vent for a particular patient.

Some examples of different types of ventilators are provided, in exhibit 26–1.

Exhibit 26–1 Types of Ventilators

Primarily Designed To Be Volume-Cycled, Pressure-Limited Vents	*Pressure-Cycled/Pressure-Limited*
Bear 1, 2, 3, and 5	Bird MK 7 and up
Bennett MA-1, MA-2, MA-2+2, and the PB 7200 series	Bennett PR 1, PR-2 and AP-4 and AP-5
Emerson Post-Op	*Time or Pressure-Cycled, Pressure-Limited*
Adult STAR	Bear Cub
Bird 6400ST and 8400	Bourns BP 200
Sieman's Servo 900B, 900C, 900E, and 300	

Please be aware that many of the previously mentioned vents can be set to respond to other cycling parameters, like time or pressure but these examples illustrate the primary design goals and classifications of each machine. Also know that this list is short and does not include all machines currently available. In fact, you probably think I just crawled out from beneath a rock. I assure you that is not the case. I'm just trying to stick with the types of ventilators that the NBRC likes.

The Modes of Ventilation

I am certain that everyone reading has heard muffled talk about such seemingly vacuous things like assist control, synchronized intermittent mandatory ventilation (SIMV), pressure support, and the like. You now will have the window to these mysteries opened for you so that you, too, can fully understand these modes. Modes of ventilation are simply different types of mechanical ventilatory support. They operate differently to achieve various ends—much like the modes of an air conditioner where different settings provide different levels of cooling or heating. By choosing a particular mode, we can begin to tailor the patient's treatment by providing the level of support we think is needed at that particular point in the therapy. Figure 27–1 illustrates the various ventilatory patterns produced by the following modes of ventilation; these modes have been included for your reference. Shall we have a closer look?

CONTROL MODE

When a vent is set to the control mode, the machine provides only the rate that is programmed into it. No additional, spontaneous breaths can be triggered by the patient. It is for precisely this reason that this mode is never used by itself. It is used in conjunction with "H" valve or blowby intermittent mandatory ventilation (IMV), but never by itself.

ASSIST-CONTROL MODE (AC)

In assist-control mode, the machine will deliver the programmed rate, but the patient may take breaths in addition to those that have been programmed; each of the additional breaths will also deliver the preset V_T. If, for example, the machine is set at a rate of 10 bpm and a V_T of 700 ml, the patient will receive those breaths without any effort on his or her part. If the patient wishes to take an additional 10 breaths, he or she may; however, each of those additional breaths will be delivered at the V_T programmed into the machine. If the V_T is 700 ml, then each of the additional 10 breaths will be 700 ml in volume—not more, not less. Spontaneous breaths are always delivered at the preset V_T in assist-control mode. AC mode on the PB 7200 series vents is called CMV mode.

ASSIST MODE

The assist mode is the same as described previously with one great difference—there is no "backup" or pre-programmed/control rate dialed into the vent. The patient must rely entirely on his or her own (spontaneous) inspiratory effort to trigger the machine and therefore get a breath. Each time the patient triggers the machine, it delivers the programmed V_T, but to get the breath, the patient *must* trigger the machine. On the PB 2800 home vent, setting the vent on assist is really setting the vent on assist-control. Why Bennett did this I can't say, but this is the only case of confusing labeling I know of. For what I hope are obvious reasons, we have relegated the assist mode to the same exile as the control mode; we never use the assist mode!

INTERMITTENT MANDATORY VENTILATION MODE

When using the IMV mode, a backup rate, or control rate is programmed into the vent to provide a minimal amount of support to the patient. To facilitate the patient's spontaneous respirations, an "H" valve is placed in the inspiratory side of the vent circuit, before the humidifier. Oxygen flows to the

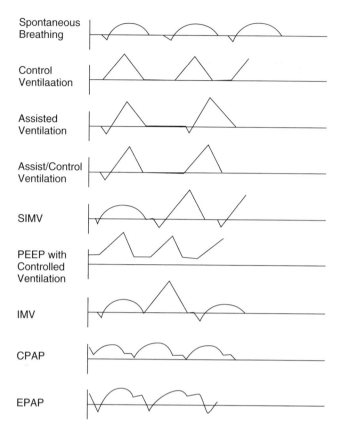

Figure 27–1 Ventilatory Patterns

"H" valve from a jet nebulizer via a long, wide bore tube. This arrangement allows the patient to take spontaneous breaths, as large or as small as he or she likes, in addition to the intermittent mandatory breaths from the vent, the volume of which is programmed into the vent. This mode is a combination of control and spontaneous breaths.

OK, let's try it this way. With the previously mentioned "H" valve in line, we set the vent at 8 bpm × 800 ml. Without any effort on the patient's part, he or she will get eight breaths/min with a volume of 800 ml/breath, for a total of 6.4 L/min in mandatory ventilation. The patient can draw additional breaths at any time and at any volume he or she wishes. These additional spontaneous breaths help to build the patient's strength, leading toward self-sufficiency. As the patient becomes better able to meet his or her own ventilatory demands, the mandatory rate is gradually decreased, hopefully to the point where the patient can be taken off the vent completely. One drawback to this is that when the patient takes a breath, the machine may then slam in another one on top of it. Not to worry—technology has an answer to this problem.

SYNCHRONIZED INTERMITTENT MANDATORY VENTILATION MODE

SIMV is built into a vent, rather than being facilitated through a "hang-on" accessory. In SIMV mode, everything operates the same as IMV, except for the following two things:

1. The patient triggers a demand valve, a device not unlike a scuba regulator, which then delivers the patient's spontaneous breath. The demand valve provides the patient with the same F_{IO_2} as the vent is set for because it is a part of the vent.
2. The vent has a delay, usually 4 sec. If the machine senses a patient-triggered breath within this 4-second window, a machine breath will be delivered at that time. This feature ensures that the machine does not jam a machine breath into the patient on top of a spontaneous one. If the machine does not sense a spontaneous breath 4 sec before the machine breath, it gives the machine breath. OK?

PRESSURE SUPPORT VENTILATION

Pressure support ventilation (PSV) was originally conceived to help patients overcome the resistance to breathing caused by the vent circuits and artificial airways. To set PSV, the vent mode selector is set to the designated mode, then the desired level of pressure support is programmed. Each time the patient triggers a spontaneous breath, the machine delivers a pressurized breath up to the preset pressure support level and no further. The objective is to make the spontaneous breath as easy as possible to obtain, without making patients expend all of their slim resources on only overcoming the resistance created by the airway and vent circuit, which would leave them little reserve to achieve a tidal breath. Conversely, it is not the goal of PSV to provide the patient's total V_T.

For example, if a patient is struggling to breathe, we set the vent to PSV mode and dial in a support level of 10 cmH_2O. With each spontaneous breath triggered by the patient, the vent will boost to 10 cmH_2O and no more, easing the patient's WOB. That's the theory.

The PSV mode can be used in conjunction with the SIMV mode as well as by itself. If mandatory breaths are programmed, those breaths will be delivered by the vent at the appropriate intervals and programmed V_T. The programmed V_T will not be delivered during the spontaneous pressure support breaths. Remember that pressure support breaths are triggered by the patient—they are not mandatory programmed machine breaths and their V_T will vary based on the patient's effort.

The original concept of PSV, as stated previously, has been modified by some to be a constant IPPB. In some cases, the level of pressure support is adjusted until the desired V_T is delivered. Once the pressure support level is set and the desired volume is being returned by the patient, the patient is left to cruise on this PSV setting. The doctors and RCPs less knowledgeable than you claim victory by saying the patient is weaned from mandatory ventilation. In such cases, PSV ceases to become a weaning tool and simply assumes the form of a basic pressure cycled ventilator. With some of the newer, sportier vents available today, PSV has become old news in its original context.

FLOW-BY

This is another mode that was devised to reduce the patient's WOB. Flow-by accomplishes this by generating a constant gas flow through the vent circuit, enabling the patient to draw from a gas supply that is slightly pressurized because of the constant flow. Because a supply of fresh gas is always available at the patient's artificial airway, airway resistance is dramatically reduced, easing the patient's WOB during spontaneous breathing. One can think of flow-by as a passive form of PSV. The machine will still deliver control breaths between the patient's spontaneous breaths. Flow-by also makes patients so comfortable, if improperly used, that they fail to wean off the vent as fast as those using an old fashion T-tube; but, this is my opinion—far be it for me to stand in the way of high technology.

Flow-by is found on the PB-7200a and 7200e vents that have become the new standard in many acute care settings. For your exam, it might be good to know that there are several caveats when programming flow-by. Flow-by cannot be used effectively while PSV is turned on; it can be one *or* the other only. If PSV and flow-by are programmed, PSV will trigger with each spontaneous breath, overriding the flow-by. Finally, flow-by can be used only, like PSV, in the SIMV mode. If you think about it, flow-by and PSV are ineffective in the assist-control (CMV on the 7200s) mode because, A/C delivers the full, preset tidal volume when a spontaneous breath triggers the vent.

Although there are other, more exotic modes of ventilation, the ones mentioned are the modes you might encounter on an exam. We will discuss weaning again, later, but for now get a grasp on the previously defined tools. Understand that these modes are meant to either provide total support to patients, or assist them in gradually developing their stamina to a point where they will no longer require mechanical support from the vent. Control, assist, and assist-control provide high levels of support, whereas IMV, SIMV, PSV, and flow-by provide methods for the gradual withdrawal of support.

AUXILIARY AIRWAY MANEUVERS

Sighs

Sighs are essentially a deep breath used to prevent atelectasis when smaller V_Ts are being used. Many vents perform these maneuvers automatically, only requiring the RCP to turn the function "on." Sighs are usually set to volumes 1.5–2 times the patient's V_T and delivered between 6–12 times/hour. An attempt should be made to keep the peak sigh pressures between 50–60 cmH_2O or lower. Use caution when setting sigh parameters on patients with badly diseased lungs because these patients may not be able to tolerate the increased pressures generated, resulting in a pneumothorax.

Expiratory Retard

Expiratory retard causes the expiratory phase of the breath to be retarded (slowed), facilitating increased mechanical bronchodilation time. This is much like pursed lip breathing. This option is rarely used because in practice it doesn't act the way theory dictates. Additionally, it decreases venous return.

Inspiratory Hold

This maneuver does exactly what its name implies—it holds inspiration, usually for 0.1 to 0.5 sec, causing inspired gas to be better distributed throughout the patient's lungs. This option is rarely used because it has a tendency to cause patient discomfort and an increase in the Pa_{CO_2}.

Positive End Expiratory Pressure and Continuous Positive Airway Pressure

Positive end expiratory pressure (PEEP) and continuous positive airway pressure (CPAP) are the same thing, except that it is called PEEP when mandatory vent breaths are programmed and CPAP when no mandatory vent breaths are involved. These options are usually applied when the patient's Pa_{O_2} is < 50 torr on 50% O_2. PEEP/CPAP functions to increase the Pa_{O_2} by increasing the functional residual capacity (FRC), compliance, and O_2 transport by increasing the resting baseline pressure.

28

Ventilator Alarms

Vent alarms are probably the most important devices we use to stave off disaster. When setting the alarms, we must set the parameters close enough to the actual vent settings to allow for patient movement while maximizing patient safety. The following list is a generalization, including those alarms found on most vents. Be aware that each manufacturer may have particular alarm combinations they are fond of. This list covers the essential alarms that must be set, if they are available. We shall approach this section in a cause and effect manner to allow better association between potential problems and their corresponding alarm responses.

1. Patient Disconnect——————Low Pressure Alarm, Low Volume (V_T or $\dot{V}E$)
   Set your low pressure alarm 5 to 10 cmH$_2$O below the peak pressure.
2. High Temperature——————High Temperature Alarm/Inline temperature probe.
   Temperature should not exceed 37°C.
3. Low Gas Source Press——————Pressure Sensor/Alarm (not an analyzer)
4. Increased Airway Resistance = High Pressure Alarm
   This could be due to secretions, bronchospasm, or other circuit or airway obstruction.
   Set your high pressure alarm 10 to 15 cmH$_2$O above your peak airway pressure.
5. I:E Ratio > 1:1——————Ratio Alarm
6. Power Failure/Vent Failure——————Vent Inoperative Alarm
7. Low/High Minute Volume——————Low/High Minute Volume
8. Low/High Respiratory Rate——————Low/High Rate
9. Low PEEP/CPAP——————Low PEEP/CPAP pressure due to leak in circuit because of a loose connection or endotracheal/tracheostomy tube cuff leak. Set the low PEEP/CPAP alarm 2 to 4 cmH$_2$O below the set level of PEEP/CPAP.

In my opinion, in order of importance, the alarm priorities are the following:

1. Patient disconnect (low pressure);
2. High pressure;
3. Low V_T or $\dot{V}_E$; and
4. all others.

The objective of these alarms is to ensure patient safety and alert the RCP to any undesirable or life-threatening situations that may arise. To optimize the effectiveness of alarms, they should be set to alert the staff to evolving problems, not set to go off only after a crisis is upon you. Some vents provide the RCP with alarm options that border on bizarre in their use and negligible in their effectiveness; although you may wish to disable them, think twice before you do. About the time you bypass an alarm, that situation will arise. Not only does bypassing an alarm cause a safety issue, it causes a liability issue as well—if the machine malfunctions, the manufacturer is not responsible because you have altered the intended function of the machine. As a rule, if the alarm is on the vent, use it! Simply set your parameters appropriately.

Basic Ventilator Controls

The basic controls, rate, tidal volume, F_{IO_2}, modes, and pressure limits are the hub of the wheel, whereas auxiliary maneuvers complement or enhance these basic functions of mechanical ventilatory support.

BASIC CONTROLS

These are rate (frequency = f), tidal volume (V_T), F_{IO_2}, flow rate (peak flow), mode selector and pressure limits. Because modes of ventilation already have been discussed, we shall not cover them here.

Rate (f)

This setting tells the vent how many breaths per minute to deliver to the patient.

Tidal Volume (V_T)

This is the volume that is delivered with each machine breath. Each time the machine cycles, a mandatory breath is delivered to the patient, the volume of which is called tidal volume.

Flow Rate (Peak Flow Rate)

The flow rate is usually set by the RCP as a rule (see why you need to know about pressure-time relationships?) and is measured in liters/minute. This determines how fast or how slow each breath fills the patient's lungs. Faster flows decrease T_I (inspiratory time), whereas slower flows increase T_I. Given a static (unchanging) rate, increasing the T_I (decreased flow) will decrease T_E (expiratory time), and vice versa. These two times compose the I:E ratio, which is a comparison of times in both phases of the breath. The faster the air goes in, the more time there is for it to come out. Remember, fast flow rates cause a lot of airway resistance, so we like to keep low rates between 40–60 L/min for adults. If the patient's inspiratory demand is high, you may need higher flow rates than those mentioned.

F_{IO_2} or $O_2\%$

This is the amount of oxygen ordered by the physician. More sophisticated vents mix the entire amount of gas required for all maneuvers internally, whereas some older vents must have additional devices attached to provide oxygenation.

Pressure Limits

These are the safety pop-offs that must be set to ensure excessive pressures are not delivered to the patient as the vent attempts to deliver the V_T and sigh volumes. Each pop-off should be set 10–15 cmH$_2$O over the observed peak airway pressure for each type of breath. The pop-offs for V_T and sigh breaths must be set independently because sigh breaths are larger and will therefore require slightly higher pressure to be delivered than a tidal breath. Most vents provide dual controls for this purpose.

Indications, Effects, and Complications of Mechanical Ventilation

Here is a quick reference list that provides you with some of the major physiologic effects of mechanical ventilation. The RCP should be intimately familiar with these because if inappropriate ventilator settings or maneuvers are ordered, it is up to us to point out the potential problems that may arise.

INCREASED BY VENTILATION

The following are increased by ventilation:

1. MAP;
2. Mean intrathoracic pressure;
3. Intracranial pressure;
4. Mechanical bronchodilation; and
5. Psychological and gastrointestinal stress.

DECREASED BY VENTILATION

The following are decreased by ventilation:

1. Venous return and cardiac output;
2. Urinary output;
3. Work of breathing; and
4. Intrapulmonary shunt

INCREASED BY PEEP

The following are increased by PEEP:

1. Intrapulmonary pressure;
2. Intrathoracic pressure;
3. Functional residual capacity;
4. Lung compliance;
5. Pa_{O_2} and Pv_{O_2};
6. Intracranial pressure;
7. Risk of barotrauma; and
8. Oxygen transport.

DECREASED BY PEEP

The following are decreased by PEEP:

1. Cardiac output;
2. Shunt; and
3. Extravascular lung H_2O.

The significance of these effects greatly depends on what your patient's problems are. For example, if your patient just underwent a craniotomy, then you will want to be judicious in the use of PEEP and high tidal volumes because you will wish to keep intracranial pressure low. This is one example of why this information is important to you for both the exam and your career.

INDICATIONS FOR THE INSTITUTION OF MECHANICAL VENTILATION

The indications for mechanical ventilation are

1. Apnea; and
2. Respiratory failure (this may include severe respiratory insufficiency).

The following parameters should be used as guidelines only. Each patient must be evaluated as a unique situation but when patients' clinical parameters slide into the following ranges, they are usually to the point where they cannot support themselves and need assistance.

1. $Pa_{O_2} < 60$ torr on $\geq 80\%$ O_2
   This *by itself* indicates a large intrapulmonary shunt and CPAP should be considered. When shunting exists, as it often does along with the following problems, it is only one of several problems and total mechanical support, possibly with PEEP, should be considered.

2. $Paco_2 > 50$ torr—This indicates that a dangerous level of CO_2 is beginning to accumulate (see item 3).
3. pH < 7.25—Decreasing pH indicates acid accumulation. This accumulation of acid is due to the patient's inability to eliminate CO_2 (inadequate ventilation), which translates into mechanical intervention to normalize CO_2 levels and, therefore, the acid content of the blood.
4. VC ≤ 15 ml/kg—normal VC is in the range of 60 to 75 ml/kg.
5. Negative inspiratory force (NIF) ≤ –20 cmH_2O—This reflects the patient's ability to draw in a breath. – 20 cmH_2O is considered to be the minimum acceptable effort required to take a barely adequate breath; anything less provides only enough tidal volume to ventilate the anatomic dead space.

SIGNS OF ACUTE RESPIRATORY FAILURE

1. Bad ABGs: See previous guidelines.
2. Patient is exchanging air poorly. Poor respiratory patterns and/or mechanics exist (see previous).
3. Fluid and/or protein build up in alveoli (white on CXR) and fills aveoli so gas exchange cannot take place.
4. Refractory hypoxemia (despite giving patient more O_2, Pao_2 stays low) exists.
5. Diffuse coarse and/or fine inspiratory crackles are present.
6. Thin, clear and white product is evident.
7. A patient who is in the throes of status asthmaticus has normal ABGs.

CAUSES OF ARDS (SHOCK LUNG)

Causes include the following:

1. Massive flail (many fractured ribs);
2. Massive trauma to body;
3. Multiple system trauma;
4. Patient was on pulmonary bypass an excessive length of time;
5. Sepsis;
6. Massive transfusion;
7. Chemical inhalation; and
8. Fat emboli (commonly seen in fractures of the long bones).

SIGNS OF ARDS:

Signs include the following:

1. Low Pao_2s;
2. High $Paco_2$s;
3. Low pH;
4. Decreasing compliance; and
5. Increasing shunt (onset occurs 24 to 48 hours after event).

CHRONIC RESPIRATORY FAILURE (AS SEEN IN PATIENTS WITH COPD)

Chronic respiratory failure includes the following:

1. High $Paco_2$s;
2. Low Pao_2s;
3. High (yes) pHs;
4. CO_2 narcosis (confusion and hallucinations);
5. Frequent headaches, sleepiness, and confusion;
6. Right ventricular hypertrophy (enlarged right ventricle);
7. Peripheral edema;
8. When you ventilate patients who live with chronic respiratory failure, remember to aim for Pao_2s in the 50–60 torr range if the patient's pH is in the normal range after he or she is ventilated. This will minimize the chance of knocking out the patient's hypoxic drive. If you give your patient too much O_2 and eliminate the stimulus to breathe (hypoxic drive), your patient will be on the vent forever. Additionally, you must remember that if the pH is normal, the corresponding CO_2 is most likely normal for that patient, even if it's outside the "normal" range.

CALCULATING COMPLIANCE

$$\text{Static Compliance} = C_S = \frac{\text{Delivered } V_T}{\text{Plateau Pressure} - \text{PEEP}}$$

$$\text{Dynamic Compliance} = C_D = \frac{\text{Delivered } V_T}{\text{Peak Pressure} - \text{PEEP}}$$

Average Tubing Compliance is 2–3 ml/cmH_2O × manometer press = total tubing compliance.

COMPLICATIONS OF VENTILATION

As with everything we do, there may be complications. Listed here for your perusal are a few of the more serious ones.

Barotrauma

This may appear in the form of a pneumothorax or pneumomediastinum. Keep an eye out for subcutaneous emphysema.

Tracheal Structural and Tissue Damage

This problem usually results from excessive cuff pressure.

Infection

With a direct path to the lungs, infection is a frequently encountered problem.

31

Implementation of Mechanical Ventilation and Ventilator Checks

Before we get into this section, I should point out that you must secure a physician's order for the implementation of mechanical ventilation. Once the decision is made to ventilate, the order should include all primary therapeutic settings. That would include the following minimum parameters:

1. Rate;
2. Tidal volume;
3. F_{IO_2};
4. Mode of ventilation;
5. PEEP/CPAP, if desired, or other auxiliary airway maneuvers;
6. Pressure support or flow-by, if desired; and
7. In specific cases, sighs may be ordered; in others, this may be up to the RCP.

The rest of the settings are usually up to you but you must secure an order for the previously mentioned parameters. You should be prepared to make recommendations on any or all of these parameters in the case the orders are inappropriate.

BEFORE PATIENT GOES ON VENT

Before your patient goes on vent, do the following:

1. Get baseline ABGs.
2. Get baseline vital signs and auscultate chest very carefully! Be sure to record your findings.
3. Calculate V_T (10–15ml/kg).
4. Decide on AC or SIMV mode. What is the immediate goal? AC gives the patient almost total rest, whereas SIMV makes patients work for their breaths to various degrees (depending on the mandatory rate, the higher that is, the less WOB the patient has).
5. Adjust flow for proper I:E ratio (use 0.5–1.5 sec if you're using time or work toward an I:E ratio of 1 to 1.5:2). Generally, you use time for children on pressure vents and look at the I:E ratio for adults on volume vents.
6. Set rate (f); evaluate need for support by the following:
   a) If you use higher than normal V_T, use lower than normal "f." This provides
      1) Better prevention of microatelectasis, and
      2) Better overall alveolar ventilation.
   b) Conversely, use higher rates with lower V_Ts.
      1) Decreased MAP is an advantage of this approach.
      2) Sighs can be programmed to combat atelectasis.

SOME TOOLS FOR SETTING FLOW RATES

$$T_I = \frac{V_T \text{ (in liters)}}{\text{Flow (in liters/second)}}$$

$$\text{Peak Flow Rate} = \frac{V_T}{T_I}$$

You may use these formulas to calculate your settings—or use your intuition—but these formulas show the theory behind the practice. On your exam, use these guidelines to set up your test vents. The peak flow calculation is useful if you work with Servo 900 series vents.

Remember that sine or tapered flow patterns provide better gas distribution and reduce both peak airway pressure and MAP.

VENTILATOR CHECKS

The following items are always checked during an RCP's q4° vent checks, as far as your exam is concerned. Some check parameters will differ, depending on the type of vent being used. In the real world, vent checks may be done at intervals from q2–q4°s, depending on a particular institution's policies.

1. Check tubes for condensate; drain PRN.
2. Check settings to ensure they correspond to doctor's orders.
3. Check exhaled volumes to ensure they are equal to V_T ordered.
4. Check inspiratory time or peak flow.
5. Check rate, V_T and F_{IO_2}.
6. Check that the vent is in the ordered mode.
7. Check the circuit temperature on the heat moisture exchanger (HME). (There should not be any secretions in the HME.)
8. Check the endotracheal and tracheostomy tube cuff pressure and the endotracheal tube position.
9. Check all alarms.
10. Check peak airway pressure, plateau pressure, and calculate C_D and C_S.
11. Check spontaneous rate, which = total rate – control rate.
12. Check spontaneous V_T and $\dot{V}_E$.
13. Check airway resistance, heart rate, blood pressure, breath sounds, and ABGs.
14. Check maintenance of Pa_{O_2} and Pa_{CO_2}; are they within limits?

AIRWAY RESISTANCE

$$RAW = \frac{\text{Peak Press} - \text{Plateau Press}}{\text{Flow Rate}}$$

You must use a square wave flow pattern to do calculation.

32

The Ventilator Set-up and Fine Tuning the Vent to the Patient

This section will attempt to summarize and clarify the application of algebra when initiating, maintaining, and withdrawing (weaning) ventilator support. I realize you have been barraged with formulas that seem to have vague applications; for your exams, however, these formulas will be the tools that will lead you to the right answers. With this (the exam) in mind, we shall, as we say, take it from the top. Please be aware that your ABG formulas will not be included here unless directly applicable to the treatment of the ventilator patient. The ABG formulas are important for exam purposes, so don't ignore them. All calculations regarding body weight use ideal, not actual, body weight.

VENTILATOR SET-UP

The physician will write an order that tells the RCP what "f," V_T, mode, F_{IO_2}, and auxiliary airway maneuver(s) he or she wishes the patient to be on. It is up to the RCP to notify the doctor if any or all of these settings are off base, so here are the guidelines you use on your exams.

1. V_T: To calculate V_T use the standard of 10–15 ml/kg with patients of average size. Use 10 ml/kg for petite patients and 15 ml/kg for those with larger frames. Remember to use ideal body weight, not actual weight, for the calculation. For example, a patient who weighs 75 kg × 15 ml = 1115 ml (1000 ml) = V_T.
2. f: Rate should be based on the patient's need for mechanical support. In other words, is there any spontaneous effort on the patient's part? The textbooks say a rate of 10 to 18 breaths per minute is a good place to start; 10 × 1000 ml = 10 L/min.
3. $\dot{V}_E$: Rule of thumb starting point is 5–10 L/min. Know these relationships:
$f \times V_T = \dot{V}_E$, $\dot{V}_E/V_T = f$, $\dot{V}_E/f = V_T$!
4. F_{IO_2}: Start low, basing your starting point on any pulse oximeter or ABG data you may have obtained before the vent set-up. When you begin to get into the > 60% range, consider using PEEP.
5. Mode: Choice of mode depends upon the patients' ability to participate in their ventilation or the amount of rest they require.
6. Sighs: Set sighs at 1.5 times the V_T. If your V_T is 1000 ml, set your sighs at 1500 ml.

Once you have the patient on the vent, wait 1/2 to 1 hour, draw ABGs, and make changes according to those results, especially the Pa_{CO_2} and pH. Adjustments in f, V_T and F_{IO_2} can be made at this point to bring the patient's acid-base balance and oxygenation within desired parameters. You have to start somewhere, and these guidelines are meant to do just that, give you a starting point. Try to get a good feel for this information in general, but be sure you understand the mathematical relationships highlighted previously.

FINE TUNING THE VENT TO THE PATIENT

Here are some notes that might help you make those clinical decisions on your exams or in real life, if you dare.

Ideas Regarding P_{CO_2} and $\dot{V}_E$

1. If the patient has normal lungs, aim for a normal Pa_{CO_2}. Adjust your minute volume accordingly (rate + $V_T = \dot{V}_E$).
2. If the patient has COPD, aim for his or her baseline P_{CO_2}; if none is available, adjust $\dot{V}_E$ to yield a normal pH.
3. Patients with head injuries or post-craniotomies usu-

ally benefit from high minute volumes for the first 12–24 hours, keeping the P_{CO_2} in the 30–35 torr range, providing vasoconstriction, thereby reducing edema (swelling).

4. If your patient has a high P_{CO_2}, you must increase ventilation. Increase the V_T first, increase the rate as a second option but use the V_T to increase $\dot{V}_E$ and improve gas distribution, preventing atelectasis.
5. If the patient has a low P_{CO_2}, decrease the rate first and decrease the V_T as the second option. By doing this, you preserve the improved gas distribution of the higher volume.
6. In the treatment of low P_{CO_2}, there is one other rarely used, but testable option—to add mechanical dead space to the vent circuit. You can do this by simply adding small (6 inch) sections of tubing, each of which is ~150 ml in volume. You keep adding tubing until the Pa_{CO_2} reaches the desired range. Adding dead space results in patients rebreathing some of their own expired CO_2, causing a slight rise in the their Pa_{CO_2}. When adding dead space, no other settings are changed.

Ideas Regarding P_{O_2}

1. 100% O_2 can cause ARDS.
2. Try to keep the F_{IO_2}s you use ≤ 0.5; 0.4 is better. Use PEEP if necessary to facilitate lowering the F_{IO_2}.
3. Use PEEP if
   a. F_{IO_2} is 0.6 to 0.7 (60%–70%), and
   b. The patient's cardiovascular status is *good*.
4. PEEP in adults: Start with 5 cm and increase in increments of 5 cm, until optimum PEEP (highest PEEP with the highest Pa_{O_2}) is reached. In children, start at 2 cm and increase by 2–3 cm.
5. After you reach optimum or peak PEEP (increasing Pa_{O_2} by 20–40 torr), start dropping F_{IO_2}.
6. If the F_{IO_2} is > 0.5, drop the F_{IO_2} by 5%–20% and recheck Pa_{O_2}. If F_{IO_2} is < 0.5, drop the F_{IO_2} by increments of 5% only at a time.

COMPLIANCE

Dynamic compliance is the relationship between how easily a lung will expand and the RAW with gas flowing through the airways. When we measure dynamic compliance, we not only measure the expandability of the lung, but the airway resistance and the resistance created by the vent circuit. Remember that when peak airway pressure rises, C_D decreases. Besides a loss of lung expandability, water in the vent tubing, retained secretions, bronchospasm, or any airway obstruction may cause a decrease in C_D.

Static compliance is the more accurate measurement of lung expandability because air flow is stopped. The higher the compliance, the easier it will be to ventilate that lung because it is less stiff. The stiffer the lung, the lower the compliance because the lung tissue has less expandability. To get a static measurement, an inspiratory hold or plateau is programmed for just one breath so the measurement can be taken. Two factors that may increase your plateau pressure, thereby decreasing C_S, are fluid in the alveoli (ARDS or pneumonia) or restrictive lung disease. Normal expected C_S on the vent is between 40 and 60 cmH_2O. C_S for normal lungs off the vent (you and I) is between 80 and 100 cmH_2O or more.

Keep in mind that optimal PEEP = the level of PEEP that results in the highest C_S.

Compliance represents the relationship between the Δ in volume versus the Δ in pressure (Δ = change). We are primarily concerned with static compliance, but dynamic compliance is also of concern, as noted in the previous paragraph. Volume measurements can be in milliliters or liters. Pressure measurements are always in cmH_2O. For the following examples, we shall assume that our vent's V_T is set at 1,000 ml, peak airway pressure is 25 cmH_2O, plateau pressure is 15 cmH_2O, and the PEEP is 5 cmH_2O.

Static Compliance

$$C_S = \frac{\text{Set } V_T \text{ in milliliters or liters}}{\text{Plateau Pressure} - \text{PEEP}} = \text{Volume/cmH2O}$$

$$C_S = \frac{1000 \text{ ml}}{15 - 5 \text{ cmH}_2\text{O}} = \frac{1000 \text{ ml}}{10 \text{ cmH}_2\text{O}} = 100 \text{ ml/cmH2O}$$

This means that for each cmH_2O of pressure applied to the lungs, 100 ml of volume is delivered. Static compliance always uses plateau pressure.

Dynamic Compliance

$$C_D = \frac{\text{Set } V_T \text{ in milliliters or liters}}{\text{Peak Airway Pressure} - \text{PEEP}} = \text{Volume/cmH2O}$$

$$C_D = \frac{1000 \text{ ml}}{25 - 5 \text{ cmH2O}} = \frac{1000 \text{ ml}}{20 \text{ cmH}_2\text{O}} = 50 \text{ ml/cmH2O}$$

We have discussed the difference between static and dynamic compliance, so I will not belabor the point, but be aware that it is the *static* compliance that most likely will appear on the test. Be prepared to do the calculation and don't forget to subtract the PEEP. As has been noted, static

compliance is of greater concern on your exam than dynamic, but be aware of both. The units of measure, as far as the exam is concerned, most likely will be ml/cmH$_2$O, but be prepared for L/cmH$_2$O.

IDEAL $\dot{V}_E$

This formula will provide you with an idea of what to change your patient's $\dot{V}_E$ in order to achieve proper acid–base balance. Always assume your desired Paco$_2$ = 40 torr, unless you are given cause to think otherwise, ie, your patient has COPD.

$$\dot{V}_E = \frac{Paco_2 \text{ (actual)} \times \dot{V}_E \text{ (actual)}}{Paco_2 \text{ (desired)}} = \text{New } \dot{V}_E \text{ (in liters)}$$

Use this formula to change your vent settings when pH and Paco$_2$ abnormalities are involved. Do try to keep your V$_T$S from getting too low, because a larger V$_T$ prevents atelectasis and improves gas distribution, also minimizing any V/Q abnormalities that may exist.

An example problem may be the following:

A 26-year-old patient with no spontaneous effort is on the following vent settings:

f = 10, V$_T$ = 600 ml, % O$_2$ = 35%, T$_I$ = 0.5 sec, mode = SIMV.

On these settings, the patient's pH = 7.30. Paco$_2$ = 59 torr. What setting(s) would you change to correct this problem?

1. Increase the f to 18.
2. Increase the V$_T$ to 900 ml.
3. Increase the f to 12.
4. Increase the V$_T$ to 750 ml.
5. Change nothing.
   A. 1 only.
   B. 1 and 4 only.
   C. 2 only.
   D. 5 only.

Now, let's do the math and talk about each option. Based on the data given to us in the problem, we know that actual Paco$_2$ = 59 torr and actual $\dot{V}_E$ = 10 × 600 ml = 6.0 L/min.

Let's plug these known numbers into our formula for desired $\dot{V}_E$.

$$\dot{V}_E = \frac{59 \text{ torr} \times 6.0 \text{ L}}{40 \text{ torr}} = \frac{354}{40} = 8.85 \text{ or } 9.0 \text{ L/min}.$$

Our new $\dot{V}_E$ should be 9.0 L/min; now, the problem is what to change to achieve this new $\dot{V}_E$. Let's analyze this.

If you choose "A," your $\dot{V}_E$ = 10.8 L. Too much!

"B" gives you a $\dot{V}_E$ of 13.5 L. Wrong again! This is way too much!

"C" yields a $\dot{V}_E$ of 9.0 L/min. Sounds good! But check them all!!

"D" is just plain goofy!

After looking at all of the options, we can (hopefully) plainly see that "C" is the most correct answer. Because our calculation brings us closest to 9.0 L/min, this would be the most correct answer.

There are several hints in the problem that tell us that we will have to raise the $\dot{V}_E$ too. We are told that the patient is 26 years old, someone not likely to be a CO$_2$ retainer, thereby telling us that our desired Paco$_2$ will be 40 torr. Low pH and high Paco$_2$ = respiratory acidosis; another hint that $\dot{V}_E$ must be increased is that without spontaneous ventilation, the patient can't compensate on his or her own.

33

Troubleshooting Tips

When confronted with a possible vent malfunction, the first thing you must do is to remove the patient from the machine and ventilate them by hand (BVM). Call another RCP or a nurse to manually ventilate the patient while you evaluate the performance of the machine.

PATIENT ASSESSMENT

After you have disconnected the patient, assess the patient and check the following:

1. Chest movement. Check for good expansion and symmetry.
2. Check that breath sounds are bilateral.
3. Note the amount of resistance encountered with BVM ventilation. If you encounter high pressure while bagging, the problem may be with the patient.
4. Check that vital signs are stable.
5. Check status of patient's respiratory distress.
   a. If the distress continues, it is a problem with the patient. This must be diagnosed and corrected through treating the patient.
   b. If BVM ventilation relieves the patient's distress, your problem is with the ventilator or the fact that the patient is fighting the machine.

ASSESSING THE VENTILATOR

Assuming the problem is with the machine and/or circuit, rather than the patient, follow these handy tips.

1. Check for leaks. Leaks can cause decreased peak pressures, low PEEP, or low pressure alarms.
2. Check the position of the endotracheal or tracheostomy tube along with the cuff pressure. If the patient has a chest tube, check that there is no leak at that site. Tracheoesophageal fistulas can cause a leak too.
3. Check the circuit. Check any points in the circuit where it could come apart, loosen, or even a small leak could occur. Press every connection and push it tightly together, even if it appears to be properly connected. Start at one end of the circuit and work your way to the other, i.e., start at the vent end or the patient end, but be systematic.
4. Do not discount the likelihood that the patient's condition has changed. An increase in compliance, decrease in RAW, improved atelectasis or infiltrates, or a change in the patient's position all can cause a decrease in peak pressures and, therefore, reflect improvement in the patient's condition.
5. Check the vent settings. It is not unlikely that someone has come along and changed the settings, either accidentally or intentionally. Doctors are notorious for this.

Increased Peak Pressures

1. Check endotracheal tube position and patency. Check for tube obstructions, herniated cuff, and proper tube position (2 cm above carina).
2. Check the patient. Increased secretions, decreased compliance, pneumothorax, pulmonary edema, and pneumonia all can cause increased peak pressures.
3. Check vent circuit. Condensate and kinks in the tubing can cause peak pressure increases.
4. Check the vent settings.

Decreased Expired Volumes

The causes are essentially the same as those for decreased peak pressure, but also may be caused by a spirometer leak if no other leaks are present.

Decreased PEEP/CPAP

These can be caused by leaks, increased patient inspiratory effort, or altered vent settings.

Increased PEEP/CPAP

These can be caused by changes in settings, decreased T_E, water in the expiratory limb of the circuit, or the patient fighting the machine.

Manometer Needle is Slow to Return to Zero

This can be caused by exhalation valve tubing being kinked (thin tube), a sticky exhalation valve, or water in the expiratory limb of the circuit.

Slow Rise in Manometer Needle

This can be caused by a leak in the circuit, insufficient peak flow setting, or increased patient inspiratory effort.

Poor I:E Ratio

This can be caused by inappropriate flow rates, high mandatory rates, or the machine being set to sensitive and autocycles.

The most important thing to remember is that if the patient is in distress, you ensure adequate ventilation via a BVM before you play Sherlock Holmes with the vent. Additionally, remember the various relationships we discussed among volume, flow, pressure, and time—this is where they come into play. Remember that flow controls the speed at which the breath goes into the lungs—if it is slower, RAW is decreased; if it is higher, RAW is increased. The higher your vent rate and/or volume, the faster the flow rate must be to provide proper T_I and T_E. Physics makes the world go round and is not hard, if you just *think*! Look at the practical application and see how it works.

Resolving problems with ventilators and the patients attached to them is a systematic process governed by science. The key to solving these problems lies in knowing the relationships among the variables involved and what occurs to each when we manipulate them. That's why gas laws are important. That's why it's important to know the physics that govern lung and thorax mechanics and the physiologic effects they yield. That's why we were so concerned with positive and negative pressure breathing, PEEP/CPAP, and blood gases. Take the time to work all of these concepts into one interrelated idea with the patient as the focal point, if you haven't already.

34

Weaning the Patient from the Ventilator

WEANING PARAMETERS

Before we start the weaning process, we must assess the patient's ability to tolerate breathing on his or her own, even for a few minutes at a time. To gain some feel for a patient's capabilities, we perform weaning parameters. By measuring these various parameters, we can determine patients' abilities to sustain themselves for the short term.

As always, these guidelines are not carved in stone and the RCP must carefully assess the patient's ability. The minimum parameters are the following:

1. Spontaneous rate: < 25 is good because it avoids undue stress that leads to muscle fatigue, but generally a rate of ≤ 32 facilitates weaning well.
2. NIF: Negative inspiratory force should be at least –20 cmH$_2$O. The normal maximal force is –70 to –100 cmH$_2$O.
3. FVC or VC Forced vital capacity should be at least 1.0 L or 10–20 ml/kg. This gives some insight into the patient's ability to take deep breaths, should the need arise.
4. ABGs should be reasonable with minimum PEEP because the patient will not be on PEEP when placed on T-piece weaning trials.
5. V$_T$: Minimum tidal volume should be 250–300 ml. The average person has ~ 150 ml of anatomic dead space, leaving a minimal amount of volume for gas exchange.
6. MVV: Maximal voluntary ventilation measures the patient's ability to ventilate under the most stressful conditions and should be three to four times the $\dot{V}_E$.
7. $\dot{V}_E$: Minimal acceptable $\dot{V}_E$ is 5–6 L/min.
8. The patient's heart rate should be kept < 120 bpm, unless tachycardia is an underlying condition.

Upon finding the patient capable of sustaining these values, we can begin weaning either in terms of decreasing the vent rate, using SIMV, etc., or starting T-piece trials.

When we begin to wean a patient, we may find it necessary to proceed slowly; by this, I mean that rather than taking a patient off the vent for short periods, we may choose to gradually decrease the amount of mandatory support. Our primary criteria for weaning will be objective patient assessment, subjective assessment, and the guidelines discussed in the following text.

WEANING TECHNIQUES

IMV and SIMV

These are the methods of choice when weaning a patient off a high level of mandatory ventilation. Operationally, we decrease the $\dot{V}_E$ by decreasing the "f" rather than the V$_T$. As the rate is decreased, the patient is forced to compensate by initiating spontaneous breaths. By leaving the V$_T$ intact at higher than spontaneous levels, atelectasis is prevented and good gas distribution is preserved. The "f" is continuously decreased to the point where the patient can tolerate being off the vent for a period.

Sink or Swim (T-Piece or Trach Collar Trials)

When the patient demonstrates, through weaning parameters, that the patient can sustain him or herself, we can begin taking the patient off the vent and placing him or her on a T-piece for increasing periods, in accordance with the patient's tolerance. There is no SIMV support, PSV, or flow-by—just patient effort—and as the patient gains strength and endurance, the length of the trials can be increased.

PSV, CPAP and Flow-By

These modes can be set to overcome the resistance the patient encounters when trying to initiate a breath through the vent circuit; this may or may not be used in conjunction with mandatory vent breaths. These modes theoretically allow the patient to take a normal spontaneous breath without additional resistance. If any mandatory breaths are programmed, the "f" can be gradually decreased until the patient becomes self-sufficient. At this point, the patient can be placed on a T-piece. Remember that CPAP, in addition to overcoming RAW, will increase O_2 transport so it must be reduced to minimal levels before placing the patient on a T-piece.

Weaning methods such as pressure support and flow-by are accompanied by a caveat. They are used to wean the patient from mandatory ventilation, but when the patient is subjected to a room air T-piece, the patient crashes because of anxiety. Normal breathing is so much more difficult than these passive weaning modes that patients become scared of failure. Ideally, as patients are weaned to these passive modes, they, in turn, should be gradually minimized (made more difficult) to help acclimate the patient to ambient breathing.

TERMINATION OF WEANING TRIAL

Terminate a weaning trial if the following conditions occur:

1. Pa_{O_2} < 70 torr (Sa_{O_2} < 92%);
2. HR >120 bpm;
3. pH < 7.25;
4. MAP changes by more than 15 cmH_2O;
5. Pa_{CO_2} increases by 1 torr/min;
6. PVCs occur; and
7. The "Q" sign develops (patient becomes obtunded).

Once again, these are guidelines, not hard and fast rules. The patient may have underlying conditions that preclude the application of one or more of these parameters. Use your assessment skills! Your assessment skills are the critical factor.

Now we shall focus on the patient who is marginally ready to come off the vent. We now will consider how to get a patient with COPD or considerable neuromuscular damage off the vent and keep them off. The point at which we find our patient is when the patient has successfully completed a 12-hour weaning trial and appears strong enough to tolerate being off 24 hours. At this point, the RCP must consider ways to improve the patient's chances of success; if indeed, the patient can go 24 hours, then we must continue to assist the patient to stay off the vent. We shall look into these methods.

TOOLS TO HELP PATIENTS STAY OFF THE VENT

IPPB and Manual Breaths via BVM

Any patient with a marginal pulmonary reserve should be a candidate for ventilatory augmentation with IPPB immediately after they wean from the vent. By using IPPB q4º, a patient can be provided with hyperinflation to prevent atelectasis, improve the cough reflex, and/or help control CO_2 accumulation.

Instead of IPPB, hyperinflation may be provided by *bagging* the patient with a BVM device q4º. Manual ventilation can achieve the same beneficial effects that IPPB produces, but usually for a shorter duration.

If your patient has copious secretions, alternate bagging with the IPPB so that the patient is being bagged or given an IPPB q2º. Two to 5 days after weaning, it should be possible to discontinue the IPPB.

After the IPPB has been discontinued, hyperinflation can be facilitated via BVM by giving 10 to 15 deep breaths q2–4º around the clock as indicated or, if the patient is up to it, q4º while awake. By bagging patients periodically, we can ensure alveolar hyperinflation, improve their cough reflex, and intermittently blow off CO_2. Manual ventilation should continue until patients become strong enough to do ISB volumes of at least 1.0 L and clear their own secretions.

Pulse Oximetry

When starting serious weaning, it is advisable to monitor the patient with an oximeter. In doing this, the RCP can continuously monitor the patient's Sa_{O_2} and heart rate. If the patient fails to maintain adequate parameters, the RCP can intervene before a crisis occurs.

As a rule, acceptable SATs are > 90% but many patients momentarily dip into the mid to high 80s during the first 10–15 minutes after they are taken off the vent. Don't panic if this happens; just watch them carefully. If their SATs drop into the low 80s and stay there, terminate the trial.

It is also a good idea to monitor patients with oximetry during the first 24 hours they are off the vent. In doing so, you will note that the SAT drops when patients are suctioned, cough, exert themselves, or try to speak (with the aid of a speaking valve). Don't get excited, these are normal events but should the SAT stay low, you can immediately hyperoxigenate patients and adjust their F_{IO_2}, PRN. Oximetry is useful whenever you have concerns about a patient's oxygenation. Don't be afraid to take a spot reading—that is the only way you assure yourself that all is well.

Patient Ventilation Monitors

Several companies make ventilation monitors that read out the patient's respiratory rate, V_T, and $\dot{V}_E$; these include alarms that can be set to warn the RCP of impending trouble. These monitors are invaluable when used on patients with a marginal pulmonary status. It is feasible to use these monitors only with endotracheal or tracheostomy tubes because the gas flow is controlled and channeled in those circumstances. If the patient tolerates being off the vent for 2 to 3 days, the monitor can be discontinued.

Speaking Valves

These valves are handy devices that allow tracheostomy patients to speak relatively normally. The valves prevent the patient from exhaling through the tracheostomy tube, forcing the air past the vocal cords. There are no flow-dependent attachments or special devices—simply a one-way valve that fits directly on the tracheostomy tube. It is necessary to deflate the cuff before placing the valve on the tracheostomy tube. These valves go a long way to boost patient morale.

There are two "big players" in speaking valves. Passey-Muir valves are more traditional one-way valves which close completely during exhalation, forcing the patient to cough through their mouth. Montgomery valves are like a halfway solution, providing enough back-pressure to force air past the vocal cords, but still allowing the patient to expectorate through their tracheostomy tube.

Choosing the proper valve requires consideration of the patient's condition. Stronger patients do well with the Passey-Muir valve because they can move their secretions up and out through their mouth. The Montgomery valve facilitates speech in the weaker patients who have not yet developed a strong cough response but are capable of speech. This valve requires only that patients cough their secretions through their tracheostomy tubes, after which they can simply reset the flap with their fingers. These issues are not likely to appear on an exam but they may be useful to you in your chosen profession to facilitate patient weaning or to improve patient quality of life.

35

Pulmonary Function Testing

The focus for your exam will test your knowledge of the various volumes and, when combined, the capacities they form; additionally, you will be asked to distinguish among test results for patients with restrictive, obstructive, or a combination of both diseases.

The first thing you must do is memorize the diagram of volumes and capacities in Figure 35–1, which are listed in the following:

- Total Lung Capacity (TLC) = (Do I really need to define this?)
- Inspiratory Capacity (IC) = Tidal Volume (T_V) + Inspiratory Reserve Volume (IRV)
- Functional Residual Capacity (FRC) = Expiratory Reserve Volume (ERV) + Residual Volume (RV)
- Vital Capacity (VC) = ERV + TV + IRV

RESTRICTIVE LUNG DISEASE

In this situation, you will observe that patients' volumes and capacities will be lower than their predicted values on a pulmonary function test (PFT) study. This occurs because in restrictive diseases, the lungs' elasticity is gradually reduced, as the disease progresses. Reduced elasticity translates into a decreased ability of the lung tissue to expand as much as it could under normal conditions. Therefore, a patient's vital capacity, tidal volume, etc., will be less than predicted because of the inability of the lungs to properly expand. Flow rates may not be greatly affected, if at all, in those individuals with restrictive lung disease, but most likely will show some decrease, again, because of the lack of elasticity/recoil. Also, you will see little, if any, change in pre and post bronchodilator studies done on patients who have restrictive lung disease. So, in a nutshell, an overall decrease in volumes and capacities, little or no improvement after bronchodilator therapy, along with a normal FEV_1 indicate *restrictive lung disease.*

OBSTRUCTIVE LUNG DISEASE (COPD)

In obstructive disease, air can get into the lungs easily, but has difficulty getting out because of airway obstruction. You can expect to see the various volumes be greater than predicted because of physiologic compensation, whereas flow rates are less than predicted because of the obstructive nature of the disease, especially the FEV_1 and the FEF_{25-75}. If the FEV_1 is < 70% of predicted, it is an indication of obstructive disease; additionally, the FEF_{25-75} (small airway flow rates are measured in L/sec, whereas other flow rates are measured in L/min) is an indicator of obstructive disease if it is decreased below predicted levels. We see improvement in the PFTs of people with obstructive disease after pre/post bronchodilator studies because of improved airflow that is facilitated by the relief of the bronchospasm that accompanies obstructive disease.

ASTHMA

Pre and post-peak expiratory flows frequently are done with a portable flow gauge, along with each aerosol therapy (AT) treatment, to assess the effectiveness of the therapy while also monitoring the patient's improvement. However, the best and most precise way to assess the reversibility and/or the degree of reversibility of bronchospasm is to perform a before and after bronchodilator PFT study/methacholine challenge test. The goal of this test is to produce a 20% decrease in the FEV_1 and determine the least amount of methacholine needed to produce this effect. The PFT will graphically demonstrate if the bronchospasm is reversible and to what extent it is reversed by inhaled bronchodilator therapy. The proof of reversibility, or the lack thereof, will be shown

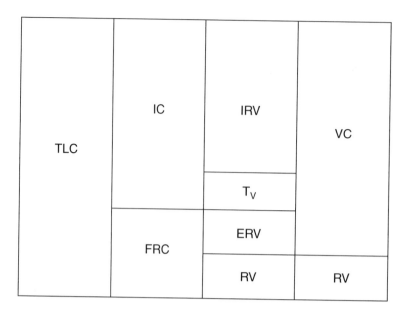

Figure 35–1 Lung Volumes and Capacities

in the amount of improvement seen in the study results. The before and after PFT (spirometry) study is the answer to the question, "What is the best way to determine the extent of reversibility of bronchospasm in a patient with COPD, asthma, or restrictive lung disease?"

ADVICE

Several bits of advice I offer regarding PFTs are as follows. It would behoove you to know what normal, obstructive, and restrictive flow-volume loops look like. Also, be sure which volumes can be added together to form a particular capacity. This probably will come up on the exam, as will questions regarding which way values move in a particular disease process. Finally, become familiar with the wave forms, or graphs, for the various volumes so you can recognize and evaluate them if needed.

There are two other subjects we should touch upon, lest they be on the exam. Let's take a few minutes to review fluidics and choice subjects regarding home care. I believe that these subjects do not routinely appear on the exam, but one can never be certain what the NBRC will do. We shall take a "snap shot" of fluidics first.

FLUIDICS

Fluidics is a term used to describe a technology that applies the characteristics of fluids in motion to achieve various control and logic functions. The most popular vents using this technology are the Bird MK7 through 14, Puritan-Bennett PR-1 and 2, and the Monaghan-225, which is a pneumatically powered, volume-cycled, pressure-limited machine.

The Coanda Effect

The principle of fluidics was discovered in 1932 by a man named Coanda. He found that gas (which is a fluid) can be diverted by placing various obstructions in its path. Positive and negative pressures can influence a fluid to change its course. He also found that, if left undisturbed, flow will continue along the same path, only changing its route with the application of positive or negative pressure influence (control signals). What's more, these control signals need be administered only in short, momentary bursts—only long enough to bump the flow in another direction. When a new flow direction is established, a separation bubble forms that creates negative pressure, pulling the gas flow toward itself (remember that). This bubble keeps the flow moving in the same direction. Additionally, once the flow switches, it will continue to follow the new path because of the separation bubble that will form, until another control signal is sent. Know the basics of the Coanda effect!

Fluidics is a technology that uses fluid characteristics, exclusively, to operate the machine. There is no electricity involved at all. There are what appear to be colored lights on the machine's panel (Monaghan-225). In reality, these are only colored shutters that indicate if a breath has been time-

or pressure-cycled. Fluidics is a powerful technology, but the advent of microprocessors has relegated it to a subordinate role. There are fluidic components in many types of equipment we use, but these are usually used in conjunction with other technologies. It is important that you become casually familiar with the previously mentioned details.

THOUGHTS ON HOME CARE

The primary goal of the home-care RCP is to help the patient become and stay as independent as possible. Convenience and portability are issues in the home environment, so you will encounter different types of equipment than you are used to seeing in hospitals.

Oxygen is a primary concern, because most people with moderate to severe pulmonary disease tend to use this drug around the clock. In the home, you won't find the convenient piped-in oxygen you are so familiar with. Oxygen is most commonly provided in the home through electrically powered oxygen concentrators, the most efficient type being those that use the molecular sieve principle. These devices concentrate oxygen by filtering out the other gases present in the room air, then store the 90% to 95% pure oxygen until it is needed. Most units can supply flow rates up to and including 5 L/min, but are not back-pressure compensated. The portability issue is resolved through the use of little "D" cylinders that are carried over the shoulder on a strap or in small liquid oxygen tanks. Either portable device can last several hours, depending on the flow rates required.

In cases when higher oxygen flow rates are required, liquid oxygen (LOX) base units are necessary. These large units can provide enough flow to power a cold steam nebulizer and can be easily refilled by the home-care provider. On the average, a large base unit can hold about 30,000 L of gas; this is practical because LOX expands about 860 times its liquid volume when it turns to gas.

IPPB and aerosol treatments are generally provided with electrically powered equipment, such as the PB AP-5 IPPB machine or one of the many electrically powered aerosol therapy compressors on the market. The circuits are provided by the home-care provider, who also will provide instruction on the care and cleaning of the equipment.

The old standby for cleaning equipment in the home is acetic acid, vinegar to neophytes. Some sources say to mix one part vinegar and two parts water to clean respiratory equipment, others recommend solutions such as diluting 1 ml of vinegar in 400 ml of water. Don't worry about particulars now. For your exam, simply be aware of the fact that an acetic acid solution is acceptable for equipment cleaning.

For your home-care concerns, keep the following in mind:

- The most efficient type of oxygen concentrators are electrically powered molecular sieves, not back-pressure compensated.
- The most practical IPPB treatment involves an electrically powered machine such as the AP-5.
- The most practical equipment for aerosol therapy is the non-adjustable electrically powered compressor designed specifically for the purpose.

On the whole, approach your exam questions logically. Start by asking yourself "What do I know to be true about this question?" Immediately eliminate the answers that you know are incorrect and work your way through the other choices step by step, comparing their degrees of correctness.

If you are interested, there are two fine publications that I use as reference sources. The first is the time-honored standard of respiratory care, *Egan's Fundamentals of Respiratory Care*. The second is a comprehensive volume on equipment, *Respiratory Care Equipment*, by Steven P. McPherson, RRT.

You are likely to be intimidated by all this information; all I can say is that familiarity breeds confidence. The more familiar you become with the material, the more confident you shall be about your ability to pass the exam. The only way to become intimately familiar with this type of information is to go over each topic until you can recite the facts in your sleep. Having said that, let me point out that simply reciting information won't do. You must be able to apply it; so, after you commit the facts to memory, work on the applications.

So, there it is. I sincerely hope that I have helped clear some of the haze and put you onto a positive track for your exam. Good luck.

SUGGESTED READING

Burton G, Hodgkin J. *Respiratory Care, A Guide to Clinical Practice*. Philadelphia, Pa: J.B. Lippincott Company; 1984.

Physicians Desk Reference. Montvale, N.J.: Medical Economics Data Inc; 1993.

Shapiro B, Harrison R, Trout C. *Clinical Application of Respiratory Care*. St. Louis, Mo: Year Book Medical Publishers Inc; 1984.

The Self-Assessment Tests

Now you shall have the chance to put all of the data you've absorbed to the test, literally, while learning more. You will soak up information like a sponge by answering the following questions and then correcting your answers, if necessary. These questions are as near to actual test questions in style and content as I could devise. Use what you've learned and think about each question carefully. There are four categories of questions: clinical data, equipment use, therapeutic procedure, and history and principles. At the end of the book, you will find the test answers and the breakdown of the number of questions in each category. You can divide the total number of questions in each category into the number you got correct in that category to evaluate your strength or weakness in that area.

Take three hours for the test.

Self-Assessment Test 1

1) When mouth-to-mouth resuscitation is being performed, it is most important to watch the patient's
   A. Abdomen.
   B. Eyes.
   C. Chest.
   D. Color.

2) You, as the respiratory practitioner, are preparing to suction a patient with an endotracheal tube. Which of the following is a necessary step in properly suctioning the patient?
   A. Rinse the catheter with water before suctioning.
   B. Use the largest catheter that will pass through the tube.
   C. Oxygenate the patient both before and after suctioning.
   D. Instill 5 cc of normal saline solution before suctioning.

3) Which of the following is the best way to determine if a patient has a pneumothorax?
   A. Sputum culture
   B. Peak flow
   C. Arterial blood gas
   D. Chest X-ray

4) A bubble humidifier is primarily used to
   A. Deliver large amounts of water to the lungs.
   B. Add molecular water to gas.
   C. Add particulate water to gas.
   D. Deliver a bronchodilator.

5) When using the Bird MK 7 for an IPPB treatment, the RCP can extend the inspiratory time by
   A. Decreasing the flow rate.
   B. Decreasing the cycling pressure.
   C. Increasing the flow rate.
   D. Decreasing the sensitivity.

6) Which of the following is not advisable immediately after a patient's tracheostomy tube has been removed?
   A. Asking the patient to cough.
   B. Suturing the stoma closed.
   C. Cleaning the stoma site with hydrogen peroxide.
   D. Applying a sterile dressing to the stoma site.

7) Which of the following is associated with the administration of epinephrine?
   A. Renal damage
   B. Laryngospasm
   C. Tachycardia
   D. Bradycardia

8) When a patient is exhibiting Kussmaul's respirations, the underlying cause most likely is
   A. Carbon dioxide narcosis.
   B. Tetanus.
   C. Diabetic acidosis.
   D. Pickwickian syndrome.

9) Which of the following best reflects adequate ventilation?
   A. Bicarb (HCO_3^-)
   B. Pa_{CO_2}
   C. Base excess
   D. Sa_{O_2}

10) Which of the following organisms is most frequently cultured from humidifiers and nebulizers?
    A. *Mycobacterium tuberculosis*
    B. *Pseudomonas aeruginosa*
    C. *Proteus vulgaris*
    D. *Staphylococcus aureus*

11) An arterial blood gas was drawn on a patient with a lung contusion. The patient is on a 70% aerosol mask. The blood gas results are the following:

pH: 7.40.
Paco₂: 42 torr
Pao₂: 49 torr
HCO₃⁻: 23.6 mEq/liter
Based on these results, which therapeutic modality would you recommend?
A. CPT
B. AT
C. CPAP
D. IPPB

12) Which of the following sterilization methods would be most effective against an organism of the genus *Clostridium*?
A. Ethyl alcohol
B. Ethylene oxide
C. Hydrogen peroxide
D. Pasteurization

13) Which are the most likely characteristics of pulmonary secretions when the patient suffers from pulmonary edema?
A. Thick and bloody
B. Thick and green
C. Pink and frothy
D. Thin and yellow

14) To ensure sterility when using acid glutaraldehyde to sterilize respiratory equipment, how long should the equipment remain in the solution bath?
A. 15 minutes
B. 2 days
C. 2 hours
D. 10 hours

15) What is the first thing the RCP must do before performing a treatment on a patient?
A. Knock on the door.
B. Wear a mask.
C. Introduce yourself.
D. Wash your hands.

16) The Clark electrode is used to determine which of the following?
A. Relative humidity
B. Arterial partial pressure of oxygen
C. Arterial partial pressure of carbon dioxide
D. Hydrogen ion concentration in the blood

17) When checking a patient's oxygen concentrator in the home, which of the following is most important as far as the RCP is concerned?
A. Check the patient's extension cord.
B. Clean or change the filter.
C. Check the high-pressure gas source.
D. Top off the liquid oxygen in the reservoir.

18) An elevated white blood cell count would be consistent with which of the following?
A. Low hemoglobin
B. Respiratory alkalosis
C. Elevated potassium levels
D. Bacterial infection

19) Collecting a sputum specimen for a culture and sensitivity would be most helpful in evaluating which of the following?
A. Pneumonitis
B. Cardiogenic pulmonary edema
C. Emphysema
D. Bronchospasm

20) When performing chest physiotherapy, the patient should be instructed to do which of the following?
A. Use an ISB device.
B. Cough constantly.
C. Cough only when instructed to do so.
D. Hold his or her breath for 90 sec when instructed to do so.

21) An active 3-year old is ordered 35%–50% Fio₂. Which of the following devices would the child tolerate the best?
A. Partial rebreathing mask
B. Oxygen tent
C. Venturi mask
D. Hyperbaric oxygen chamber

22) Breathing techniques used to relieve dyspnea in patients with COPD include which of the following?
 I. Exhaling through the nose
 II. Pursed lip breathing
 III. Inhaling through the nose
 IV. Abdominal (diaphragmatic) breathing
A. I only
B. III only
C. IV only
D. II, III, and IV only

23) If the drug beclomethasone is administered via metered dose inhaler, which of the following may occur?
A. Cardiac dysrhythmia
B. Immediate bronchodilation
C. Nervousness
D. Oral candidiasis (thrush)

24) If an "H" cylinder of oxygen has 1,200 psig and the flow is set at 12 L/min, how long will this cylinder last at this flow rate?
A. 47 minutes
B. 12 hours
C. 5 hours
D. 3 hours

25) If an endotracheal tube is inserted too far, which of the following is the most likely result?
   A. Right mainstem bronchus intubation
   B. Esophageal intubation
   C. Left mainstem bronchus intubation
   D. None of the above

26) The mechanical dead space associated with a positive pressure ventilator is related to the
   A. I:E ratio
   B. Patient's size
   C. Volume of the circuit
   D. Respiratory rate

27) A patient who is recovering from abdominal surgery is ordered incentive spirometry breathing. The patient does not seem to be putting forth a maximum effort. Which of the following may help the patient reach the ISB goal?
   A. Instruct the patient to breathe faster.
   B. Place a pillow over the incision and exert light pressure.
   C. Instruct the patient to do the ISM on his or her own.
   D. All of the above.

28) Adding 6 inches of tubing between the patient and the "Y" in the ventilator circuit of a volume-cycled ventilator set to the "control" mode would have what, if any, effect on the patient's arterial blood gas results?
   A. No change
   B. Increase the P_{ACO_2}
   C. Increase the S_{aO_2}
   D. Increase the pH

29) Which of the following most frequently causes airway obstruction during cardiac arrest?
   A. The uvula
   B. The larynx
   C. Dentures
   D. The tongue

30) While performing CPR, you have difficulty ventilating a patient who is not intubated. Which of the following is the most likely problem?
   A. Abnormal anatomy of the airway.
   B. The patient is trying to speak.
   C. Excessive gastric air is present.
   D. The patient's head is improperly positioned.

31) Which of the following bronchodilators would be contraindicated if the patient's secretions were tenacious?
   A. Albuterol
   B. Metaproterenol
   C. Atropine
   D. Isoetharine

32) What is the best way to determine if adequate humidification is being provided to an adult who is being mechanically ventilated?
   A. Perform nasotracheal suctioning.
   B. Check the ventilator circuit for adequate condensation.
   C. Perform and induce sputum.
   D. Weigh the patient.

33) A 34-year-old man presents in the emergency department and has the following blood gas results:

   pH: 7.15

   P_{aCO_2}: 75 torr

   P_{aO_2}: 48 torr

   HCO_3^-: 24 mEq/l

   These blood gases can be said to be which of the following?
   A. Fully compensated respiratory acidosis with hypoxemia
   B. Uncompensated respiratory acidosis with moderate hypoxemia
   C. Partially compensated metabolic alkalosis with severe hypoxemia
   D. Uncompensated respiratory alkalosis with mild hypoxemia

34) The physician orders a patient to be mechanically ventilated and states that the patient has stiff lungs. Which type of ventilator would be most appropriate?
   A. Manual resuscitator
   B. Volume-cycled ventilator
   C. Pressure-cycled ventilator
   D. Negative pressure ventilator

35) Which of the following most likely would be true if a pressure ventilator was used on the patient in question 34?
   A. There is no danger of pneumothorax when high ventilating pressures are present.
   B. No alarms need to be set on the ventilator at this time.
   C. The patient's peak airway pressure would decrease as volume increases.
   D. The patient may not receive adequate volume because of excessive pressure requirements.

36) A spontaneously breathing, intubated patient weighs 70 kg (154 lb) and generates the following weaning parameters:

   V_T: 456 ml

   VC: 1220 ml (1.22 L)

   NIF: −44 cmH$_2$O

As the RCP on duty, you would recommend which of the following?
A. Start bronchodilator therapy.
B. Place the patient back on the ventilator.
C. Maintain current therapy.
D. Extubate the patient.

37) When setting up CPAP on an adult, using a mask, which of the following alarms is most important to ensure proper therapy?
A. Pulse monitor.
B. Low pressure alarm.
C. High respiratory rate.
D. I:E ratio.

38) A patient states that he has difficulty sleeping and prefers to use two pillows to help him breathe easier. Which of the following does this best describe?
A. Bradypnea
B. Eupnea
C. Tachypnea
D. Orthopnea

39) Monitoring the airway pressures of mechanically ventilated patients is important because it enables the RCP to monitor which of the following?
A. Pulmonary compliance
B. Intercranial pressure
C. Tissue perfusion
D. Arterial oxygen tension

40) To facilitate adequate tissue perfusion in the tracheal mucosa, tracheostomy tube cuff pressure should not exceed which of the following?
A. Carotid artery pressure
B. Tissue capillary pressure
C. Pulmonary wedge pressure
D. Central venous pressure

41) Which of the following is true regarding the care of a patient with a tracheostomy tube?
A. The tube always should have a high pressure, low volume cuff, and it should be fully inflated.
B. The inner cannula isn't necessary and may be discarded.
C. An extra tracheostomy tube should be kept at the patient's bedside.
D. The patient should be suctioned at least every half hour.

42) Which of the following is the primary reason a spacer device is used with metered-dose inhalers?
A. To fill the chamber with the total number of puffs ordered before inhalation.
B. To decrease the patient's inspiratory effort.
C. To overcome coordination difficulties between actuation and inhalation.
D. To increase the patient's inspiratory effort.

43) A patient is receiving oxygen via non-rebreathing mask and is emptying the reservoir bag completely on inspiration. Which course of action is most appropriate?
A. Change the delivery device to a nasal cannula.
B. Suggest the patient be started on bronchodilator therapy.
C. Increase the flow of oxygen to the mask.
D. Intubate the patient because the patient's work of breathing is too high.

44) After obtaining an arterial blood gas sample, the RCP should do which of the following?
A. Lay the sample on the bed and observe the patient for 5 minutes.
B. Remove your gloves and recap the needle.
C. Slowly roll the sample and place it in ice.
D. Remove your gloves and roll the sample.

45) If a patient damages his or her vocal cords during accidental extubation, which of the following most likely will be heard upon auscultation?
A. Rales
B. Wheezing
C. Stridor
D. Rhonchi

46) What is the maximum time a blood gas sample should remain on ice and still reflect accurate values when analyzed?
A. 2 hours
B. 30 minutes
C. 5 minutes
D. 1 hour and 15 minutes

47) When an RCP asks a patient what day of the week it is and the facility they are in, the RCP is assessing which of the following?
A. The patient's willingness to socialize
B. The patient's orientation to time and place
C. The patient's intelligence
D. The patient's emotional status

48) A patient is being ventilated in the assist-control mode. After reviewing the patient's chest X-ray and blood gas results, you, the RCP, decide to increase the patient's alveolar ventilation. Which of the following is the most appropriate way to do this?
A. Increase the mechanical dead space.
B. Increase the F_{IO_2}.
C. Decrease the PEEP.
D. Increase the tidal volume.

49) Cromolyn sodium administration should be terminated at the time of administration if which of the following occurs?
   A. Increased sputum is produced.
   B. Acute bronchospasms occur upon administration.
   C. Urine output drops.
   D. Breath sounds improve.

50) A spontaneously breathing patient with COPD, on a F_{IO_2} of 0.6, becomes sleepy and unresponsive. This is most likely due to which of the following?
   A. An increase in Pa_{CO_2}
   B. An increase in the bicarb
   C. An increase in cardiac output
   D. A decrease in Pa_{CO_2}

51) Which of the following would you consider to be the best tool to measure a patient's inspiratory muscle strength?
   A. Bird MK 7
   B. A negative inspiratory pressure gauge
   C. A Wright's spirometer
   D. A Passey-Muir valve

52) Which term best describes water that is free of microorganisms and other contaminants?
   A. Normal saline solution
   B. Sterile water
   C. Distilled water
   D. Hypertonic saline

53) A physician has written an order for one of your patients that is not appropriate. You, as the RCP, should do which of the following?
   A. Rewrite the order yourself because you know what the physician means.
   B. Contact the physician and ask him or her to clarify the order.
   C. Go ahead and administer the therapy properly anyway.
   D. Ignore the order and do nothing. Continue previous orders.

54) If an RCP has difficulty obtaining a blood gas sample, after the first attempt the RCP should do which of the following?
   A. Make one more attempt. If unsuccessful, contact another practitioner to draw the blood.
   B. Stick the patient as many times as necessary to obtain the sample.
   C. Attempt a carotid artery stick.
   D. Forget about the order and continue your rounds.

55) What is the NaCl content of normal saline solution?
   A. 1.0%
   B. 0.45%
   C. 0.9%
   D. 0.09%

56) You, as the RCP on call for the emergency room, are asked to assist in the selection of an airway. It appears to you that the patient most likely will require mechanical ventilation. Which of the following would be the airway of choice under these circumstances?
   A. An oral endotracheal tube
   B. An esophageal obturator
   C. A Shiley tracheostomy tube
   D. A Jackson tracheostomy tube

57) Which of the following airways would be most appropriate for a patient who will likely need mechanical ventilation shortly?
   A. An oral endotracheal tube
   B. An esophageal obturator
   C. A tracheostomy tube
   D. A Jackson tracheostomy tube

58) All of the following are goals associated with pulmonary rehabilitation of the patient with COPD except:
   A. Improved diet
   B. Complete reversal of the disease
   C. Decreased frequency and length of hospitalizations
   D. Increased exercise tolerance

59) A patient has completed a pulmonary function test, with the following results:

   VC (vital capacity): 2,600 ml

   FRC (functional residual capacity): 3,000 ml

   ERV (expiratory reserve volume): 1,000 ml

   What is the patient's TLC (total lung capacity)?
   A. 5,600 ml
   B. 4,600 ml
   C. 3,600 ml
   D. 6,600 ml

60) What is the approximate, normal Sv_{O_2} (venous oxygen saturation) of a person at sea level?
   A. 55%
   B. 60%
   C. 75%
   D. 95%

61) You, as an RCP, are starting a new patient on aerosolized bronchodilators. Your instructions to the patient would include which of the following to ensure the treatment is taken properly?
   A. Here's your treatment; I'll be back in 15 minutes.
   B. Put this in your mouth and breathe real deep.
   C. This will make you breathe easier.
   D. Put the mouth piece in your mouth and breathe normally through it. Take a deep breath every fourth or

fifth breath only and hold that breath for about 5 seconds. The treatment will last about 10 to 15 minutes.

62) A patient has stridor. This is due to edematous vocal cords caused by a traumatic extubation. Which of the following would provide the most effective relief of this condition?
   A. Beta 2 sympathomimetics
   B. Mast cell stabilizers
   C. Mucolytics
   D. Alpha sympathomimetics

63) When breathing room air at sea level, what is the amount of oxygen physically dissolved in 100 ml of blood?
   A. 0.3 ml
   B. 03.14 ml
   C. 1.2 ml
   D. 2.1 ml

64) While reviewing a patient's chart, you, the RCP, notice that the previous RCP documented that the patient had crackles in both bases. Which of the following terms would also describe this condition?
   A. Wheezes
   B. Rales
   C. Rhonchi
   D. Stridor

65) All of the following may cause a decrease in a patient's $Paco_2$ except
   A. Increased physiologic dead space
   B. Increased respiratory rate
   C. Increased minute ventilation
   D. Increased tidal volume

66) Which of the following statements is true about cromolyn sodium (Intal)?
   A. It provides immediate relief of bronchospasm.
   B. It does not interact well with albuterol sulfate.
   C. It will not relieve acute bronchospasm.
   D. It should not be mixed with any other drugs.

67) Which of the following is most likely to cause a restrictive lung disorder that will be revealed on a pulmonary function study?
   A. Influenza
   B. Tracheitis
   C. Kyphoscoliosis
   D. Acute bronchitis

68) Which of the following sputum characteristics are most likely to present themselves in the presence of an acute bacterial pulmonary infection?
   A. Thin clear sputum
   B. Thick yellow sputum
   C. Frothy pink secretions
   D. Little or no sputum production

69) A patient aspirates an unknown quantity of food during a meal. The first thing that you, as the RCP, should do is
   A. Perform an emergency tracheostomy.
   B. Place the patient on 4 L/min via nasal cannula.
   C. Auscultate the patient's chest.
   D. Mechanically ventilate the patient.

70) When PEEP is instituted on a mechanically ventilated patient, which of the following parameters should be most closely monitored?
   A. Spontaneous respiratory rate
   B. Pao_2
   C. $Paco_2$
   D. Tidal volume

71) Which of the following best describes an accumulation of grossly purulent fluid in a patient's pleural space?
   A. Empyema
   B. Hemoptysis
   C. Neoplasm
   D. Granuloma

72) For a patient to receive an effective IPPB treatment, all of the following should be true except
   A. Good, precise instructions from the RCP.
   B. A well trained RCP.
   C. The patient should be cooperative.
   D. The patient must be able to assemble the machine's parts.

73) Which of the following terms best describes a respiratory rate of eight breaths per minute in a spontaneously breathing patient?
   A. Tachypnea
   B. Bradypnea
   C. Eupnea
   D. Hypoventilation

74) What site is commonly used to assess a patient's pulse?
   A. Popliteal
   B. Apical
   C. Femoral
   D. Radial

75) Which of the following men is known as the father of inhalation therapy?
   A. von Clauswitz
   B. Aristotle
   C. Sylvester
   D. Beddoes

76) "Dephlogisticated air" (oxygen) was discovered by whom?
   A. Galen
   B. Clinton
   C. Priestly
   D. Hippocrates

77) Which of the following are variables in Poiseuille's law?
   I. Viscosity
   II. Tubing length
   III. Flow
   IV. Tubing radius
   V. Velocity
   A. I, III, and IV only
   B. I, II, III, and IV only
   C. IV and V only
   D. None of the above

78) Which of the following is true about Bernoulli's principle?
   A. It describes resistance to flow through a tube.
   B. An increase in forward velocity produces an increase in lateral wall pressure.
   C. As forward velocity decreases, lateral wall pressure decreases.
   D. As forward velocity increases, lateral wall pressure decreases.

79) If the radius of a tube is decreased from 4 mm to 1 mm, what happens to resistance (R) to the gas flow?
   A. R would increase by a factor of 256.
   B. R would decrease by a factor of 4.
   C. R would increase by a factor of 16.
   D. None of the above.

80) Which of the following factors promotes laminar flow through a tube?
   I. Increased velocity
   II. Increased viscosity
   III. Decreased fluid density
   IV. Doubling the tube diameter
   A. II only
   B. II and III only
   C. III and IV only
   D. I, III, and IV only

81) The descent of the diaphragm greatly increases the available volume in the thorax. Which of the following gas laws describes this relationship?
   A. Charles' law
   B. Boyle's law
   C. Dalton's law
   D. Graham's law

82) The force required to convert a gas back to its liquid state, at its critical temperature, is called what?
   A. Boiling point
   B. Vapor pressure
   C. Critical pressure
   D. Partial pressure

83) Which of the following statements is true regarding a flagged chart?
   A. There is a sticker listing allergies on the front.
   B. There is a new physician's order that awaits implementation.
   C. Isolation precautions are necessary.
   D. There is a sticker denoting the type of insurance the patient has.

84) The point at which a liquid turns into its gaseous state, at atmospheric pressure, is best characterized by which of the following terms?
   A. Boiling point
   B. Vapor pressure
   C. Critical temperature
   D. Critical pressure

85) Which of the following statements about pressure compensated Thorpe tubes are correct?
   I. They are accurate only in the upright position.
   II. Accuracy is not affected by downstream back pressure.
   III. They are used to indicate and control flow.
   IV. They use variable pressure and a fixed orifice to control and measure flow.
   A. I and III only
   B. I, II, and III only
   C. I and II only
   D. III and IV only

86) Which of the following statements are true about Bourdon gauge flowmeters?
   I. They are accurate when back pressure is applied.
   II. They use a fixed orifice and variable pressure to measure flow rates.
   III. They may indicate lower than actual flow rates.
   IV. They use a variable orifice with fixed pressure to regulate flow.
   A. I and IV only
   B. II and III only
   C. II only
   D. IV only

87) Which of the following nebulizer types create output known to have consistently small particles and the highest water output?
   A. Babbington nebulizers
   B. Ultrasonic nebulizers
   C. Jet nebulizer
   D. Both B and C

88) All of the following are humidifiers except
   A. Passover
   B. Bubble diffusion
   C. Heated cascade
   D. All of the above

89) Which of the following statements are true of ultrasonic nebulizers?
   A. They are powered by pneumatic gas source.
   B. Amplitude setting changes particle size.
   C. Particle size is adjustable.
   D. None of the above.

90) Which of the following factors *does not* affect aerosol deposition and penetration?
   A. Gravity
   B. Inertial impaction
   C. Ciliary activity
   D. Ventilatory pattern

91) Which of the following is true of heated nebulizers?
   A. The gas' ability to carry water increases.
   B. Droplet size increases.
   C. Aerosol water content decreases.
   D. Heat has no effect on nebulizer function.

92) Which of the following is true regarding low flow oxygen delivery devices?
   A. Less than 100% oxygen is delivered to the patient under most circumstances.
   B. They can be worn while smoking.
   C. There is no fire hazard.
   D. They provide the total inspiratory gas needs of the patient.

93) Which of the following is true of high flow oxygen delivery devices?
   A. All are pressure compensated.
   B. They are designed to eliminate the entrainment of room air by the patient.
   C. They are more comfortable than low flow devices.
   D. All are appropriate for all patients.

94) The recognized hazards of aerosol therapy include which of the following?
   I. Nosocomial infection
   II. Bronchospasm
   III. Fluid overload in infants
   IV. Swelling of dehydrated secretions
   A. I only
   B. I and II only
   C. II, III, and IV only
   D. I, II, III, and IV

95) Which of the following statements is true about oxygen content?
   A. It is the total amount of oxygen carried in the blood.
   B. It is measured in volumes %.
   C. It is normally 97%.
   D. Both A and B

96) To maintain a patent airway during CPR in a patient who has a suspected neck injury, the RCP should use which of the following techniques?
   A. Stabilize the patient's head and use a chin lift.
   B. Flex the patient's head on the neck.
   C. Turn the patient's head face down.
   D. Hyperextend the patient's neck.

97) A 1:200 contains how many milligrams per milliliter?
   A. 1.0 mg/ml
   B. 0.5 mg/ml
   C. 5.0 mg/ml
   D. 0.25 mg/ml

98) You notice that a patient has marked intercostal retractions. Which of the following is the most likely cause?
   I. Asthma
   II. Tracheal obstruction
   III. Infant respiratory distress syndrome
   IV. Emphysema
   A. I only
   B. II only
   C. II and IV only
   D. II and III only

99) Arterial blood gases have been drawn on a patient who is being ventilated on a volume-cycled machine. The ABGs reveal that uncompensated respiratory acidosis is present. Which corrective action would you recommend?
   A. Decrease the minute ventilation.
   B. Increase the minute ventilation.
   C. Decrease the inspiratory flow.
   D. Increase the F_{IO_2}.

100) You, as the RCP, would recommend which of the following treatments for a patient who is producing small to moderate amounts of thick, purulent sputum?
   A. Incentive spirometry breathing (ISB)
   B. Intubation
   C. Ultrasonic nebulizer therapy
   D. A centrifugal humidifier

101) How is the static compliance of a patient who is on a mechanical ventilator determined?
   A. Tidal volume divided by the peak airway pressure
   B. Peak airway pressure divided by the tidal volume
   C. Peak airway pressure divided by the plateau pressure
   D. Tidal volume divided by the plateau pressure

102) To make sure that no foreign matter from an oxygen cylinder is introduced into a regulator, the RCP should take which of the following steps?
   A. Carefully examine the cylinder valve.
   B. Clean the cylinder valve with a cloth.
   C. Lightly grease the cylinder valve.
   D. Turn the tank on and off quickly, before attaching the regulator.

103) A patient is on a 40% T-piece with 6 inches of reservoir tube attached to the Brigg's ("T") adapter. What would be the result of the reservoir tube being removed?
   I. The patient's F_{IO_2} would decrease.
   II. Mechanical dead space would increase.
   III. The patient would entrain more room air.
   A. I only
   B. I and II only
   C. I and III only
   D. II and III only

104) Which of the following is generally recommended for cleaning respiratory equipment in the home environment?
   A. An ammonia and bleach solution
   B. Ethyl alcohol
   C. Glutaraldehyde
   D. Acetic acid

105) Which of the following correctly defines vital capacity?
   A. A maximal exhalation performed after a maximal inhalation.
   B. Breathing in as fast and as deep as possible.
   C. The forced exhalation volume after a normal tidal breath.
   D. Breathing as fast and as deep as possible for 20 seconds.

106) Which of the following is most desirable when a head trauma patient is placed on a volume ventilator?
   A. Hyperoxygenate the patient.
   B. Use expiratory resistance.
   C. Hyperventilate the patient.
   D. Use accelerating flow patterns.

107) If a patient's blood pressure is extremely low, which of the following positions would be most beneficial?
   A. Reverse Trendelenburg
   B. Trendelenburg
   C. Fowler's
   D. Semi-Fowler's

108) Which of the following terms accurately describes hypoxia that is caused by circulatory failure and decreased venous return?
   A. Stagnant
   B. Anemic
   C. Cytotoxic
   D. Histotoxic

109) Which of the following is true regarding oxygen's affinity for hemoglobin when arterial pH decreases?
   A. It increases.
   B. It stays the same if there is an increase in carbon dioxide.
   C. It remains the same.
   D. It decreases.

110) You, as the RCP, encounter a patient who refuses to wear their 21% trach collar. What should you do?
   I. Tell the patient it's OK as long as the patient breathes through his or her nose.
   II. Explain the importance of humidity.
   III. Suggest the use of a heat moisture exchanger.
   IV. Recommend a tracheostomy plug or button be used.
   A. I only
   B. I and II only
   C. I, II, and III only
   D. II, III, and IV only

111) What method does the P_{O_2} electrode in a blood gas analyzer use to obtain a result from a blood sample?
   A. Spectrophotometry
   B. Polarography
   C. Galvanic cells
   D. Severinghaus

112) A barometer is used to measure which of the following?
   A. Barometric pressure
   B. Blood pressure
   C. Relative humidity
   D. Pleural fluid pressure

113) While suctioning a patient, you notice a significant decrease in blood pressure. Which of the following would be the most likely cause of this complication?
   A. The catheter is causing the patient to cough.
   B. This is a vagal reflex response.
   C. Hypoxia
   D. Hypercarbia

114) Which of the following is true regarding the set-up procedure of a non-rebreathing mask?
   A. The bag will empty during exhalation.
   B. Always use a bubble humidifier with this device.
   C. A high amount of room air should be entrained during inspiration.
   D. The reservoir bag should not collapse, but should remain about one-third full during inspiration.

115) All of the following are contraindications for postural drainage in Trendelenburg position except
   I. If a patient has moderate to severe dyspnea
   II. When hypotension is present
   III. If rhonchi are present during auscultation
   IV. After a recent craniotomy
   A. I and II only
   B. III and IV only
   C. I and III only
   D. II and III only

116) All of the following are relevant information when reviewing a patient's chart except
   A. Sputum culture results
   B. Blood gas results
   C. Hobbies
   D. Drug allergies

117) Who discovered oxygen in 1774?
    A. Torricelli
    B. Priestly
    C. Beddoes
    D. von Linde

118) All of the following are true statements about charting except
    A. Charting can be used for billing purposes.
    B. Charting keeps employees occupied when they have no work.
    C. A chart is a legal document.
    D. A chart can be useful in medical research.

119) All of the following are good charting techniques except
    A. Spelling and syntax accuracy
    B. Legibility
    C. Documenting without your signature, time, and date
    D. Writing on consecutive lines, leaving no lines blank

120) If you make a mistake while charting, you should
    A. Use a pencil so you can erase your mistake.
    B. Write over the error so it is not visible.
    C. Draw a single line through your mistake, write error beside it, and initial it.
    D. Leave the error intact.

121) All of the following is true regarding oxygen cylinder storage except
    A. Cylinders may be stored in high traffic areas.
    B. The area should be properly labeled and NO SMOKING signs posted.
    C. Cylinders should be secured by chains.
    D. There should be separate, designated areas for full and empty cylinders.

122) The approximate F_{IO_2} of a patient who is on a 3 L/min nasal cannula is
    A. 32%
    B. 36%
    C. 24%
    D. 28%

123) Cheyne-Stokes breathing is usually associated with which of the following?
    A. Pneumonia
    B. Brain stem injuries
    C. Asthma
    D. Diabetic acidosis

124) What is the unit of measure used when measuring blood pressure with a sphygmomanometer?
    A. mg/ml
    B. mm Hg
    C. joule
    D. cm

125) All of the following are characteristic of subcutaneous emphysema except
    A. Crepitus
    B. Air under the skin
    C. May be caused by an alveolar rupture
    D. Similar to asthma

126) All of the following are true about patients with alpha 1 antitrypsin deficiency except
    A. It may lead to a mild form of emphysema.
    B. It does not affect pulmonary function test results.
    C. It may lead to a mild case of bronchitis.
    D. It is the cause of 10–20% of all emphysema cases.

127) All of the following terms are acceptable when documenting breath sounds except
    A. Wheezes
    B. Rhonchi
    C. Junky
    D. Rales

128) A patient with bullous emphysema is being mechanically ventilated. The peak airway pressure rises above 50 cmH$_2$O. This patient is in danger of developing which of the following?
    A Bronchitis
    B. Lung abscess
    C. Pneumothorax
    D. Atelectasis

129) While reviewing a patient's chart, you notice that the patient has undergone a thoracotomy recently. Which therapeutic procedure would not be recommended at this time?
    A. CPT
    B. Incentive spirometry
    C. Bronchodilator therapy via aerosol
    D. IPPB

130) Nosocomial infection is usually caused by which of the following?
    A. Steroids
    B. Improper hand washing
    C. Tracheostomy tubes
    D. None of the above

131) When using ethylene oxide sterilization, which of the following should be a concern?
    A. Vent the gas to the outside atmosphere.
    B. Control the temperature and humidity of the equipment.
    C. Aerate the equipment after sterilization for 24 hours.
    D. All of the above

132) A patient's completed pulmonary function study has the following results:
VC: 53% of predicted
FEV_1: 55% of predicted
FEV_1/FVC: 83%
Peak flow: 115% of predicted
TLC: 71% of predicted
MVV: 124% of predicted
You, as an RCP, would interpret these results as which of the following?
A. Within normal limits
B. A restrictive disease only
C. An obstructive disease only
D. Both a restrictive and obstructive disease

133) When a patient complains of numbness and tingling after bronchodilator therapy, the most likely cause is
A. This is psychosomatic and should be overlooked.
B. The patient was holding his or her breath.
C. The patient hyperventilated during the treatment.
D. The medication

134) Which of the following problems may arise when high concentrations of oxygen are given to newborns?
I. Retrolental fibroplasia
II. Increased hair loss
III. Decreased surfactant production
IV. Pulmonary edema
A. I only
B. I and II only
C. I and III only
D. I, III, and IV only

135) A jet nebulizer can be used to do which of the following?
A. Increase gas density.
B. Hydrate secretions.
C. Hyperinflate the lungs.
D. Add molecular humidity to the gas stream.

136) A patient in the ER is in acute distress. Room air ABG results are as follows:
pH: 7.23
P_{CO_2}: 60 torr
P_{O_2}: 40 torr
HCO_3^-: 25 mEq/l
S_{aO_2}: 76%
You, as the RCP, would interpret these results as:
A. Compensated respiratory acidosis with hypoxemia
B. Uncompensated metabolic acidosis with severe hypoxemia
C. Uncompensated respiratory acidosis with moderate hypoxemia
D. Compensated respiratory alkalosis without hypoxemia

137) The physician orders the patient mentioned in question 136 to be placed on oxygen. You would recommend which of the following?
A. 2 L/min
B. 100% non-rebreather mask
C. 28% venti mask
D. 70% venti mask

138) After placing the patient on oxygen, you notice the SpO_2 has risen to 96% and upon auscultation you hear bilateral wheezes and decreased breath sounds throughout all fields. Which of the following would you recommend?
A. Ultrasonic nebulizer therapy
B. IPPB with normal saline
C. A room humidifier
D. An aerosolized bronchodilator

139) The patient is comfortable, because of your suggestion, for approximately 2 hours. Suddenly, the patient's heart rate increases, the patient becomes dyspneic and cyanotic, and the SpO_2 drops to 68%. A stat ABG reveals the following:

pH: 7.22

P_{CO_2}: 68 torr

P_{O_2}: 45 torr

H_{CO_3}: 26 mEq/l

S_{aO_2}: 65%

Which of the following would you recommend?
A. IPPB treatments q 2 hours
B. CPAP mask at 10 cmH_2O
C. Intubate and mechanically ventilate with a volume-cycled ventilator.
D. Intubate and mechanically ventilate with a pressure-cycled ventilator.

140) Your patient has been ventilated for ½ hour. ABGs reveal the following:

pH: 7:43

P_{CO_2}: 45 torr

P_{O_2}: 280 torr

H_{CO_3}: 25

S_{aO_2}: 100%

Which of the following changes would be appropriate at this time?
A. Increase the tidal volume.
B. Add 5 cmH_2O of PEEP.
C. Decrease the F_{IO_2}.
D. Make no changes.

Test 1: Answer key and category breakdown

The categories are AP = anatomy and physiology, TP = therapeutic procedures, CD = clinical data, E = equipment selection and use, and H and HP = history and principles.

1)	C	TP	36)	D	TP	71)	A	CD
2)	C	TP	37)	B	E	72)	D	E
3)	D	CD	38)	D	CD	73)	B	CD
4)	B	E	39)	A	CD	74)	D	TP
5)	A	E	40)	B	CD	75)	D	H
6)	B	TP	41)	C	CD	76)	C	H
7)	C	TP	42)	C	E	77)	B	H
8)	D	TP	43)	C	E	78)	D	H
9)	B	CD	44)	C	TP	79)	A	H
10)	B	CD	45)	C	CD	80)	B	H
11)	C	TP	46)	B	TP	81)	B	H
12)	B	E	47)	B	TP	82)	C	H
13)	C	CD	48)	D	TP	83)	B	TP
14)	D	E	49)	B	TP	84)	A	H
15)	D	TP	50)	A	CD	85)	B	E
16)	B	E	51)	B	E	86)	C	E
17)	B	E	52)	B	E	87)	B	E
18)	D	CD	53)	B	TP	88)	D	E
19)	A	CD	54)	A	TP	89)	D	E
20)	C	TP	55)	C	E	90)	C	H
21)	B	E	56)	D	CD	91)	A	E
22)	D	TP	57)	A	E	92)	A	E
23)	D	TP	58)	B	CD	93)	B	E
24)	C	E	59)	B	CD	94)	D	CD
25)	A	TP	60)	C	CD	95)	D	H
26)	C	TP	61)	D	TP	96)	A	TP
27)	B	TP	62)	D	TP	97)	B	TP
28)	B	E	63)	A	CD	98)	D	CD
29)	D	TP	64)	B	CD	99)	B	TP
30)	D	TP	65)	A	CD	100)	C	TP
31)	C	TP	66)	C	TP	101)	D	TP
32)	B	TP	67)	C	CD	102)	D	E
33)	B	CD	68)	B	CD	103)	C	TP
34)	B	E	69)	C	TP	104)	D	E
35)	D	CD	70)	B	TP	105)	A	CD

106)	C	TP	118)	B	H	130)	B	TP
107)	B	TP	119)	C	TP	131)	D	E
108)	A	CD	120)	C	TP	132)	B	CD
109)	D	H	121)	A	E	133)	C	TP
110)	D	TP	122)	A	E	134)	D	TP
111)	B	E	123)	B	CD	135)	B	E
112)	A	E	124)	B	CD	136)	C	TP
113)	B	TP	125)	D	CD	137)	B	TP
114)	D	E	126)	B	CD	138)	D	TP
115)	D	TP	127)	C	TP	139)	C	TP
116)	C	CD	128)	C	TP	140)	C	TP
117)	B	H	129)	D	TP			

Self-Assessment Test 2

1) Which of the following persons is credited with developing the process of fractional distillation?
   A. von Linde
   B. Priestly
   C. von Richthofen
   D. von Hindenburg

2) It would be most appropriate to recommend which of the following drugs as a substitute for isoetharine (Bronkosol) for a patient who has bronchospasm and whose heart rate increases by 60 beats/minute?
   A. Acetylcysteine (Mucomyst)
   B. Beclomethasone (Vanceril)
   C. Racemic epinephrine (Vaponefrin)
   D. Albuterol (Ventolin)

3) Which of the following is NOT generally advisable immediately after tracheal decannulation?
   A. Suturing the stoma closed
   B. Application of a sterile dressing to the site
   C. Cleaning the site with hydrogen peroxide
   D. Having the patient cough

4) A pulmonary wedge pressure (PWP) is considered normal in which of the following ranges?
   A. 0–2 mm Hg
   B. 5–25 mm Hg
   C. 15–22 mm Hg
   D. 27–34 mm Hg

5) Immediately after a tracheostomy, which of the following complications may occur?
   I. Postoperative bleeding
   II. Subcutaneous and/or mediastinal emphysema
   III. Tracheal stenosis
   A. I only
   B. III only
   C. I and II only
   D. II and III only

6) It would be most appropriate to recommend which of following for a patient with moderate dyspnea who is known to have a 40% pneumothorax?
   A. Administer a nebulized bronchodilator.
   B. Administer IPPB.
   C. Insert an endotracheal tube.
   D. Recommend that a chest tube be inserted.

7) An endotracheal tube that is inserted too far will most likely enter the
   A. Right upper lobe bronchus
   B. Left upper lobe bronchus
   C. Right mainstem bronchus
   D. Left mainstem bronchus

8) A patient is on a 60% cold steam mask. You notice that upon inspiration the mist disappears completely. Your most appropriate course of action would be to
   A. Increase the oxygen flow rate.
   B. Increase the F_{IO_2}.
   C. Decrease the F_{IO_2} to increase system flow rate.
   D. Add a second nebulizer at the same flow rate and F_{IO_2}.

9) Which of the following persons is credited with the discovery of oxygen in 1774?
   A. Mengele
   B. Beddoes
   C. Spock
   D. Priestly

10) A patient who is wearing a 35% venti mask becomes dyspneic during meals. Your most appropriate course of action would be to
    A. Explain to the patient that he or she will not receive a meal tray.
    B. Place the patient on a 2 L/min nasal cannula for meals.
    C. Recommend that tube feedings be started.
    D. Place the patient on a nasal cannula @ 4–5 L/min.

11) Who invented the first mercury barometer?
   A. von Manstein
   B. Bennett
   C. Torricelli ✓
   D. Fahrenheit

12) A patient is on a dual 40% cold steam set-up, with an additional 8 L/min titrated into the system. Both flow-meters are running at 8 L/min. What is the total flow of this system?
   A. 64 L/min
   B. 36 L/min
   C. 48 L/min
   D. 72 L/min

13) The F_{IO_2} of the system mentioned in question 12 is increased to 60%, with only 5 L/min titrated into it; both flowmeters are increased to 10 L/min. What is the total flow of this system?
   A. 40 L/min
   B. 55 L/min
   C. 45 L/min
   D. 60 L/min

14) An "H" cylinder, with 1,500 psig, is running a non-rebreathing mask @ 15 L/min. How long will the cylinder last?
   A. 11 hours
   B. 300 hours
   C. 24 hours
   D. 5 hours

15) Which of the following individuals is not commonly associated with respiratory care?
   A. Bert
   B. Beddoes
   C. Lavoisier
   D. Guderian

16) After the instillation of 3 ml of acetylcysteine into a patient's endotracheal tube, you notice the onset of diffuse, audible wheezes. The most appropriate course of action would be which of the following?
   A. Give an aerosol treatment with Vaponefrin immediately.
   B. Notify the doctor and recommend the immediate administration of a beta 2 drug.
   C. Give another dose of Mucomyst to clear the mucous plug.
   D. Increase the F_{IO_2} to 40%.

17) An "E" cylinder with 1,800 psig is running @ 6 L/min. How long will it last?
   A. 2 hours
   B. 1.5 hours
   C. 0.75 hours
   D. 10 hours

18) Which of the following is/are true of the central chemoreceptors?
   I. They are located in the medulla.
   II. They are stimulated MOST strongly by changes in the pH.
   III. Stimulation causes an increase in ventilation.
   IV. They tend to continue to function long after other receptors have been "burned out."
   A. I only
   B. II and IV only
   C. I, II, and III only
   D. III only

19) The pulmonary wedge pressure generated from a Swan-Ganz catheter is the direct reflection of
   A. Pulmonary artery pressure
   B. Right ventricular filling pressure
   C. Central venous pressure
   D. Left ventricular pressure

20) Which of the following is/are true of antibiotics?
   I. Some interfere with cell wall synthesis.
   II. Some interfere with DNA replication.
   III. Organisms may develop a tolerance to the antibiotics.
   IV. Antibiotics attack only the targeted organism, leaving desirable organisms intact.
   A. I only
   B. I and IV only
   C. I and II only
   D. I, II, and III only

21) Which of the following is true of the peripheral chemoreceptors?
   I. They react most strongly to changes in Pa_{CO_2}.
   II. They function long after the central receptors have been "burned out."
   III. They react most strongly to Pa_{O_2}.
   IV. If excessive amounts of oxygen are given to patients with COPD, they may signal the brain to stop breathing completely.
   A. I and II only
   B. I, II, and IV only
   C. III only
   D. II, III, and IV only

22) Who is considered to be the father of respiratory care because of his use of gases to treat disease?
   A. Beddoes
   B. Bert
   C. Lavoisier
   D. von Linde

23) In ultrasonic nebulizers, electricity is passed through the piezoelectric crystal to set up the mist-producing vi-

brations. What happens to the crystal to cause this vibration?
A. It produces electrical shocks.
B. It changes shape.
C. It operates on the Bernoulli principle.
D. It uses the venturi effect.

24) A cold-steam jet nebulizer is set at 80% and is connected to an oxygen flowmeter running at a flow rate of 9 L/min. What is the O_2:air entrainment ratio?
A. 1:1
B. 4:1
C. 1:3
D. 3:1

25) Refer to question 24. What is the total flow from this system?
A. 12 L/min
B. 27 L/min
C. 36 L/min
D. 18 L/min

26) Refer to questions 24 and 25. If the patient's minute volume is 20 L/min, the system from question 25 can be said to have which of the following effects on the patient?
I. The system is providing the desired F_{IO_2}.
II. The system is providing an F_{IO_2} less than what is desired.
III. The system is providing a flow rate that meets the patient's demand.
IV. The system is providing less flow than the patient requires.
V. The system is providing a higher F_{IO_2} than the patient needs.
A. I and IV only
B. I, IV, and V only
C. II and IV only
D. I, III, and V only

27) Refer to questions 24, 25, and 26. To ensure that the patient is receiving adequate flow and F_{IO_2} from the system from question 25, you would
I. Do nothing.
II. Set up a double nebulizer system to increase flow, setting both nebulizers at 80%.
III. Increase the output of the flowmeter to 12 L/min.
IV. Run the nebulizer off air and titrate 5 L/min O_2 into the system.
V. Titrate additional O_2 into the original system.
A. I only
B. II and IV only
C. IV only
D. II only

28) Of the following solutions, which will produce particles that will tend to generally remain the same size as they enter the patient's airway?
A. Isotonic solutions
B. Hypotonic solutions
C. Hypertonic solutions
D. Ginantonic solutions

29) An 18-year-old woman is admitted to the emergency room with multiple rib fractures. An arterial blood gas sample, obtained while the patient is breathing room air, reveals the results below.
pH: 7.48
$Paco_2$: 32 torr
HCO_3^-: 23 mEq/l
Pao_2: 40 torr
These data indicate which of the following?
I. Respiratory alkalosis
II. Hyperventilation
III. Increased $P(A-a)O_2$
A. I only
B. III only
C. I and II only
D. I, II, and III

30) Oxygen therapy has been initiated on the patient in question 29. Which of the following changes can be expected?
I. Increase in $Paco_2$
II. Decrease in minute ventilation
III. Increase in pulse rate
IV. Increase in pH
A. I and II only
B. I and III only
C. II and IV only
D. III and IV only

31) A respiratory care practitioner is preparing to suction a patient and finds a partially empty 1 L bottle of saline for irrigation at the patient's bedside. Which of the following statements is relevant to this situation?
A. Saline should not be used as a rinse solution.
B. Saline should be no less concentrated than 3% NaCl if it is to be used as a rinse solution.
C. Saline to be used as a rinse solution should be labeled "saline for injection."
D. The saline may be used if it has been opened within the previous 24 hours and the date and time are recorded on the bottle.

32) An asthmatic patient in acute respiratory distress presents to the emergency room with markedly diminished breath sounds. After bronchodilator therapy, auscultation of the chest reveals coarse breath sounds and

wheezing. This change suggests which of the following?
A. Development of a pneumothorax
B. Improvement of the air flow in the lungs
C. Worsening of the asthmatic condition
D. Onset of pulmonary edema
E. Development of a pulmonary embolism

33) Which of the following should be prescribed to provide adequate humidification to the patient?
A. Inspired gas with 50% relative humidity
B. Tracheobronchial suctioning
C. Inspired gas through a cold bubble diffusion humidifier
D. Inspired gas with an absolute humidity of 43.8 mg/L

34) When a patient who is receiving oxygen via a non-rebreathing mask inhales, the reservoir bag on the mask does not deflate. Probable causes of this situation include which of the following?
I. The flowmeter setting is too low.
II. The mask is not tight enough.
III. The one-way valve is sticking in the closed position.
A. I only
B. III only
C. I and II only
D. II and III only

35) The therapeutic use of oxygen might help accomplish which of the following?
I. Prevent absorption atelectasis
II. Decrease the myocardial workload
III. Decrease the work of breathing
IV. Increase the patient's respiratory rate
A. I only
B. II and III only
C. III and IV
D. I, II, and III only

36) Which of the following would indicate that a patient has suddenly developed a complete upper airway obstruction?
I. Supraclavicular retraction
II. Inability to speak
III. Marked increase in use of accessory muscles of ventilation
A. I only
B. III only
C. I and II only
D. I, II, and III

37) When inspecting the chest of a patient with emphysema, a respiratory care practitioner would most likely find which of the following?
A. Obesity
B. Barrel chest
C. Funnel chest
D. Central cyanosis

38) Which of the following is used by the ultrasonic nebulizer to produce droplets from the water reservoir?
A. Heat
B. Steam
C. Baffling
D. Vibration

39) A patient with COPD who is spontaneously breathing an F_{IO_2} of 0.5 becomes sleepy and unresponsive. The patient's reaction, most likely, is a result of
A. Increased Pa_{CO2}
B. Insufficient oxygenation
C. Decreased cardiac output
D. Excessive ventilation

40) A patient's arterial blood gas study reveals increased acidity (decreased pH) along with a decreased HCO_3^- measurement; otherwise, all values are within normal limits. This is most likely an indication of
A. Acute respiratory acidosis
B. Compensated respiratory acidosis
C. Acute metabolic alkalosis
D. Acute metabolic acidosis

41) A young, previously healthy patient has the following arterial blood gas results:
pH: 7.15
Pa_{CO_2}: 75 torr
HCO_3^-: 25 mEq/l
Pa_{O_2}: 70 torr
On the basis of this information, which of the following would be correct?
I. Mild hypoxemia is present.
II. The situation is chronic.
III. The situation is acute.
IV. Metabolic acidosis exists.
V. Respiratory acidosis exists.
A. I and IV only
B. II and V only
C. I and V only
D. I, III, and V

42) A Venturi mask is most likely to deliver an F_{IO_2} higher than intended if
A. The flow is set 5 L/min too high.
B. Nebulized water is being added through the air entrainment ports.
C. The holes in the mask are too large.
D. The air entrainment ports have been blocked.

43) A patient is receiving oxygen via a 32% Venti mask, but becomes dyspneic when she removes it to eat. The

respiratory care practitioner should recommend delivering the oxygen via
A. Nasal cannula @ 1 L/min
B. Nasal cannula @ 3 L/min
C. Nasal cannula @ 5 L/min
D. Nasal cannula @ 6 L/min

44) Alveolar humidity levels in healthy individuals are characterized by which of the following?
   I. Relative humidity = 100%
   II. Water vapor pressure = 47 torr
   III. Absolute humidity = 43.9 mg H$_2$O/L of air
   IV. Humidity deficit = 0 mg/L of air
A. III only
B. I and II only
C. I, II, and III only
D. I, II, III, and IV

45) An "H" cylinder is placed in service at 10 L/min. The gauge reads 1,800 psig. What is the tank's approximate duration?
A. 6 hours
B. 3 hours
C. 9 hours
D. 12 hours

46) A patient who is being mechanically ventilated with an F$_{IO_2}$ of 0.8 and 5 cm H$_2$O of PEEP has the following arterial blood gas results:
pH: 7.37
Pa$_{CO_2}$: 38 torr
Pa$_{O_2}$: 52 torr
Based on this data, the RCP should recommend which of the following?
A. Increase the F$_{IO_2}$ to 1.0 only.
B. Increase PEEP to 10 cm H$_2$O only.
C. Increase the F$_{IO_2}$ to 1.0 and the PEEP to 10 cm.
D. Decrease the PEEP and increase the F$_{IO_2}$.

47) Which of the following is LEAST important to evaluate, before changing the patient's therapy from mechanical ventilation to a T-piece?
A. Gag reflex
B. P(A-a)O$_2$
C. Vital capacity
D. V$_D$/V$_T$

48) While examining a patient's chest, the RCP palpates inspiratory and expiratory vibrations which clear when the patient coughs effectively. This indicates which of the following?
A. The patient has emphysema.
B. The airways are functioning normally.
C. Secretions were present in the airways.
D. The patient has pneumonia.

49) Which of the following nerves controls the function of the diaphragm?
A. Phrenic
B. Diaphragmatic
C. Vagus
D. Glossopharyngeal

50) Which of the following is/are functions of the respiratory tract?
A. Humidification
B. Heating
C. Conduction
D. All of the above

51) Which of the following is immediately true of left heart failure?
A. Breath sounds are clear.
B. Pedal edema
C. Onset of pulmonary edema
D. Blood pressure decreases.

52) In general, crackles starting in the bases and gradually becoming diffuse during a short period indicate the onset of
A. Myocardial infarction
B. Hepatic failure
C. Emphysema
D. Congestive heart failure

53) The only component of the respiratory tract specifically designed to take part in gas exchange is/are the
A. Respiratory bronchioles
B. Small airways
C. Alveoli
D. Bronchi

54) The vocal cords are located in the
A. Larynx
B. Glottis
C. Epiglottis
D. Carina

55) A strong cough reflex is caused by accumulation of secretions or direct stimulation to which of the following?
A. Epiglottis
B. Carina
C. Alveoli
D. Tongue

56) Diuretic therapy is helpful in the treatment of which of the following?
A. Pneumonia
B. Cystic fibrosis
C. Epiglottis
D. Congestive heart failure

57) An "infiltrate" on a CXR report probably indicates that the patient suffers from
   A. COPD
   B. Emphysema
   C. Pneumonia
   D. Pleural effusion

58) The maximum depth that suspended particles can be carried into the pulmonary tree by inhaled tidal gas is referred to as
   A. Deposition
   B. Penetration
   C. Stability
   D. Rain-out

59) A Puritan-Bennett all-purpose nebulizer is set at 10 L/min and 40% O_2. As a result of the large bore tubing being partially filled with condensate, which of the following will probably occur?
   A. The pressure relief valve will make an audible signal.
   B. The oxygen flowmeter reading will be less than actual because of back pressure.
   C. The system's F_{IO_2} will increase.
   D. The system's F_{IO_2} will decrease.

60) The two primary variables that control the amount of pressure exerted by a gas are
   A. The volume of the gas and the number of gas particles present
   B. The volume and temperature of the gas
   C. The number of gas particles present and their respective densities
   D. The absolute humidity and temperature of the gas

61) Legionnaires' disease is caused by:
   A. Viruses
   B. Bacteria
   C. Dust
   D. Allergies

62) Sputum culture and sensitivity would be most helpful for evaluating which of the following clinical conditions?
   A. Cardiogenic pulmonary edema
   B. Pneumonitis
   C. Empyema
   D. Suspected bronchogenic carcinoma

63) Which of the following devices will provide 100% body humidity?
   A. Heated cascade humidifier
   B. Bubble humidifier
   C. Spinning disc humidifier
   D. Pneumatic nebulizer

64) A patient receiving continuous heated aerosol therapy with air via "T" adapter (Briggs), develops subcutaneous emphysema around the tracheostomy site, neck, and chest. To obtain additional pertinent data, the most appropriate diagnostic procedure would be which of the following?
   A. NIF measurement
   B. Chest radiograph
   C. Hemoglobin and red blood cell count
   D. Timed forced expiratory volumes

65) Chronic hypoxia is associated with pulmonary hypertension leading to
   A. Emphysema
   B. Left ventricular failure
   C. Endobronchial carcinoma
   D. Cor pulmonale

66) The actual amount of water vapor in a gas is called
   A. Relative humidity
   B. Total humidity
   C. Absolute humidity
   D. Percent actual humidity

67) A cold steam jet nebulizer is set on the 40% dilution mode and connected to an air flowmeter running at a flow rate of 6 lpm. Downstream there is 5 L/min of O_2 being bled in. What is the delivered F_{IO_2}?
   A. 0.30
   B. 0.35
   C. 0.40
   D. 0.45

68) Refer to question 67. What is the total flow rate through the system?
   A. 32 L/min
   B. 48 L/min
   C. 24 L/min
   D. 29 L/min

69) Which of the following influence glutaraldehyde's effectiveness?
   I. pH
   II. Temperature
   III. Exposure time
   IV. Flammability
   A. I and III only
   B. II and IV only
   C. I, II, and III
   D. II, III, and IV

70) The amount of water that the respiratory tract must add to inspired air to equal 43.9 mg/L of water is called the
   A. Humidity deficit
   B. Body humidity
   C. Relative humidity
   D. Absolute humidity

71) Of the following solutions, which will produce particles that tend to evaporate and shrink in size as they enter the patient's airway?
   A. Hypotonic solutions
   B. Hypertonic solutions
   C. Isotonic solutions
   D. Hygrotonic solutions

72) What is/are the advantage(s) of gas sterilization over aldehyde solutions?
   I. Items may be packaged before sterilizing.
   II. It has superior penetrating abilities.
   III. It has nonexplosive characteristics.
   IV. It ensures sterility.
   A. II only
   B. I and III only
   C. II and IV only
   D. I, II, and IV only

73) Bland aerosols are believed to have optimum stability when the particle diameter ranges are approximately
   A. < 0.25 microns
   B. 4–5 microns
   C. 2–3 microns
   D. 0.2–0.7 microns

74) The most important property of helium, with respect to its use in helium-oxygen therapy, is its
   A. Density
   B. Viscosity
   C. Flammability
   D. Specific gravity

75) A patient with a venti mask set at 40% and running at 8 L/min has a peak inspiratory demand of 40 L/min. Therefore
   I. The patient is receiving less than 40% O_2.
   II. The patient is receiving more than 40% O2.
   III. The patient's peak inspiratory demand is being met by the mask.
   IV. The patient is exceeding the mask's ability to provide adequate flow.
   A. III only
   B. IV only
   C. I and IV only
   D. II and III only

76) A patient states that he has trouble sleeping unless he uses two pillows. This comment is indicative of which of the following conditions?
   A. Dysphagia
   B. Anorexia
   C. Orthopnea
   D. Eupnea

77) Which of the following statement(s) is/are true regarding the body's normal, initial response to acute hypoxemia?
   I. Cardiac output increases.
   II. Pulmonary artery pressure increases.
   III. A significant ventilatory response occurs.
   IV. Bradycardia and hypotension occur.
   A. I only
   B. I and II only
   C. I, II, and III only
   D. II, III, and IV only

78) A patient comes to the emergency room with a chief complaint of shortness of breath. ABGs are drawn while the patient is breathing room air, with the following results:
   pH = 7.38
   P_{CO_2} = 65 torr
   P_{O_2} = 48 torr
   HCO_3^- = 33 mEq/l
   S_{AO_2} = 90%
   The safest medical gas therapy device would be a
   A. Partial rebreathing mask @ 12 L/min
   B. Non-rebreathing mask @ 12 L/min
   C. Venti mask @ 28%
   D. Nasal cannula @ 51 L/min

79) The reciprocal relationship between volume and pressure of a gas was determined by
   A. Lavoisier
   B. Harvey
   C. Boyle
   D. Fudd

80) Upon discovery, the element OXYGEN, was named "dephlogisticated air" by
   A. Sheele
   B. Priestly
   C. Gore
   D. Goring

81) An "H" cylinder is set up on a wing. It is running at 12 L/min and has 1,900 psi remaining in the tank. How long will it last?
   A. 3 hours
   B. 8 hours
   C. 16 hours
   D. 1.6 hours

82) What theory states that the approximate distance between molecules is 300 times > than their diameter?
   A. Theory of relativity
   B. Kinetic theory of gas
   C. The boss has gas
   D. Mary Shelly's theory of electrocellular stimulation

83) Whose law of gases is the following: The pressure of a gas is equal to the sum of the pressures of all the gases that compose it OR the pressure of a gas is equal to the sum of its partial pressures?
   A. Charles' law
   B. Boyle's law
   C. Bernoulli's law
   D. Dalton's law

84) If a gas has a total pressure of 760 mm Hg, what is the partial pressure of O_2 if it composes 21% of the total?
   A. 100.3 torr
   B. 243.6 mm Hg
   C. 159.6 torr
   D. 105.4 mm Hg

85) O_2 and CO_2 differ in their diffusion characteristics in that
   A. They are different gases, but their diffusion rates are the same.
   B. O_2 diffuses approximately 40 times faster than CO_2.
   C. CO_2 diffuses 19 times faster than O_2.
   D. Shelly's theory states that diffusion is determined by the patient's HGB.

86) Who theorized that gas diffusion is proportionate to the solubility of a gas?
   A. Shelly
   B. Gramm
   C. Henry
   D. Priestly

87) Fraction distillation of oxygen was developed by
   A. von Raab
   B. Clinton
   C. Priestly
   D. von Linde

88) According to Bernoulli, as the forward velocity of a gas flowing through a tube increases, lateral wall pressure
   A. Remains constant
   B. Increases
   C. Decreases
   D. Creates a jet

89) A cold steam nebulizer is running @ 10 L/min and is set at 40%. According to your knowledge of air to O_2 entrainment ratios, what is the total flow to the patient?
   A. Entrainment ratio is 3:1 so the total flow is 40 L/min.
   B. It is 10 L/min because there is no entrainment.
   C. It is 20 L/min because the ratio is 1:1 for 40%.
   D. Cold steams don't entrain air, they entrain O_2.

90) Right heart failure can lead to which of the following?
   A. Hemoptysis
   B. Hematuria
   C. Pedal edema
   D. Diaphoresis

91) Which of the following is the functional unit of gas exchange?
   A. Alveoli
   B. Torricelli
   C. Respiratory bronchioles
   D. Pulmonary arteries

92) The term "dead space ventilation" refers to
   A. The patient is dying.
   B. Unperfused parts of the lung are moving air.
   C. Parts of the lungs are being perfused but not ventilated.
   D. Ventilation and perfusion are less than normal in some areas.

93) Peripheral chemoreceptors are MOST EFFECTIVELY stimulated by
   A. Rise in P_{CO_2}
   B. Elevation in the H^+ ion concentration (drop in pH)
   C. Both A and B
   D. A fall in the P_{O_2} (fall in oxygen tension)

94) The walls of arteries are
   A. Always responsible for carrying blood that is oxygenated
   B. Essentially the same in construction
   C. Used to working under less pressure than veins
   D. Thicker and more elastic than veins

95) The human heart is
   A. Four-chambered
   B. Three-chambered
   C. Only capable of an output of 2.0 L/min, max
   D. Responsible for extracting its oxygen from the superior vena cava

96) The NBRC is the organization that
   A. Lobbies politicians in Washington, D.C. on behalf of RTs.
   B. Is responsible for RT national credentialing exams.
   C. Something I made up
   D. A multifaceted RT organization

97) Alveolar disintegration is most commonly an effect in
   A. Emphysema
   B. Asthma
   C. Bronchiectasis
   D. Orchiditis

98) Effective incentive spirometry will change which of the following?
   A. P_{CO_2}
   B. Secretion consistency
   C. Relative humidity
   D. Gag reflex

99) How many milligrams of a drug are in 1 ml of a 0.5% solution?
   A. 0.5 mg
   B. 5 mg
   C. 50 mg
   D. None of the above

100) Which of the following drugs affects both alpha and beta receptors?
   A. Beclomethasone
   B. Albuterol
   C. Racemic epinephrine
   D. Isoetharine

101) A patient is, according to ECG monitor, suffering from ventricular fibulation. Which course of action should you follow as an RCP?
   A. Initiate the steps required to start CPR.
   B. Tell the charge nurse.
   C. Do nothing; this is normal for that patient.
   D. Call the physician.

102) A common complication of lobar pneumonia may be which of the following?
   A. Pneumothorax
   B. Emphysema
   C. Endocarditis
   D. Empyema

103) If a Collins water seal spirometer is used, the residual volume would be determined by using which of the following equations?
   A. $T_V + VC$
   B. $TLC - T_V$
   C. $FRC - ERV$
   D. $ERV - IC$

104) After assisting with a fiber optic bronchoscopy on a ventilator patient, the RCP notices that there is a significant increase in peak airway pressure. Which of the following may be responsible for this pressure increase?
   I. Bronchospasm
   II. Pneumothorax
   III. Pulmonary hemorrhage
   IV. Laryngospasm
   A. I and II only
   B. I and IV only
   C. II and III only
   D. I, II, and III only

105) An intubated patient in ICU is on a 35% cold steam nebulizer via a Brigg's adapter (T-piece). Each time the patient inhales, the mist disappears completely. Which of the following is an appropriate action for an RCP to take?
   I. Add a reservoir tube to the T adapter.
   II. Increase the flow of oxygen to the nebulizer.
   III. Decrease the F_{IO_2} set on the nebulizer.
   A. I only
   B. III only
   C. I and II only
   D. II and III only

106) The dynamic compliance of a patient suffering from status asthmaticus and on a ventilator has decreased dramatically during a 30-minute period. Which of the following medications should provide the fastest improvement in the dynamic compliance?
   A. Acetylcysteine
   B. Theophylline
   C. Beclomethasone
   D. Inhaled atropine

107) When a pneumatic aerosol generator is being used, the RCP should reduce the aerosol output for which of the following?
   I. A patient with dried, retained secretions who becomes dyspneic on the aerosol
   II. An infant who has pulmonary edema
   III. A patient who has just received a tracheostomy tube
   A. I only
   B. II only
   C. III only
   D. I and II only

108) The following are the results of a PFT study performed on a 45-year-old male patient who weighs 150 lbs and is 6 ft 2 in tall.

	actual	predicted
FVC	2.76 L	4.43 L
FEV1	2.16 L	2.25 L
FEV1/FVC	90%	
D_{CO} (diffusion)	51%	

   There was no significant response to the bronchodilator.
   These data are indicative of which of the following?
   A. Pulmonary fibrosis
   B. Chronic bronchitis
   C. Emphysema
   D. Normal lungs

109) Which of the following is the most effective way to increase alveolar ventilation on a patient who is on a ventilator?

A. Increase the peak flow rate.
B. Increase the mechanical dead space.
C. Increase the tidal volume.
D. Add PEEP.

110) The following volumes were taken from a PFT report.
VC = 4,500 ml
FRC = 1,000 ml
ERV = 1,300 ml
IC = 3,800 ml
Based on these data, what is the patient's TLC?
A. 5,100 ml
B. 3,800 ml
C. 4,800 ml
D. 5,800 ml

111) After reducing the PEEP on a ventilator from 10 cm H_2O to 5 cm H_2O, the RCP notices that the ventilator cycles on continuously, without the patient triggering the machine. Which of the following is causing this malfunction?
A. The rate control should have been reset after the change.
B. The sensitivity should have been adjusted after the change.
C. The tidal volume should have been adjusted.
D. The peak flow should have been adjusted.

112) A coldsteam jet nebulizer is set at 80% and is connected to an oxygen flowmeter running at a flow rate of 9 L/min. What is the O_2:air entrainment ratio?
A. 1:1
B. 4:1
C. 1:3
D. 3:1

113) Refer to question 112. What is the total flow from this system?
A. 12 L/min
B. 27 L/min
C. 36 L/min
D. 18 L/min

114) Refer to questions 112 and 113. If the patient's minute volume is 20 L/min, the system can be said to have which of the following effects on the patient?
I. It provides the desired F_{IO_2}.
II. It provides an F_{IO_2} less than what is desired.
III. It provides a flow rate that meets the patient's demand.
IV. It provides less flow than the patient requires.
V. It provides a higher F_{IO_2} than the patient needs.
A. I and IV only
B. I, IV, and V only
C. II and IV only
D. I, III, and V only

115) Refer to questions 112, 113, and 114. To ensure the patient is receiving adequate flow and F_{IO_2} from the system, you would
I. Do nothing.
II. Set up a double nebulizer system to increase flow, setting both nebulizers at 80%.
III. Increase the output of the flowmeter to 12 L/min.
IV. Run the nebulizer off air and titrate 5 L/min O_2 into the system.
A. I only
B. II and IV only
C. IV only
D. II only

116) Of the following solutions, which will produce particles that will tend to generally remain the same size as they enter the patient's airway?
A. Isotonic solutions
B. Hypotonic solutions
C. Agrotonic solutions
D. Hypertonic solutions

117) An 18-year-old woman is admitted to the emergency room with multiple rib fractures. An arterial blood gas sample, obtained while the patient is breathing room air, reveals the following results:
pH: 7.48
Pa_{CO_2}: 32 torr
HCO_3^-: 23 mEq/l
Pa_{O_2}: 40 torr
These data indicate which of the following?
I. Respiratory alkalosis
II. Hyperventilation
III. Increased $P(A-a)O_2$
A. I only
B. III only
C. I and II only
D. I, II, and III

118) Oxygen therapy has been initiated on the patient in question 117. Which of the following changes can be expected?
I. Increase in Pa_{CO_2}
II. Decrease in minute ventilation
III. Increase in pulse rate
IV. Increase in pH
A. I and II only
B. I and III only
C. II and IV
D. III and IV

119) A respiratory care practitioner is preparing to suction a patient and finds a partially empty 1 L bottle of saline for irrigation at the patient's bedside. Which of the following statements is relevant to this situation?

A. Saline should not be used as a rinse solution.
B. Saline should be no less concentrated than 3% NaCl if it is to be used as a rinse solution.
C. Saline to be used as a rinse solution should be labeled "saline for injection."
D. The saline may be used if it has been opened during the previous 24 hours and the date and time are recorded on the bottle.

120) An asthmatic patient in acute respiratory distress presents to the emergency room with markedly diminished breath sounds. After bronchodilator therapy, auscultation of the chest reveals coarse breath sounds and wheezing. This change suggests which of the following?
A. Development of a pneumothorax
B. Improvement of the air flow in the lungs
C. Worsening of the asthmatic condition
D. Onset of pulmonary edema

121) Which of the following should be prescribed to provide adequate humidification to the patient?
A. Inspires gas with 50% relative humidity
B. Tracheobronchial suctioning
C. Inspired gas through a cold bubble diffusion humidifier
D. Inspired gas with an absolute humidity of 44 mg/L

122) When a patient who is receiving oxygen via a nonrebreathing mask inhales, the reservoir bag on the mask does not deflate. Probable causes of this situation include which of the following?
I. The flowmeter setting is too low.
II. The mask is not tight enough.
III. The one-way valve is sticking in the closed position.
A. I only
B. III only
C. I and II only
D. II and III only

123) The therapeutic use of oxygen might help accomplish which of the following?
I. Prevent absorption atelectasis.
II. Decrease the myocardial workload.
III. Decrease the work of breathing.
IV. Increase the patient's respiratory rate.
A. I only
B. II and III only
C. III and IV only
D. I, II, and III only

124) Which of the following would indicate that a patient has suddenly developed a complete upper airway obstruction?
I. Supraclavicular retraction
II. Inability to speak
III. Marked increase in use of accessory muscles of ventilation
A. I only
B. III only
C. I, II, and II
D. II and III only

125) A patient with *Pneumocystis carinii* pneumonia has an SpO_2 of 85% and experiences dyspnea upon mild exertion. Which of the following would you recommend?
A. IPPB therapy
B. Oxygen therapy
C. Incentive spirometry
D. Inhaled steroids

126) The following ABGs were obtained from a patient who is being mechanically ventilated on an F_{IO_2} of .85 and 5 cmH_2O of PEEP.
pH: 7.38
P_{CO_2}: 39 torr
P_{O_2}: 50 torr
Which of the following changes would you suggest?
A. Increase the respiratory rate.
B. Increase the PEEP to 10 cmH_2O.
C. Increase the F_{IO_2} to 1.0.
D. Keep the current settings.

127) Refer to question 126. The patient's ABGs have improved because of your excellent care and the doctor orders bedside weaning parameters with the following results:
RR: 35
Tidal volume: 150 ml
NIF: –20 cmH_2O
Minute volume: 5.25 L
Using this data, you do which of the following?
A. Recommend extubation.
B. Let the patient rest and try later.
C. Do weaning parameters q 1 hour until you see better results.
D. Recommend CPT.

128) When coordinating the sequence of therapies for a patient who requires bronchopulmonary toilet, which of the following should the RCP do last?
A. Medicated aerosol therapy
B. Instruct the patient in deep breathing and coughing
C. Chest percussion
D. Postural drainage

129) To determine if a patient, who is intubated, is receiving adequate humidity, the RCP should evaluate which of the following?

A. Skin turgor
B. Urine output
C. Sputum consistency
D. Sputum color
E. Chest radiograph

130) Upon performing a ventilator check on a patient, you obtain the following data:

Peak Inspiratory (Airway) Pressure 50 cmH$_2$O
Plateau Pressure 46 cm H$_2$O
Tidal Volume 800 ml
Peak Flow Rate 60 lpm
Frequency (f) 10 breaths/min
PEEP 5 cmH$_2$O

Based on this information, you, the RCP, should conclude that
A. The patient's compliance is normal.
B. Compliance is decreased.
C. Compliance is increased.
D. Dynamic compliance is increased while the static compliance is normal.

131) The RCP instructs the patient to take a maximum inhalation from a resting exhalation. Which of the following is measured by this maneuver?
A. TLC
B. RV
C. IC
D. MVV

132) Which of the following is the first priority in the treatment of a patient with a known tension pneumothorax?
A. Releasing trapped air from the thorax
B. Stat CXR
C. Stat IPPB tx
D. Administering CPAP

133) There is a leak in a nasal CPAP system on an infant. Which of the following most likely will solve the problem?
A. Triple the flow rate.
B. Reduce the flow rate.
C. Adjust the position of the nasal prongs.
D. Increase CPAP pressure.

134) Which of the following pulmonary function measurements is the largest when within the normal range for any patient?
A. FRC
B. Respiratory rate
C. NIF
D. FVC

135) The RCP most likely would notice which of the following in a patient who has sustained a right phrenic nerve injury?
A. Asymmetric chest movement
B. Nothing
C. Bronchospasm
D. Tracheal shift

136) In relation to a tracheostomy tube or endotracheal tube, the outside diameter of a suction catheter should be
A. About the same diameter
B. No greater than one quarter the diameter
C. No greater than one half the diameter
D. Whatever is handy

137) You receive an order to percuss a patient's left lower lobe, lateral basal segment. Which area would you percuss?
A. Below the left scapula
B. The left lower ribs on the patient's side
C. Over the left clavicle
D. None of the above

138) Percussion and drainage are ordered in the left lateral decubitus. Which of the following positions would you place the patient in?
A. Left side up on the patient's side
B. Right side up on the patient's side
C. Sitting up, leaning left
D. None of the above

139) A patient who has received aerosolized Mucomyst has become dyspneic after the treatment. The most likely cause is
  I. Bronchospasm
 II. Sensitivity to the medication
III. Shock lung
 IV. No bronchodilator was given with, or before, the Mucomyst.
A. I only
B. I and III only
C. II and IV only
D. I, II, and IV only

140) A ventilator alarm is sounding intermittently during the inspiratory cycle. The most likely problem is
A. Patient disconnect
B. Accumulated pulmonary secretions
C. Battery malfunction
D. Blender/accumulator malfunction

Test 2: Answer key and category breakdown

The categories are AP = anatomy and physiology, TP = therapeutic procedures, CD = clinical data, E = equipment selection and use, and H and HP = history and principles.

1)	A	H	36)	D	TP	71)	A	AP
2)	D	TP	37)	B	TP	72)	D	E
3)	A	TP	38)	D	E	73)	D	TP
4)	B	CD	39)	A	CD	74)	A	HP
5)	C	CD	40)	D	CD	75)	C	TP
6)	D	TP	41)	D	CD	76)	C	CD
7)	C	TP	42)	D	E	77)	C	AP
8)	D	TP	43)	B	E	78)	C	TP
9)	D	H	44)	D	HP	79)	C	HP
10)	D	E	45)	C	E	80)	B	HP
11)	C	H	46)	B	TP	81)	B	E
12)	D	E	47)	A	TP	82)	B	HP
13)	C	E	48)	C	CD	83)	D	HP
14)	D	E	49)	A	AP	84)	C	HP
15)	D	H	50)	D	AP	85)	C	HP
16)	B	TP	51)	C	AP	86)	B	HP
17)	B	E	52)	D	CD	87)	D	HP
18)	C	TP	53)	C	AP	88)	C	HP
19)	D	CD	54)	A	AP	89)	A	E
20)	D	TP	55)	D	AP	90)	C	AP
21)	D	TP	56)	D	TP	91)	A	AP
22)	A	H	57)	C	CD	92)	B	TP
23)	B	E	58)	B	HP	93)	D	AP
24)	D	E	59)	C	E	94)	D	AP
25)	A	E	60)	B	HP	95)	A	AP
26)	C	E	61)	B	CD	96)	B	HP
27)	D	E	62)	B	CD	97)	A	CD
28)	A	TP	63)	A	CD	98)	A	TP
29)	D	TP	64)	B	TP	99)	B	TP
30)	A	TP	65)	D	CD	100)	C	TP
31)	D	TP	66)	C	HP	101)	A	TP
32)	B	TP	67)	B	E	102)	D	TP
33)	D	TP	68)	D	E	103)	C	TP
34)	D	E	69)	A	E	104)	D	TP
35)	B	TP	70)	A	AP	105)	C	TP

106)	D	TP	118)	A	TP	130)	B	TP
107)	D	TP	119)	D	E	131)	C	TP
108)	A	TP	120)	B	TP	132)	A	TP
109)	C	TP	121)	D	HP	133)	C	E
110)	C	TP	122)	D	E	134)	D	CD
111)	B	TP	123)	B	TP	135)	A	CD
112)	D	E	124)	C	TP	136)	C	TP
113)	A	E	125)	B	TP	137)	B	TP
114)	C	TP	126)	B	TP	138)	B	TP
115)	D	E	127)	B	TP	139)	D	TP
116)	A	TP	128)	B	TP	140)	B	CD
117)	D	TP	129)	C	TP			

Self-Assessment Test 3

Note: If you thought the last two tests were difficult, have fun with this one, because I think this is the hardest one. If you thought the last two tests were easy, perhaps you will like this one a bit more.

1) The maximum level of aerosol particle penetration of the bronchial tree is which of the following?
   A. Alveoli
   B. Mainstem bronchi
   C. Segmental bronchioles
   D. None of the above

2) Which of the following lung segments is being drained when the patient is lying slightly prone on his or her right side, in Trendelenburg?
   A. Apical segment of the left upper lobe
   B. Left lower lobe, posterior basilar segment
   C. Right lower and middle lobe
   D. None of the above

3) Hemoptysis can be defined as
   A. Coughing up or suctioning blood
   B. A collapsed lung
   C. A nose bleed
   D. Bloody chest tube drainage

4) Elevating a patient's left shoulder and rotating their head to the right during suctioning may do which of the following?
   A. Prevent a vagal response
   B. Ensure proper secretion drainage
   C. Increase chances of inserting the catheter into the left mainstem
   D. Decrease airway trauma

5) Which of the following may be complications of airway suctioning?
   A. Atelectasis
   B. Hypoxia
   C. Hemoptysis
   D. All of the above

6) Which of the following defines a PEEP compensated sensitivity control on a ventilator?
   A. As PEEP increases, sensitivity decreases.
   B. Sensitivity does not change when PEEP is changed.
   C. Sensitivity increases as PEEP increases.
   D. None of the above

7) Venous return to the heart may be increased by
   A. Mechanical ventilation
   B. IPPB therapy
   C. Incentive spirometry
   D. PEEP

8) Which of the following is true of IPPB therapy?
   A. It provides mechanical bronchodilation.
   B. It facilitates optimum aerosol particle deposition.
   C. It increases venous return.
   D. None of the above

9) Where is the innominate artery located?
   A. The neck
   B. The lungs
   C. The heart
   D. The trachea

10) Which of the following is/are considered to be an undesirable effect(s) of PEEP?
    A. Reduced cardiac output
    B. Increased cardiac output
    C. Increased functional residual capacity
    D. All of the above

11) Blood is considered to be acidotic when
    A. The hydrogen ion concentration increases
    B. The pH drops
    C. None of the above
    D. A and B only

12) Administration of 100% oxygen may cause atelectasis because
    A. The nitrogen that keeps the alveoli inflated is no longer present.

B. The acini are dysfunctional.
C. Carbon dioxide cannot be exchanged.
D. All of the above are pure nonsense and untrue.

13) Ideal endotracheal tube position in the trachea is
    A. Resting on the right mainstem bifurcation
    B. 2 cm above the carina
    C. With the cuff of the tube resting just below the vocal cords
    D. With the tip of the tube resting on the carina

14) The actual amount of water vapor carried by a gas is known as
    A. Relative humidity
    B. Absolute humidity
    C. Total humidity
    D. Body humidity

15) The visible gas stream flowing from the end of a cold stream T–piece reservoir tube disappears with each patient breath. The proper corrective action would be to
    A. Increase the flow rate of the system.
    B. Do nothing, it's no problem.
    C. Change the patient to a non-rebreathing mask.
    D. Put the patient back on the vent.

16) Which of the following is a primary goal of volume–oriented IPPB therapy?
    A. To relieve the stress associated with mechanical ventilation
    B. To reduce excessive carbon dioxide levels
    C. To provide mechanical bronchodilation
    D. To improve cough reflexes

17) Aerosol particles are said to have optimum penetration in which of the following ranges?
    A. Less than 0.3 μm
    B. 0.1–10 μm
    C. 0.3–5.0 μm
    D. 1.0–2.0 μm

18) Which of the following solutions cause the greatest increase in total airway resistance?
    A. 3% saline solution
    B. 0.45% saline solution
    C. Normal saline solution (0.9%)
    D. Sterile water

19) Which of the following is a contraindication to Trendelenburg?
    A. Bronchiectasis
    B. Pneumonia
    C. Morbid obesity
    D. Severe atelectasis

20) Effective incentive spirometry will change which of the following?
    A. pH
    B. Pa_{O_2}
    C. Vital capacity
    D. None of the above

21) Which of the following devices reads flow by measuring the back pressure of a gas moving through a fixed orifice?
    A. Pressure compensated Thorpe tubes
    B. Uncompensated Thorpe tubes
    C. Bourdon gauge
    D. Diameter–dependent Thorpe tube

22) What is the minimum time that should elapse after a tube feeding is turned off before it is safe to place a patient into the Trendelenburg position?
    A. 30 minutes
    B. 1 hour
    C. 45 minutes
    D. No waiting period is necessary.

23) The peak airway pressure read on the manometer of a Bird MK 7 is a reflection of the pressure in
    A. The patient's alveoli
    B. The mainstem bronchi
    C. The ventilator mouth piece
    D. The ventilator pressure chamber (side)

24) Which of the following microorganisms reproduce by invading a healthy cell and reprogramming its RNA to replicate itself?
    A. *Euglena*
    B. Viruses
    C. Bacterial spores
    D. Gram negative rods

25) How many milliliters are in 1.65 L of gas?
    A. 1,650 ml
    B. 16.5 ml
    C. 165 ml
    D. 16,500 ml

26) Which of the following factors affect the effectiveness of glutaraldehyde sterilization?
    A. pH
    B. Exposure time
    C. A and B only
    D. Temperature

27) Which of the following solutions produce aerosol particles that shrink when they enter the patient's airway?
    A. Isotonic solutions
    B. Hypertonic solutions
    C. Therapeutic aerosols
    D. Hypotonic solutions

28) How many milligrams of a drug are found in 1 milliliter of a 2% solution?

A. 20 mg/ml
B. 2 mg/ml
C. 0.2 mg/ml
D. None of the above

29) Which of the following is true about the term "pH"?
   A. No units of measure are associated with it.
   B. It indicates that the number associated with it denotes hydrogen ion concentration.
   C. The pH scale goes from 1 to 14.
   D. All of the above

30) Hyperventilation could be a compensatory response to which of the following?
   A. Hypoventilation
   B. Hypoxemia
   C. Oxygen toxicity
   D. Crohn's disease

31) To which of the following structures does the Bundle of His feed electrical impulses?
   A. The ventricles of the heart
   B. The SA node
   C. The medulla oblongata
   D. The AV node

32) Aerosolized steroids are indicated in the treatment of which of the following pathologies?
   A. Empyema
   B. Cor pulmonale
   C. Asthma
   D. Emphysema

33) All of the following are physical characteristics of oxygen except
   A. Colorless gas
   B. Odorless gas
   C. Supports combustion
   D. Explosive properties

34) Albuterol sulfate is
   A. A beta 2 bronchodilator with no significant beta 1 effects
   B. A strong beta 2 drug with moderate alpha effects
   C. A strong beta 1 and beta 2 drug
   D. A strong beta 1 and moderate beta 2

35) All of the following are true of acetylcysteine except
   A. That it has a mild beta 2 effect
   B. That it should be given with or directly after a bronchodilator
   C. That it breaks down the disulfide bonds in mucous
   D. That patients allergic to sulfa should not be given this drug

36) All of the following are potential side effects of sympathomimetic drugs except
   A. Increased heart rate
   B. Tremor
   C. Dyspnea
   D. Palpitations

37) Which of the following drugs is a beta blocker?
   A. Terbutaline sulfate
   B. Propranolol
   C. Metaproterenol sulfate
   D. Isoetharine

38) Beta 2 receptor stimulation generally causes which of the following responses?
   A. Smooth muscle tissue relaxation
   B. Increased heart rate
   C. Vasoconstriction
   D. None of the above

39) Which of the following is true about aerosolized steroids?
   A. They are absorbed systemically.
   B. They are effective in relieving acute bronchospasm.
   C. Failure to rinse the mouth after administration may lead to candidiasis (thrush).
   D. They are rarely useful in the treatment of reactive airway diseases.

40) If an object is aspirated, the most likely area of deposition will be
   A. The right lower lobe
   B. The left lower lobe
   C. Either apical segment
   D. None of the above

41) Bronchiectasis in children and young adults may be a result of
   A. Farmer's lung
   B. Emphysema
   C. Cystic fibrosis
   D. None of the above

42) The treatment of choice for *Pneumocystis carinii* pneumonia is which of the following?
   A. Incentive spirometry breathing
   B. Inhaled pentamidine
   C. Inhaled steroids
   D. Inhaled acetylcysteine

43) All of the following are true about congestive heart failure except
   A. Pedal edema may be present.
   B. Rhinorrhea may be present.
   C. Rales may be present upon auscultation.
   D. Dyspnea may be present.

44) All of the following are true of Atrovent (ipratropium bromide) except

A. It is an atropine derivative.
B. It works through the parasympathetic nervous system.
C. It has a strong beta 2 effect.
D. It should be used in conjunction with a sympathomimetic agent.

45) Vital capacity equals
A. $IRV + T_V + ERV$
B. $IRV + T_V$
C. $IRV + FRC + ERV$
D. $T_V + IC$

46) Upon auscultation, wheezing usually indicates which of the following?
A. Bronchospasm
B. Congestive heart failure
C. Consolidation
D. Empyema

47) All of the following are true about Portex adult endotracheal tubes except
A. That they are graduated in 2-cm increments
B. That they have no cuff
C. That they have removable 15-mm adapters
D. That the largest standard size is 10 mm

48) Which of the following medications provides an alpha response as well as a mild beta 2 response?
A. Albuterol sulfate
B. Isoetharine
C. Beclomethasone
D. Racemic epinephrine

49) The application of PEEP facilitates which of the following?
A. Increased functional residual capacity
B. Increased alveolar ventilation
C. Recruitment of collapsed alveoli
D. All of the above

50) Which of the following is considered to be a satisfactory home sterilization method for respiratory equipment?
A. Isopropyl alcohol
B. A vinegar and water solution
C. Ethylene oxide
D. Activated glutaraldehyde

51) Which of the following is a direct result of increased alveolar ventilation?
A. Increased Pa_{CO_2}
B. Increased Pa_{O_2}
C. Decreased Pa_{CO_2}
D. None of the above

52) Which of the following does not indicate the patient's ability to wean from mechanical ventilation?
A. Negative inspiratory force of -13 cmH_2O
B. FVC of 1.3 L
C. Respiratory rate of 24
D. Tidal volume of 368 ml

53) Which of the following best indicates that compliance is decreasing in a patient who is being ventilated on a volume-cycled machine?
A. Increase in the spontaneous rate
B. The minute volume begins to drop
C. There are no measurable changes.
D. The system pressure increases.

54) A venturi mask is most likely to deliver an F_{IO_2} higher than intended if
A. The flow is set 5 L/min too high.
B. Nebulized water is being added through the air entrainment ports.
C. The holes in the mask are too large.
D. The air entrainment ports have been blocked.

55) A patient is receiving oxygen via a 32% venti mask, but becomes dyspneic when she removes it to eat. The respiratory care practitioner should recommend delivering the oxygen via
A. Nasal cannula @ 1 L/min
B. Nasal cannula @ 3 L/min
C. Nasal cannula @ 5 L/min
D. Nasal cannula @ 6 L/min

56) Alveolar humidity levels in healthy individuals are characterized by which of the following?
I. Relative humidity = 100%
II. Water vapor pressure = 47 torr
III. Absolute humidity = 43.9 mg H_2O/L of air
IV. Humidity deficit = 0 mg/L of air
A. III only
B. I and II only
C. I, II, III, and IV
D. II, III, and IV only

57) An "H" cylinder is placed in service at 10 L/min. The gauge reads 1,800 psig. What is the tank's approximate duration?
A. 6 hours
B. 3 hours
C. 9 hours
D. 12 hours

58) When coordinating the sequence of therapies for a patient who requires bronchopulmonary toilet, which of the following should the RCP do last?
A. Medicated aerosol therapy
B. Instruct the patient in deep breathing and coughing
C. Chest percussion
D. Postural drainage

59) A ventilator patient is on a F_{IO_2} of 80% and 5 cm H_2O of PEEP and has the following ABG results:
pH: 7.39
Pa_{CO_2}: 40 torr
Pa_{O_2}: 50 torr
Based on this information, you, as the RCP on duty, should suggest
A. Increase the F_{IO_2} to 1.0.
B. Increase the F_{IO_2} to 1.0 and increase the PEEP to 10 cm.
C. D/C the PEEP and increase the F_{IO_2} to 1.0.
D. Increase the PEEP to 10 cm.

60) To determine if a patient who is intubated is receiving adequate humidity, the RCP should evaluate which of the following?
A. Skin turgor
B. Urine output
C. Sputum consistency
D. Sputum color
E. Chest radiograph

61) Upon performing a ventilator check on a patient, you obtain the following data:
Peak Inspiratory (Airway) Pressure   50 cmH_2O
Plateau Pressure   46 cmH_2O
Tidal Volume   800 ml
Peak Flow Rate   60 lpm
Frequency (f)   10 breaths/min
PEEP   5 cmH_2O
Based on this information, you, the RCP, should conclude that
A. The patient's compliance is normal.
B. Compliance is decreased.
C. Compliance is increased.
D. Dynamic compliance is increased while the static compliance is normal.

62) The RCP instructs the patient to take a maximum inhalation and then exhale to maximum exhalation. Which of the following is measured by this maneuver?
A. TLC
B. RV
C. FVC
D. MVV

63) Which of the following is the first priority in the treatment of a patient with a known tension pneumothorax?
A. Releasing trapped air from the thorax.
B. Stat CXR
C. Stat IPPB tx
D. Administering CPAP

64) A patient's SpO_2 is 87% on room air. Which course of action would you recommend?
A. Start the patient on a 3 L/min nasal cannula.
B. Start a 6 L/min nasal cannula.
C. Start a 24% venti mask.
D. Start a simple mask at 4 L/min.

65) If a Collins water seal spirometer is used, the residual volume would be determined by using which of the following equations?
A. T_V + VC
B. TLC – T_V
C. FRC – ERV
D. ERV – IC

66) After assisting with a fiberoptic bronchoscopy on a ventilator patient, the RCP notices that there is a significant increase in peak airway pressure. Which of the following may be responsible for this pressure increase?
I. Bronchospasm
II. Pneumothorax
III. Pulmonary hemorrhage
IV. Laryngospasm
A. I and II only
B. I and IV only
C. II and III only
D. I, II, and III only

67) An intubated patient in ICU is on a 35% cold steam nebulizer via a Brigg's adapter (T-piece). Each time the patient inhales, the mist disappears completely. Which of the following is an appropriate action for an RCP to take?
I. Add a reservoir tube to the T-adapter.
II. Increase the flow of oxygen to the nebulizer.
III. Decrease the F_{IO_2} set on the nebulizer.
A. I only
B. III only
C. I and II only
D. II and III only

68) The dynamic compliance of a patient suffering from status asthmaticus, and on a ventilator, has decreased dramatically over a 30-min period. Which of the following medications should provide the fastest improvement dynamic compliance?
A. Acetylcysteine
B. Theophylline
C. Beclomethasone
D. Inhaled atropine

69) When a pneumatic aerosol generator is being used, the RCP should reduce the aerosol output for which of the following?
I. A patient with dried, retained secretions who becomes dyspneic on the aerosol.
II. An infant who has pulmonary edema.

III. A patient who has just received a tracheostomy tube.
A. I only
B. II only
C. III only
D. I and II only

70) The following are the results of a PFT study performed on a 45-year-old male patient who weighs 150 lbs and is 6 ft 2 in tall.

	actual	predicted
FVC	2.76 L	4.43 L
FEV1	2.16 L	2.25 L
FEV1/FVC	90%	
D CO (diffusion)	51%	

There was no significant response to the bronchodilator.
These data are indicative of which of the following?
A. Pulmonary fibrosis
B. Chronic bronchitis
C. Emphysema
D. Normal lungs

71) Which of the following is the most effective way to increase alveolar ventilation on a patient who is on a ventilator?
A. Increase the peak flow rate.
B. Increase the mechanical dead space.
C. Increase the tidal volume.
D. Add PEEP.

72) What is your first course of action if a ventilator suddenly stops cycling?
A. Check the circuit for leaks.
B. Check the ventilator settings.
C. Ventilate the patient with a bag valve mask device.
D. Change ventilators.

73) Which of the following will affect a patient's F_{IO_2} when the patient is set up on a high flow system?
A. The patient's minute volume
B. The patient's inspiratory capacity.
C. Whether the patient is breathing through his or her mouth or nose
D. None of the above

74) A cold steam jet nebulizer is set at 80% and is connected to an oxygen flowmeter running at a flow rate of 9 L/min. What is the O_2:air entrainment ratio?
A. 1:1
B. 4:1
C. 1:3
D. 3:1

75) Refer to question 74. What is the total flow from this system?

A. 12 L/min
B. 27 L/min
C. 36 L/min
D. 18 L/min

76) Refer to questions 74 and 75. If the patient's minute volume is 20 L/min, the system can be said to have which of the following effects on the patient
I. It provides the desired F_{IO_2}.
II. It provides an F_{IO_2} less than what is desired.
III. It provides a flow rate that meets the patient's demand.
IV. It provides less flow than the patient requires.
V. It provides a higher F_{IO_2} than the patient needs.
A. I and IV only
B. I, IV, and V only
C. II and IV only
D. I, III, and V only

77) Refer to questions 74, 75, and 76. To ensure the patient is receiving adequate flow and F_{IO_2} from the system, you would
I. Do nothing.
II. Set up a double nebulizer system to increase flow, setting both nebulizers at 80%.
III. Increase the output of the flowmeter to 12 L/min.
IV. Run the nebulizer off air and titrate 5 L/min O_2 into the system.
V. Titrate additional O_2 into the original system.
A. I only
B. II and IV only
C. IV only
D. II only

78) Of the following solutions, which will produce particles that will tend to generally remain the same size as they enter the patient's airway?
A. Isotonic solutions
B. Hypotonic solutions
C. Agrotonic solutions
D. Hypertonic solutions

79) An 18-year-old woman is admitted to the emergency room with multiple rib fractures. An arterial blood gas sample, obtained while the patient is breathing room air, reveals the results below.
pH: 7.48
$Paco_2$: 32 torr
HCO_3^-: 23 mEq/L
Pao_2: 40 torr
These data indicate which of the following?
I. Respiratory alkalosis
II. Hyperventilation
III. Increased $P(A-a)O_2$

A. I only
B. III only
C. I and II only
D. I, II, and III

80) Oxygen therapy has been initiated on the patient in question 79. Which of the following changes can be expected?
   I. Increase in Paco₂
   II. Decrease in minute ventilation
   III. Increase in pulse rate
   IV. Increase in pH
   A. I and II only
   B. I and III only
   C. II and IV only
   D. III and IV only

81) A respiratory care practitioner is preparing to suction a patient and finds a partially empty 1–L bottle of saline for irrigation at the patient's bedside. Which of the following statements is relevant to this situation?
   A. Saline should not be used as a rinse solution.
   B. Saline should be no less concentrated than 3% NaCl if it is to be used as a rinse solution.
   C. Saline to be used as a rinse solution should be labeled "saline for injection."
   D. The saline may be used if it has been opened during the previous 24 hours and the date and time are recorded on the bottle.

82) An asthmatic patient in acute respiratory distress presents to the emergency room with markedly diminished breath sounds. After bronchodilator therapy, auscultation of the chest reveals coarse breath sounds and wheezing. This change suggests which of the following?
   A. Development of a pneumothorax
   B. Improvement of the air flow in the lungs
   C. Worsening of the asthmatic condition
   D. Onset of pulmonary edema

83) Which of the following should be prescribed to provide adequate humidification to the patient?
   A. Inspired gas with 50% relative humidity
   B. Tracheobronchial suctioning
   C. Inspired gas through a cold bubble diffusion humidifier
   D. Inspired gas with an absolute humidity of 43.8 mg/L

84) When a patient who is receiving oxygen via a nonrebreathing mask inhales, the reservoir bag on the mask does not deflate. Probable causes of this situation include which of the following?
   I. The flowmeter setting is too low.
   II. The mask is not tight enough.
   III. The one-way valve is sticking in the closed position.
   A. I only
   B. III only
   C. I and II
   D. II and III only

85) The therapeutic use of oxygen might help accomplish which of the following?
   I. Prevent absorption atelectasis.
   II. Decrease the myocardial workload.
   III. Decrease the work of breathing.
   IV. Increase the patient's respiratory rate.
   A. I only
   B. II and III only
   C. III and IV only
   D. I, II, and III only

86) Which of the following would indicate that a patient suddenly has developed a complete upper airway obstruction?
   I. Supraclavicular retraction
   II. Inability to speak
   III. Marked increase in use of accessory muscles of ventilation
   A. I only
   B. III only
   C. I and II only
   D. I, II, and III

87) When inspecting the chest of a patient with emphysema, a respiratory care practitioner most likely would find which of the following?
   A. Obesity
   B. Barrel chest
   C. Funnel chest
   D. Central cyanosis

88) Which of the following is used by the ultrasonic nebulizer to produce droplets from the water reservoir?
   A. Heat
   B. Steam
   C. Baffling
   D. Vibration

89) A patient with COPD who is spontaneously breathing an F$_{IO_2}$ of 0.5 becomes sleepy and unresponsive. The patient's reaction, most likely, is a result of
   A. Increased Paco₂
   B. Insufficient oxygenation
   C. Decreased cardiac output
   D. Excessive ventilation
   E. Increased intracranial pressure

90) A patient's arterial blood gas study reveals increased acidity (decreased pH) along with a decreased HCO_3^- measurement; otherwise, all values are within normal limits. This is most likely an indication of
   A. Acute respiratory acidosis
   B. Compensated respiratory acidosis
   C. Acute metabolic alkalosis
   D. Acute metabolic acidosis

91) A young, previously healthy patient has the following arterial blood gas results:
   pH: 7.15
   $Paco_2$: 75 torr
   HCO_3^-: 25 mEq/L
   Pao_2: 70 torr
   On the basis of this information, which of the following would be correct?
   I. Mild hypoxemia is present.
   II. The situation is chronic.
   III. The situation is acute.
   IV. Metabolic acidosis exists.
   V. Respiratory acidosis exists.
   A. I and IV only
   B. II and V only
   C. I and V only
   D. I, III, and V only

92) A venturi mask is most likely to deliver an F_{IO_2} higher than intended if
   A. The flow is set 5 L/min too high.
   B. Nebulized water is being added through the air entrainment ports.
   C. The holes in the mask are too large.
   D. The air entrainment ports have been blocked.

93) A patient is receiving oxygen via a 32% venti mask, but becomes dyspneic when she removes it to eat. The respiratory care practitioner should recommend delivering the oxygen via
   A. Nasal cannula @ 1 L/min
   B. Nasal cannula @ 3 L/min
   C. Nasal cannula @ 5 L/min
   D. Nasal cannula @ 6 L/min
   E. Nasal cannula @ 8 L/min

94) Alveolar humidity levels in healthy individuals are characterized by which of the following?
   I. Relative humidity = 100%
   II. Water vapor pressure = 47 torr
   III. Absolute humidity = 43.9 mg H_2O/L of air
   IV. Humidity deficit = 0 mg/L of air
   A. III only
   B. I and II only
   C. I, II, and III only
   D. I, II, III, and IV

95) An "H" cylinder is placed in service at 10 L/min. The gauge reads 1,800 psig. What is the tank's approximate duration?
   A. 6 hours
   B. 3 hours
   C. 9 hours
   D. 12 hours

96) A patient who is being mechanically ventilated with an F_{IO_2} of 0.8 and 5 cmH_2O of PEEP has the following arterial blood gas results:
   pH: 7.37
   $Paco_2$: 38 torr
   Pao_2: 52 torr
   Based on these data, the RCP should recommend which of the following?
   A. Increase the F_{IO_2} to 1.0 only.
   B. Increase PEEP to 10 cmH_2O only.
   C. Increase the F_{IO_2} to 1.0 and the PEEP to 10 cm.
   D. Decrease the PEEP and increase the F_{IO_2}.

97) Which of the following is LEAST important to evaluate, before changing the patient's therapy from mechanical ventilation to a T-piece?
   A. Gag reflex
   B. $P(A-a)O_2$
   C. Vital capacity
   D. V_D/V_T

98) While examining a patient's chest, the RCP palpates inspiratory and expiratory vibrations which clear when the patient coughs effectively. This indicates which of the following?
   A. The patient has emphysema.
   B. The airways are functioning normally.
   C. Secretions were present in the airways.
   D. The patient has pneumonia.

99) You have obtained the following blood gas results from a patient who is on 2 L/min:
   pH: 7.22
   Pco_2: 58 torr
   Po_2: 55 torr
   HCO_3^-: 31 mEq/L
   Which of the following would be a correct statement about this blood gas?
   A. This is an acute respiratory problem.
   B. This is a chronic respiratory problem.
   C. This is a metabolic problem.
   D. This patient is compensated.

100) Refer to the blood gas in question 99. Based on this blood gas, which of the following is most correct?
   A. No hypoxia exists.
   B. Moderate hypoxia exists.

C. The patient definitely retains CO_2.
D. Severe hypoxemia exists.

101) Refer to the blood gas in question 99. This patient's acid base status is
   A. Fully compensated
   B. Uncompensated
   C. Partially compensated
   D. All of the above, depending on your point of view

102) Refer to the blood gas in question 99. Based on these results, which of the following would be the best corrective action?
   A. Start q 2° IPPB therapy.
   B. Intubate the patient and mechanically ventilate.
   C. Increase the O_2 to 4 L/min.
   D. Change to a 24% venti mask.

103) Refer to the blood gas in question 99. This result would be most correctly interpreted as a
   A. Partially compensated respiratory acidosis with moderate hypoxemia
   B. Fully compensated respiratory acidosis with severe hypoxemia
   C. Partially compensated metabolic acidosis with moderate hypoxemia
   D. Respiratory alkalosis, uncompensated and without hypoxemia

104) You place the patient mentioned in question 103 on a vent with an F_{IO_2} of 0.4 and get the following blood gas:
   pH: 7.31
   P_{CO_2}: 51 torr
   P_{O_2}: 66 torr
   HCO_3^-: 28 m/Eq/L
   Which of the following is true?
   A. The patient's acid base status is now within normal limits and no further adjustment is needed.
   B. This is a fully compensated result.
   C. Mild hypoxemia is present.
   D. None of the above

105) Refer to the blood gas in question 104. Which course of action would you recommend?
   A. Increase the patient's tidal volume.
   B. Increase the F_{IO_2}.
   C. The patient is stable.
   D. Add 5 cm of PEEP.

106) Refer to the blood gas in question 104. Which of the following is true about the ABG in question?
   A. The patient definitely retains carbon dioxide.
   B. Fully compensated respiratory acidosis exists.
   C. Partially compensated respiratory alkalosis now exists.
   D. None of the above

107) You have made some vent changes and gotten the following ABG results after 1 hour. The F_{IO_2} is now 80%.
   pH: 7.37
   P_{CO_2}: 44 torr
   P_{O_2}: 51 torr
   HCO_3^-: 26 mEq/L
   Which of the following corrective actions would be appropriate at this time?
   A. Increase the oxygen concentration to 100%.
   B. Add 5 cm of PEEP.
   C. Increase the minute volume.
   D. Add 150 ml of mechanical dead space.

108) Refer to the blood gas in question 107. All of the following are true except
   A. Severe hypoxemia exists.
   B. A shunt exists.
   C. The patient may have ARDS.
   D. The patient may have pulmonary emboli.

109) Refer to the blood gas in question 107. Which of the following is true about these ABG results?
   A. A respiratory alkalosis is beginning.
   B. Mild hypoxemia has set in.
   C. They are normal with moderate hypoxemia.
   D. None of the above

110) Refer to the blood gas in question 107. A chest radiograph shows patchy white densities throughout all lung fields. Which of the following is the most likely pathology causing the problem?
   A. Pulmonary emboli
   B. Mucous plugging
   C. ARDS
   D. Pneumothorax

111) On 80% and 5 cm of PEEP (among other vent settings) ABGs after 3 hours are
   pH: 7.49
   P_{CO_2}: 31 torr
   P_{O_2}: 88 torr
   HCO_3^-: 25 mEq/l
   Which of the following changes would you now recommend?
   A. Decrease the PEEP to 0 cm and decrease the minute volume.
   B. Decrease the F_{IO_2} to 0.7 and decrease the minute volume.
   C. Decrease the F_{IO_2} to 0.75 and decrease the PEEP to 0 cm.
   D. Decrease the minute volume.

112) Refer to the blood gas in question 111. Which of the following is true about the ABG results in question?
   A. An uncompensated respiratory alkalosis is present with no hypoxemia.

B. A fully compensated respiratory alkalosis is present without hypoxemia.
C. Uncompensated metabolic alkalosis is present with mild hypoxemia.
D. Partially compensated metabolic alkalosis is present without hypoxemia.

113) Refer to the blood gas in question 111. The gases were drawn with the patient in the assist/control mode, on 80% and 5 cm of PEEP. Before considering switching the patient to SIMV mode, which of the following would be an advisable step?
A. Obtain weaning parameters.
B. Recheck the gases and get a chest radiograph.
C. Insert a left chest tube to drain excess fluid.
D. Do a 15-min T-piece trial to determine if the patient can tolerate SIMV.

114) Adding a 6-in flex tube to the circuit between the "Y" and the patient will have which of the following effects?
A. Make the circuit more flexible.
B. Adds about 300 ml of mechanical dead space.
C. Adds about 150 ml of mechanical dead space.
D. Facilitates installation of temperature probes.

115) Which of the following is true when an alarm sounds intermittently during the inspiratory phase of the ventilator cycle?
A. The ventilator has become disconnected.
B. There has been a power failure.
C. The patient's respiratory rate is too high.
D. There is an airway obstruction.

116) All of the following are true of the assist/control mode except
A. The patient controls the amount of volume in a tidal breath.
B. The patient may trigger as many breaths as the patient needs in addition to the preset rate.
C. The patient will receive the ventilator's preset volume each time the patient triggers the machine.
D. None of the above

117) Which of the following nerves controls the function of the diaphragm?
A. Phrenic
B. Diaphragmatic
C. Vagus
D. Glossopharyngeal

118) Which of the following is/are a function(s) of the respiratory tract?
A. Humidification
B. Heating
C. Filtration
D. All of the above

119) Which of the following is immediately true of left heart failure?
A. Breath sounds are clear.
B. Pedal edema exists.
C. Onset of pulmonary edema occurs.
D. Blood pressure decreases.

120) In general, crackles starting in the bases and gradually becoming diffuse during a short period indicates the onset of
A. Myocardial infarction
B. Hepatic failure
C. Emphysema
D. Congestive heart failure

121) The only components of the respiratory tract specifically designed to take part in gas exchange are the
A. Respiratory bronchioles
B. Small airways
C. Alveoli
D. Bronchi

122) The vocal cords are located in the
A. Larynx
B. Glottis
C. Epiglottis
D. Carina

123) A strong cough reflex is caused by accumulation of secretions or direct stimulation to which of the following?
A. Epiglottis
B. Carina
C. Alveoli
D. Tongue

124) Diuretic therapy is helpful in the treatment of which of the following?
A. Pneumonia
B. Cystic fibrosis
C. Epiglottitis
D. Congestive heart failure

125) An "infiltrate" on a CXR report probably indicates that the patient suffers from
A. COPD
B. Emphysema
C. Pneumonia
D. Pleural effusion

126) A cold-steam jet nebulizer is set at 80% and is connected to an oxygen flowmeter running at a flow rate of 9 L/min. What is the O_2:air entrainment ratio?
A. 1:1
B. 4:1

C. 1:3
D. 3:1

127) Refer to question 126. What is the total flow from this system?
   A. 12 L/min
   B. 27 L/min
   C. 36 L/min
   D. 18 L/min

128) Refer to questions 126 and 127. If the patient's minute volume is 20 L/min, the system can be said to have which of the following effects on the patient:
   I. It provides the desired F_{IO_2}.
   II. It provides an F_{IO_2} less than what is desired.
   III. It provides a flow rate that meets the patient's demand.
   IV. It provides less flow than the patient requires.
   V. It provides a higher F_{IO_2} than the patient needs.
   A. I and IV only
   B. I, IV, and V only
   C. II and IV only
   D. I, III, and V only

129) Refer to questions 126, 127, and 128. To ensure the patient is receiving adequate flow and F_{IO_2} from the system, you would
   I. Do nothing.
   II. Set up a double nebulizer system to increase flow, setting both nebulizers at 80%.
   III. Increase the output of the flowmeter to 12 L/min.
   IV. Run the nebulizer off air and titrate 5 L/min O_2 into the system.
   V. Titrate additional O_2 into the original system.
   A. I only
   B. II and IV only
   C. IV only
   D. II only

130) Of the following solutions, which will produce particles that will tend to generally remain the same size as they enter the patient's airway?
   A. Isotonic solutions
   B. Hypotonic solutions
   C. Agrotonic solutions
   D. Hypertonic solutions

131) A 24-year-old woman is admitted to the emergency room with multiple rib fractures. An arterial blood gas sample, obtained while the patient is breathing room air, reveals the following results:
   pH: 7.50
   Pa_{CO_2}: 28 torr
   HCO_3^-: 23 mEq/L
   Pa_{O_2}: 40 torr

These data indicate which of the following?
   I. Respiratory alkalosis
   II. Hyperventilation
   III. Increased $P(A-a)O_2$
   A. I only
   B. III only
   C. I and II only
   D. I, II, and III

132) Oxygen therapy has been initiated on the patient in question 131. Which of the following changes can be expected?
   I. Increase in Pa_{CO_2}
   II. Decrease in minute ventilation
   III. Increase in pulse rate
   IV. Increase in pH
   A. I and II only
   B. I and III only
   C. II and IV only
   D. III and IV only

133) A respiratory care practitioner is preparing to suction a patient and finds a partially empty 1–L bottle of saline for irrigation at the patient's bedside. Which of the following statements is relevant to this situation?
   A. Saline should not be used as a rinse solution.
   B. Saline should be no less concentrated than 3% NaCl if it is to be used as a rinse solution.
   C. Saline to be used as a rinse solution should be labeled "saline for injection."
   D. The saline may be used if it has been opened during the previous 24 hours, and the date and time are recorded on the bottle.

134) An asthmatic patient in acute respiratory distress presents to the emergency room with markedly diminished breath sounds. After bronchodilator therapy, auscultation of the chest reveals coarse breath sounds and wheezing. This change suggests which of the following?
   A. Development of a pneumothorax
   B. Improvement of the air flow to the lungs
   C. Worsening of the asthmatic condition
   D. Onset of pulmonary edema

Which of the following should be prescribed to provide adequate humidification to the patient?
   A. Inspired gas with 50% relative humidity
   B. Tracheobronchial suctioning
   C. Inspired gas through a cold bubble diffusion humidifier
   D. Endotracheal intubation

135) When a patient who is receiving oxygen via a non-rebreathing mask inhales, the reservoir bag on the mask

does not inflate. Probable causes of this situation include which of the following?
   I. The flowmeter setting is too low.
   II. The mask is not tight enough.
   III. The one-way valve is sticking in the closed position.
   A. I only
   B. III only
   C. I and II only
   D. II and III only

136) The therapeutic use of oxygen might help accomplish which of the following?
   I. Prevent absorption atelectasis.
   II. Decrease the myocardial workload.
   III. Decrease the work of breathing.
   IV. Increase the patient's respiratory rate.
   A. I only
   B. II and III only
   C. III and IV only
   D. I, II, and III only

137) Which of the following would indicate that a patient suddenly has developed a complete upper airway obstruction?
   I. Supraclavicular retraction
   II. Inability to speak
   III. Marked increase in use of accessory muscles of ventilation
   A. I only
   B. III only
   C. I and II only
   D. I, II, and III

138) When inspecting the chest of a patient with emphysema, a respiratory care practitioner most likely would find which of the following?
   A. Obesity
   B. Barrel chest
   C. Funnel chest
   D. Central cyanosis

139) Which of the following is used by the ultrasonic nebulizer to produce droplets from the water reservoir?
   A. Heat
   B. Steam
   C. Baffling
   D. Vibration

140) Which of the following is true about the NBRC?
   A. It is responsible for the credentialing of the RCPs.
   B. It runs conventions for RCPs.
   C. It organizes seminars.
   D. It lobbies Congress.

Test 3: Answer key and category breakdown

The categories are AP = anatomy and physiology, TP = therapeutic procedures, CD = clinical data, E = equipment selection and use, and H and HP = history and principles.

1)	A	TP	36)	C	TP	71)	D	TP
2)	B	TP	37)	B	TP	72)	C	TP
3)	A	CD	38)	A	TP	73)	A	E
4)	C	TP	39)	D	TP	74)	D	E
5)	D	CD	40)	A	TP	75)	A	E
6)	B	E	41)	C	AP	76)	C	E
7)	C	AP	42)	B	AP	77)	D	E
8)	A	TP	43)	B	AP	78)	A	TP
9)	D	AP	44)	C	TP	79)	D	CD
10)	A	AP	45)	A	CD	80)	A	TP
11)	D	AP	46)	A	CD	81)	D	TP
12)	A	AP	47)	B	E	82)	B	TP
13)	B	TP	48)	D	TP	83)	D	TP
14)	B	HP	49)	D	TP	84)	D	TP
15)	A	E	50)	B	E	85)	B	TP
16)	B	TP	51)	C	AP	86)	D	CD
17)	C	E	52)	A	TP	87)	E	CD
18)	D	CD	53)	D	CD	88)	D	E
19)	C	TP	54)	D	E	89)	A	AP
20)	B	TP	55)	B	E	90)	D	CD
21)	C	E	56)	C	HP	91)	D	CD
22)	A	TP	57)	C	E	92)	D	E
23)	D	E	58)	B	TP	93)	B	E
24)	B	AP	59)	D	TP	94)	D	CD
25)	A	HP	60)	C	TP	95)	C	E
26)	C	E	61)	B	CD	96)	B	TP
27)	D	TP	62)	C	CD	97)	A	TP
28)	A	TP	63)	A	TP	98)	C	TP
29)	D	HP	64)	A	TP	99)	A	CD
30)	B	AP	65)	C	CD	100)	B	CD
31)	A	AP	66)	D	TP	101)	C	CD
32)	C	TP	67)	C	E	102)	B	CD
33)	D	HP	68)	D	TP	103)	A	CD
34)	A	TP	69)	D	CD	104)	D	CD
35)	A	TP	70)	A	CD	105)	A	CD

106)	D	CD	118)	D	AP	130)	A	TP
107)	B	TP	119)	C	AP	131)	D	CD
108)	A	TP	120)	D	AP	132)	A	TP
109)	C	CD	121)	C	AP	133)	D	E
110)	C	AP	122)	A	AP	134)	B	TP
111)	B	TP	123)	C	AP	135)	D	E
112)	A	CD	124)	D	AP	136)	B	TP
113)	A	CD	125)	C	CD	137)	D	AP
114)	C	TP	126)	D	E	138)	B	AP
115)	D	E	127)	A	E	139)	D	E
116)	A	E	128)	C	E	140)	A	HP
117)	A	AP	129)	D	E			

Index

A

A, defined, 53
a, defined, 53
A-a gradient, 40
A/A ratio, 40
Abbreviations, 4–5
    qualification, 5
Acetylcysteine, 70
Acid-base balance, 29–32
    compensation, 30
    correction, 30
    defined, 29
    Henderson-Hasselbalch equation, 30–31
    non-respiratory parameters, 30
    normal values, 30
    parameter regulation, 30
    pathology, 29
Acidemia, defined, 29
Acidosis, defined, 29
Acute bronchitis, 18
Acute respiratory failure, signs, 110
Adrenocorticosteroid, 71
Adult respiratory distress syndrome, 17–18
    causes, 110
    signs, 110
Aerosol generator, humidity, 57–61
Aerosol therapy, small volume nebulizer, 83–84
Air capacity, 27
Air entrainment, oxygen delivery system, 55
Airway, 8–9
Airway resistance, mechanical ventilation, 114
Albuterol, 69, 70
Algebra, 39–40
Alkalemia, defined, 29
Alkalosis, defined, 29
Alveolar air equation, 39
Alveolar-arterial PO_2S gradient, 40

Alveoli, 8
Anemic hypoxia, 14
Anticholinergic drug, 71
Asthma, 17
    pulmonary function testing, 125–126
Atelectasis, 18, 81
Atropine sulfate, 69, 71
Atrovent, 69, 71
Auscultation, 42
Avogadro's Law, 25, 26

B

Babbington nebulizer, 57–58, 59
Barometric pressure, molecular activity, 4
Barotrauma, mechanical ventilation, 110
Base excess, 30
Bernoulli principle, 25, 55
Beta agonist, 70–71
Bird MARK (MK) 7, 78–79
Blood, symbols, 5
Blood gas analysis, 31–32
    interpretation, 32
Blue bloater, 18
Body humidity, 8, 27
    body humidity deficit, 27
    relative humidity, 59–60
Body position, inspection, 41
Boiling point, defined, 4
Bourdon gauge, 51
Boyle's Law, 25
Breath sound
    abnormal, 42–43
    complete absence in an area, 43
    crackles, 43
    decreased, 43
    A to E egophony, 42–43

increased, 43
normal, 42
rales, 43
rhonchi, 43
rumbles, 43
wheezes, 43
Breathing
   breathing pattern, 41–42
   work of breathing, 75
Broncheiolitis, 22
Bronchiectasis, 18
Bronchitis, 18
Bronchopneumonia, 19
Bronchopulmonary dysplasia, 22–23
Buffer system, 31
Bulk oxygen system, government regulations, 65–66

C

Carbon monoxide poisoning, 19, 32
Cardiac output, 8
Cardio-respiratory system
   anatomy, 7–9
   physiology, 7–9
Carina, 8–9
Cascade humidifier, 61
Central sleep apnea, 19–20
Charles' Law, 25–26
Chest examination, 41–42
Chest percussion, 85–86
   contraindications, 85–86
   goals, 85
   indications, 86
Chest shape, 41
Chronic bronchitis, 18
Chronic obstructive lung disease, 9
   pulmonary function testing, 125
Chronic respiratory failure, 110
Clark electrode, 31
Coanda effect, 126–127
Cold steam nebulizer, 55, 58, 60
Compensated flowmeter, 50–51
Compliance, ventilator, 116–117
   dynamic compliance, 116–117
   static compliance, 116
Continuous positive airway pressure, 12, 103
   ventilator weaning, 122
Cough, intermittent positive pressure breathing, 76
Crackles, 43
Critical pressure, defined, 4
Critical temperature, defined, 4
Cromolyn sodium, 70
Croup, 21
Cyanosis, 13–14
   clinical signs, 14
Cylinder duration, 39
Cylinder markings, 65–66

D

Dalton's Law, 25
Digits, inspection, 42
Dry heat, 63

E

Electro-chemical analyzer, 95–96
Electrode, 31–32
Emphysema, 18
Empyema, 18
Endotracheal tube
   cuff characteristics, 90
   cuff pressure, 91
   intubation, 91
   tracheostomy tube, compared, 89
   tube size, 91
Epiglottis, 21–22
Equipment cleaning, 63
Ethylene oxide, 63
Evaporation, defined, 4
Expiratory retard, 103
External respiration, 7

F

Face, inspection, 41
Flail chest, 18–19
Flow rate, mechanical ventilation, 113
Flow regulator, 47
   adjustable, 47, 49
   preset, 47, 48
   standardized connections, 47
Flow-by
   ventilation, 103
   ventilator weaning, 122
Flowmeter, 47–52. *See also* Specific type
   compensated, 50–51
   uncompensated, 50
Flow-volume loop, 126
Fluidics, 126–127
   Coanda effect, 126–127
   defined, 126
Foreign body aspiration, 22
Freezing point, defined, 4
Functional residual capacity, 125

G

Gas laws, 25–27, 31
Gay-Lussac's Law, 25, 26
Glucocorticoid, 71
Glutaraldehyde, 63
Government regulations, bulk oxygen system, 65–66

H

HCO$_3^-$, 30
   mechanism, 34
Hemodynamics, 11–12
Henderson-Hasselbalch equation, 30–31
Hgb, 33
High flow device, 54–55. *See also* Specific type
Histotoxic hypoxia, 15
Home care, 127
Humidification, factors, 60–61
Humidity
   aerosol generator, 57–61
   factors, 54
   water temperature, 55
Hyaline membrane disease, 22
Hydrosphere, 57–58
Hyperoxemia, 9
Hypovolemia, 11
Hypoxemia, 9, 13–15. *See also* Specific type
   cardiovascular and respiratory symptoms, 13
   chronic, 14
      symptoms, 14
   defined, 13
   physiologic causes, 13
   symptoms, 14
Hypoxemic hypoxia, 14
Hypoxia, suctioning, 92

I

Ideal Gas Law, 26
Ideal minute volume, 117
Incentive spirometry breathing, 81
   frequency, 81
Infant respiratory distress syndrome, 22
Inspiratory capacity, 81, 125
Inspiratory hold, 12, 103
Intermittent mandatory ventilation, 101–102
Intermittent positive pressure breathing, 12, 75–79
   clinical goals, 76–77
   compliance, 77
   cough, 76
   elastance, 77
   flow, 77
   hazards, 76
   indications, 79
   mean airway pressure, 77–78
      flow rate control, 78
      pressure control, 77–78
      pressure-time relationships, 78
      sensitivity, 77
   medication delivery, 76
   physiologic effects, 77
   resistance, 77
   ventilation distribution, 76
   ventilator weaning, 122

Internal respiration, 7–8
Interstitial pneumonia, 19
Ion, 31
Isoproterenol, 69

J

Jet nebulizer, 58, 60

L

Laryngo-tracheo bronchitis, 21
Left ventricle, 11
Lobar pneumonia, 19
Low flow device, 53–54. *See also* Specific type
   simple mask, 53

M

Mainstem bronchi, 8
Manual ventilation, ventilator weaning, 122
Mass spectrometer, 95
Mean airway pressure, intermittent positive pressure breathing, 77–78
   flow rate control, 78
   pressure control, 77–78
   pressure-time relationships, 78
   sensitivity, 77
Mechanical ventilation, 109–111
   airway resistance, 114
   barotrauma, 110
   compliance, 110
   complications, 110–111
   effects increased by, 109
   flow rate, 113
   implementation, 113–114
   indications, 109–110
   infection, 111
   tracheal structural and tissue damage, 111
   ventilator check, 114
Melting point, defined, 4
Metabolic acidosis, 30
Metabolic alkalosis, 30
Metaproterenol sulfate, 70
Methyl-xanthine, 70
Minimal leak technique, 91
Minute volume, ventilator, 115–116
Mist control, 57, 58
Molecular activity, barometric pressure, 4
Molecular humidity, 59
Montgomery valve, 123
Mucocilliary escalator, 8
Mucolytic agent, 69–70

N

Nasal cannula, 53
Neck, inspection, 41
Nervous system, 69–70
Neuromuscular blocking agent, 69
Non-rebreather mask, 54

O

O_2 content formula, 39
O_2 transport, 33–34
Obstructive sleep apnea, 19
Oxi-hemoglobin dissociation curve, 33–34
    factors, 34
    shifted left, 33
    shifted right, 33
Oxygen analyzer, 95–96
    chemical (Scholander) analyzers, 95
    electric analyzers, 95
    electro-chemical analyzer, 95–96
    mass spectrometer, 95
    physical analyzers, 95
Oxygen delivery system, 53–55. *See also* Specific type
    air entrainment, 55
Oxygen therapy, 13

P

P_{50}, 34
$PaCO_2$, 33–34
Palpitation, 42
Parasympathetic nervous system, 69–70
Partial rebreather mask, 54
Particulate humidity, 58–59
Passey-Muir valve, 123
Passover humidifier, 61
Pasteurization, 63
Pathogenic organisms, 35–37
    diagnostic tools, 35
    indicators, 35
    sputum, 36
    techniques, 35
Patient ventilation monitor, ventilator weaning, 122–123
PCO_2
    defined, 29
    ventilator, 115–116
PCO_2 electrode, 31
Peak airway pressure, 12
Pediatric pulmonary pathology, 21–23
Percussion, 42
pH, defined, 29
pH electrode, 31
Pharmacology, 69–71, 73–74
Phentolamine, 69

Phenylephrine, 69
Pink puffer, 18
Pleural effusion, 19
Pneumonia, 19
Pneumothorax, 19
PO_2 electrode, 31
PO_2, ventilator, 116
Poiseuille's Law, 25, 26
Positive end expiratory pressure, 11, 103
    effects decreased by, 109
    effects increased by, 109
Postural drainage, 86
    indications, 86
    positions, 86
Pressure conversion, 3–4
Pressure support ventilation, 12, 102–103
Pressurized steam autoclave, 63
Prolonged expiratory retard, 12
Propranolol, 69
PSIA, defined, 4
PSIG, defined, 4
PSV, ventilator weaning, 122
Pulmonary artery catheter, normal values, 11
Pulmonary artery wedge pressure, 11
Pulmonary embolism, 19
Pulmonary function testing, 125–127
    asthma, 125–126
    chronic obstructive lung disease, 125
    restrictrive lung disease, 125
Pulmonary hypertension, 11
Pulmonary pathology, 17–20
Pulmonary wedge pressure, 11
Pulse oximetry, ventilator weaning, 122

Q

Qualification, 5

R

Racemic epinephrine, 71
Rales, 43
Relative humidity, 27
    body humidity, 59–60
Respiration
    external, 7
    internal, 7–8
Respiratory acidosis, 29
Respiratory alkalosis, 29
Respiratory bronchiole, 8
Respiratory care
    historical aspects, 3
    pioneers, 3
Respiratory infection, treatment, 35–36
Respiratory pharmacology, 69–71, 73–74

Respiratory status, assessment, 41–43
Restrictrive lung disease, pulmonary function testing, 125
Retrolental fibroplasia, 22
Reynold's Number, 25
Rhonchi, 43
Right ventricle, 11
Robinul, 69, 71
Rumbles, 43

S

Sanz electrode, 31
Serevent, 71
Severinghaus electrode, 31
Shock lung. See Adult respiratory distress syndrome
Shrader QC device, 47
Sighs, 103
Simple mask, 53
Skin, inspection, 42
Sleep apnea, 19–20
Small volume nebulizer, aerosol therapy, 83–84
Smoke inhalation, 19, 32
Solo, 57–58
Speaking valve
    tracheostomy tube, 123
    ventilator weaning, 123
Sputum
    characteristics, 36
    currant jelly, 36
    gross blood, 36–37
    hemoptysis, 36
    mucopurulent, 36
    pathogenic organisms, 36
    purulent, 36
    rust color, 36
    types, 36
Stagnant hypoxia, 15
Status asthmaticus, 17
    children, 22
Sterilization, 63
Steroid, 70
Suctioning, 91–93
    airway to catheter size ratio, 92
    catheter types, 91–92
    hypoxia, 92
    pressures, 91
    procedure, 92
Sustained maximal inhalation, 81
Sympathetic nervous system, 69
Synchronized intermittent mandatory ventilation, 102

T

Temperature conversion, 3–4
Terminology, 9
Thorpe tube, 49–50
    compensated, 50
    uncompensated, 51
Tissue hypoxia, 14
Total lung capacity, 125
Trachea, 8
Tracheostomy tube
    cuff characteristics, 90
    cuff pressure, 91
    cuffless, 90
    disposable inner cannula, 90
    endotracheal tube, compared, 89
    fenestrated, 90
    intubation, 91
    speaking valve, 123
    troubleshooting, 90–91
    tube size, 91
    types, 90–91

U

Ultrasonic nebulizer. See USN
Uncompensated flowmeter, 50
Universal precautions, 63
USN, 57

V

Vagal response, 8–9
Vapor pressure, defined, 4
Venti mask, 54–55
Ventilation
    assist mode, 101
    assist-control mode, 101
    auxiliary airway maneuvers, 103
    control, 9
    decreased expired volumes, 119
    flow-by, 103
    increased peak pressures, 119
    intermittent mandatory ventilationi mode, 101–102
    modes, 101–103
    troubleshooting
        decreased positive end expiratory pressure/continuous positive airway pressure, 120
        increased positive end expiratory pressure/continuous positive airway pressure, 120
        manometer needle slow rise, 120
        manometer needle slow to return to zero, 120
        patient assessment, 119
        poor I:E ratio, 120
        synchronized intermittent mandatory ventilation mode, 102
        troubleshooting, 119–120
        ventilator assessment, 119–120
        ventilatory patterns, 101, 102

Ventilator
    classification, 99–100
    compliance, 116–117
        dynamic compliance, 116–117
        static compliance, 116
    controls, 107
    fine tuning, 115–116
    FIO_2, 107
    flow rate, 107
    minute volume, 115–116
    O_2 %, 107
    parameters, 99
    PCO_2, 115–116
    peak flow rate, 107
    PO_2, 116
    pressure limits, 107
    pressure vent, 99
    rate, 107
    set-up, 115
    tidal volume, 107
    volume vent, 99
Ventilator alarm, 105
Ventilator weaning, 121–123
    continuous positive airway pressure, 122
    flow-by, 122
    intermittent positive pressure ventilation, 122
    manual ventilation, 122
    patient ventilation monitor, 122–123
    PSV, 122
    pulse oximetry, 122
    speaking valve, 123
    techniques, 121–122
        IMV, 121
        SIMV, 121
        sink or swim (T-piece or trach collar trials), 121
    trial termination, 122
    weaning parameters, 121
Vital capacity, 125

W

Water temperature, humidity, 55
Weaning. *See* Ventilator weaning
Wheezes, 43
Work of breathing, 75